PLAYS ONE

J B Priestley

PLAYS ONE

LABURNUM GROVE
WHEN WE ARE MARRIED
MR KETTLE AND MRS MOON

Introduction by Tom Priestley

Foreword by Roy Hattersley

OBERON BOOKS
LONDON

Contents

Foreword

I suppose that J B Priestley came into my life during the war, when I listened to his 'Postscripts' and rejoiced that someone with a Yorkshire accent, even more pronounced than my own, was allowed to broadcast on the BBC. But it was a little volume of *Essays by Modern Masters*, given to me with a pile of other books when I arrived at grammar school, which made me a Priestleyite for life. It included some of his best-known journalism and convinced me that writing for newspapers was just as respectable an occupation as writing for anything else.

The plays and the novels came to me later, and the literary criticism later still. They combined to convince me of what I still believe is the most important quality which Priestley brought to literature: the belief that writing was a trade in itself and that men and women who had the talent to construct elegant sentences around interesting ideas should not limit their creative impulses to any one literary form.

Priestley is now enjoying a great literary revival, stimulated by the remarkable success of the undeniably outré production of *An Inspector Calls* and the rediscovery of his time plays. His comic genius – as displayed here in *When We Are Married* – continues to delight audiences all over the English-speaking world. I have no doubt that his novels – profound, profane and prophetic – are destined for a new wave of general popularity.

In the pseudo-sophistication of the last quarter of the twentieth century Priestley was often mistakenly described as a Yorkshire writer. In fact, he was a writer of genius who happened to have been born in Yorkshire and often (though not invariably) wrote about what he had learned in his boyhood. E M Forster said that to describe *The Seven Pillars of Wisdom* as a book about the war in the desert was like describing *Moby Dick* as a book about whaling. The same applies to J B Priestley. He does not write about any particular time or place. He writes about life.

Roy Hattersley
August 2002

Introduction

Tom Priestley

J B Priestley was, in old-fashioned terms, a 'man of letters'. Beginning as an essayist and critic, he moved inexorably from literary biography to fiction and, once success gave him the freedom to experiment, from fiction to drama. He once said of his writing, in a conversation with me for a film we made together, 'How can I expect other people to enjoy it, if I don't enjoy it myself?' We can easily sense his enjoyment in these three comedies.

Needless to say he had a great sense of humour, loved telling jokes, even wonderfully silly ones, and was adept at the one-liner, an ironical parting shot, a witty comment or a reflection on the absurdity of life; in his book *English Journey* he describes a poignant moment at a reunion where the remembrance of fallen comrades is made ridiculous by the misplaying of the regimental march on a tinny piano, and concludes, 'I suppose that is why I am at heart a comic writer.' He could not help seeing the humour in a situation or finding situations which were essentially comic. Comedy often consists in taking the ordinary and turning it on its head, as we will see here.

It is important to remember that plays are written to be performed, not just read on the page: this is a point my father stressed when introducing his plays. The text can be a fine first taste of the work, an initial meeting with the characters and their story, and of course can serve as an excellent reminder of past productions. But it can no more replace performance than a manuscript sheet of music can a concerto. Both need the interpretation of skilled artists – musicians or actors, conductors or directors – who will add their own individual touches to flesh out the indications the writer has given.

Most important is the addition of the element of time – the pauses, the interruptions, the sweep and flow of the piece – not to mention the vital interaction between cast and audience, because the audience too is a key part of any performance, a group of individuals strangely blended into a single entity.

Nowhere is this more crucial than in comedy, where the timing is everything, and, in playing, the rhythm may have to be adjusted to suit a particular audience. This can only be hinted at in a written text, and sometimes, in the plays collected here, you will see that certain details are left to the judgement of the actors anyway.

Laburnum Grove opened in London at the Duchess Theatre (my father's favourite) on 28 November 1933 and played for 335 performances; it later opened in New York at the Booth on 14 January 1935, where it played for 131 performances. I have never seen it on stage myself, though I did view the film version on a Steinbeck at the BFI. The film had substantially the same cast as the London stage production, with the interesting exception of Cedric Hardwicke, who had directed the stage version and for the film took over the part of Bernard Baxley, perhaps overplaying this principal comic role. The film was made by ATP at Ealing Studios, produced by Basil Dean and directed by Carol Reed; I suspect it was a 'quota quickie'. (In the 1930s cinemas were obliged to show a fixed quota of British films, so many films were made quickly and cheaply to fill the bill.) It was released in 1936.

Perhaps unusually for my father's plays, *Laburnum Grove* is set in a suburban house somewhere in North London; it is a quiet respectable area where nothing much happens, the smooth underbelly of Mike Leigh territory. But this tranquillity is an illusion. The scene throughout is the living-room, as in many of his plays. The central character is George Radfern, himself quiet and seemingly respectable, even dull; round him are grouped a variety of characters hoping to coax money out of him, and the comedy comes from their reactions to a revelation about the source of his income – is he or isn't he a crook, this gentle unassuming man? The theme, then, is greed and aspects of dishonesty; when the others reject the money, considering it tainted, are they not just as dishonest as he might be, or more so? Radfern at least tells the truth throughout. In the world where making money is the principal aim in life, he takes it to its logical conclusion. There is fine ensemble writing in this piece – a speciality of JBP – and rich character work. It is a concise and coherent comic piece.

When We Are Married opened at the St Martin's Theatre in London on 11 October 1938 and ran for 175 performances, then transferred to the Prince's Theatre on 27 March 1939, where it ran for another 102 performances; it opened in New York at the Lyceum on 25 December 1939 and ran for 156 performances. My father described the origins of the plot in his book *Rain Upon Godshill*; my mother was reading a book of French short stories on an Atlantic crossing and found an amusing tale of a couple who, celebrating the anniversary of their wedding, suddenly discovered they had never been married at all. Setting the play in his native Yorkshire and making it three couples rather than only one, my father wrote his most successful comedy: as he describes it, *A Yorkshire Farcical Comedy.*

It is a satire on provincial pomposity, with a rich local vocabulary and characters remembered from his childhood: again, a wonderful piece for ensemble acting. But what lifts it to another dimension is the character of the drunken photographer, Henry Ormonroyd, who stumbles in and out of the action, bemused and bewildered, flotsam of life's storm. The story is well known of how JBP had to play that part himself. Early in the play's London run, when the actor playing Henry Ormonroyd was injured in a car crash, they suddenly needed someone who could play the piano, who could do a Yorkshire accent and who knew the words. Only my father fitted the bill, so reluctantly he took over – or was he reluctant? He had had ambitions to be a performer in his youth, but the ten performances he gave now cured him of all acting ambition; he found it strangely frustrating. Photos remain of him in his make-up with an untidy false moustache and a wry expression on his face.

It is the most Yorkshire of all his writings, for though he came from Yorkshire and sometimes wrote about it, he was by no means a 'Yorkshire Writer'. Though my favourite production with a dream cast was that of Ron Eyre in 1986, which seemed subtly near the heart of the play and did not let the need for laughter swamp the characters, it is a special experience to see a performance in Yorkshire where individual words have a particular reverberation. My aunt Winnie, who was secretary for years to the Bradford Civic Playhouse, now the Priestley Centre for the Arts, said that performances there were judged on the reading of individual lines, so well was the text known.

Mr Kettle and Mrs Moon played at the Duchess Theatre from 1 September 1955. Also known as *The Scandalous Affair of Mr Kettle and Mrs Moon*, it was one of his later plays, when fashion in the theatre was changing and his popularity had waned. I never saw it because I was living abroad at the time. It is perhaps interesting to compare these three plays, from the beginning of his dramatic career, the apex and nearer the end, spanning over twenty years. They all fall into the category of the 'well-made play'. The essence of the well-made play is unity – unity of time, unity of place and unity of action. If it seemed to be the convention of a particular period of the drama, with the suggestion that new forms could and should replace it, that does not make it wrong in itself. With the unities went the satisfaction of the audience, who felt themselves escorted and guided throughout the experience, rather than floundering to find their own way, though this could on occasion give a greater feeling of freedom – freedom from the constraints of convention. All three of these belong firmly to the tradition of the well-made play and one might add to the list of advantages the ease of production. A professional dramatist not only wants to see his work performed as widely as possible, he also depends on it for his livelihood. So a play with a single set and a cast of mixed ages can be more easily presented in smaller or repertory theatres on a limited budget with a standard cast.

Laburnum Grove and *Mr Kettle and Mrs Moon* each have three women and six men and could almost be cross-cast with one exception; I am not suggesting that my father deliberately set out to do this, but such was his skill that he provided a practical mixture of characters. *When We Are Married* requires a larger cast with an even balance between the sexes: seven women and seven men.

In the character of Mr Kettle it is possible to see in embryo a favourite character who appears in several of his later novels.

When I pointed this out to my father he was surprised, indicating that it had not happened on the conscious level. Maybe this character was a kind of JBP alter ego. We find him in *Low Notes on a High Level*, *Festival at Farbridge* and especially in the two leading characters of *The Image Men*. He is middle-aged, a free thinker, unconventional, and enjoys the good life when he can afford it – good food and drink, cigars and the company of women. George Kettle is emerging from the chrysalis of convention, the boredom of routine and a life dedicated to other people's problems on a practical rather than emotional level. This character emerges from another regular theme, Englishness, which again permeates these three plays – as so much else of his work, especially his film *Last Holiday*. Perhaps it anchors him to his period, but it remains pertinent even today, because it stems from an analysis of the English character, which he often found inhibited from discovering its full potential. I remember once he derided modesty, or at least a kind of false modesty which is secretly pleased with itself. If he felt he had done something well, he recognised it publicly. Though basically a shy man, he did not believe in pretence. The overly modest, he felt, were pretentious and disguising their true selves. So his ideal was the character who spoke his own mind, went his own way and lived a full life. George Kettle suddenly realises this and flies in the face of dull convention, rediscovers the child in himself and fights to escape to a richer and fuller life. In this he is helped by the essential woman, Delia Moon, and the spirit of youth and adventure, Monica Twigg. The other George, George Radfern, would have approved, and so would Henry Ormonroyd.

London
March 2003

Author's Preface

J B Priestley

James Agate, when called upon once to give a short list of his likes and dislikes, included my serious plays among his likes and my comedies among his dislikes. On the other hand, I know an equally distinguished man of the Theatre who greatly prefers my comedies to my serious plays. The playgoing public appears to have no preference one way or the other, and this seems to me very sensible of it, and here I applaud its sound judgment. There are some men who should never try to be funny and there are others who are least effective when they are in grim earnest. But most of us are somewhere between these two extremes. And for my part I would bitterly resent being compelled to restrict my writing for the stage to either one form or the other. On the whole I think I find it easier to plan and then to write a serious play than I do a comedy (and to this point I shall return), but I enjoy the actual staging of a comedy more than I do that of a serious play, and if asked to produce one of my own plays I would certainly choose a comedy. Nor do I think it difficult to explain these preferences. There is about a serious play that is properly constructed a natural sweep forward, an inevitable progress, that makes it easier to write, so that often a big scene of considerable technical intricacy will almost write itself. But in the detailed presentation of a comic scene on the stage, where inflections and timing are all-important, I find myself more at home and happier on the job than I do with the more serious plays. And it is, of course, far easier to test the value of your work in comedy, if only because the laughter of the audience tells you what is happening.

There is, however, an important point to be made here. To my mind it is only in the broadest farce that 'anything for a laugh' is legitimate. In the production of comedy this can be a very dangerous policy. Many productions of Shakespeare's comedies have been ruined for me by antics more suitable to the Crazy Gang at the Victoria Palace. The fun was there, of course, but it was not the fun that Shakespeare intended. For example, in the glorious orchard scene in *Henry IV: Part Two* it is easy enough to provoke laughter by turning Shallow and Silence into knockabout buffoons, but it is equally easy in this way to ruin one of the finest scenes in all comic literature. The producer of comedy should set himself the task of discovering and then exploiting to the full the particular kind of comic effect the author intended, instead of going anywhere and doing anything for a laugh. Falling about or throwing custard pies will always produce bigger laughs than the most adroit examples of mental absurdity. I delight in wild clowning myself, but it is delightful only in its own place. Actors are often at fault here, because, having been given a comic part, they feel that every laugh, no matter how obtained, is a personal contribution of value to the production in hand, whereas they may easily be sacrificing the whole structure and value of a scene, and any lasting impression it can make, by these dubious triumphs. Every comedy worth playing has its own particular atmosphere, flavour and appeal, and these should not be sacrificed to the dangerous notion that 'every laugh is worth five pounds'. It is always possible that a few five-pound laughs may finally cost several thousands.

I have already suggested that – to me at any rate – the writing of a comedy is not as easy as pie. The point is worth making if only because more than once when a comedy of mine has been produced, some critics have told their readers in effect that I have merely been filling in a gap with a hasty bit of fooling, probably knocked off in a few days. Nothing could be further from the truth. I have usually spent far more time and trouble, done far more re-constructing and re-writing, demanded far more additional rehearsals, in the comedies than in the serious plays. During the provincial try-out of *When We Are Married* I wrote and re-wrote many scenes, and we were actually presenting one version of the play in the evenings while we were rehearsing an altered version of it during the day.

These comedies are of various kinds, and I shall try to give some indication of how I see them myself in discussing two of them here. But they all more or less fall into one large division of comedy, although that again can be easily sub-divided. These large divisions, I fancy, are High, Light and Broad. High Comedy, which has a particular appeal to Latin and Central European minds, has never been popular with English writers and audiences, though I think we might fairly claim Somerset Maugham's *The Circle* as a successful example of this form. The preference here, especially among the stalls public, has been for Light Comedy, partly because it is a form that provides admirable vehicles for popular and highly skilled star performers, without whom these flimsy pieces are apt to look very thin indeed. (This is a fact that Repertory and amateur producers ignore at their peril.) It is a form of comedy that I do not much care about myself. My own choice is Broad Comedy, which is stronger in situation and richer in its characterisation than Light Comedy, and more frankly farcical and less austerely intellectual in its approach than High Comedy. It is, I believe, peculiarly suitable to the English temperament, and as I consider I possess a fairly thick slab of this temperament, this is the field of comedy in which I have chosen to work.

Laburnum Grove

This comedy of suburban life, which brought back that fine actor, Edmund Gwenn, to the stage after some years' absence in films, was originally produced at the Duchess Theatre in the autumn of 1933. It had a very long run, which I deliberately broke (for I was the management too) to send the company to New York, where the play did reasonably well. It is a great favourite with Repertory and amateur companies here, but, perhaps because it is very English in atmosphere and humour, it has not been as widely and successfully produced abroad as many of my other plays have. The droll business with the bananas, which has amused thousands of audiences and appears to remain in their memory, owes nothing to me but was a happy invention of my friend, Sir Cedric Hardwicke, who produced the play. At the time I wrote it, when I was also gathering material for *English Journey*, I was very suspicious about our financial system, if only because the banks appeared to flourish when industry was failing, and this explains certain references in the text. Frequently in the Theatre, as most people who work in it will agree, either everything goes right or everything goes wrong. With *Laburnum Grove,* which I planned in a nursing home and wrote rapidly during convalescence, everything went right. We had a good cast, headed by Edmund Gwenn and Mary Jerrold, Ethel Coleridge and Melville Cooper; and this production brought me to the Duchess Theatre and a long and happy association with its owner, J P Mitchelhill.

When We Are Married

When We Are Married was produced at the St Martin's in October 1938, and transferred to the Prince's at the end of March 1939. It has been very popular ever since. I enjoyed writing this broadly farcical comedy because I had a lot of fun remembering and then using various aspects of West Riding life and manners known to my boyhood. The plot is nonsensical but the characters and their attitudes and their talk are all authentic. The play was magnificently cast and produced by Basil Dean, who in my opinion has a great flair for this kind of comedy. It was during the early part of its run that I had to take over, at twenty-four hours' notice, the part of Henry Ormonroyd, the drunken photographer, and thus did some acting, of a sort, about which I have boasted ever since.

January 1949

LABURNUM GROVE

An Immoral Comedy in Three Acts

to Edmund Gwenn

Characters

ELSIE RADFERN

MRS LUCY BAXLEY

BERNARD BAXLEY

GEORGE RADFERN

HAROLD RUSS

JOE FLETTEN

MRS DOROTHY RADFERN

INSPECTOR STACK

SERGEANT MORRIS

Laburnum Grove was first performed on 28 Novemeber 1933 at the Duchess Theatre, London, with the following cast:

ELSIE RADFERN, Margery Pickard

MRS LUCY BAXLEY, Ethel Coleridge

BERNARD BAXLEY, Melville Cooper

GEORGE RADFERN, Edmund Gwenn

HAROLD RUSS, Francis James

JOE FLETTEN, James Harcourt

MRS DOROTHY RADFERN, Mary Jerrold

INSPECTOR STACK, David Hawthorne

SERGEANT MORRIS, Douglas Payne

Producer, Cedric Hardwicke

Act One – Sunday Evening
Act Two, Scene 1 – Early Monday Morning
Act Two, Scene 2 – Monday Afternoon
Act Three – Monday Evening

The whole action takes place in the living-room of the Radferns' house, Ferndale, Laburnum Grove, Shooters Green, a suburb of North London.

ACT ONE

The Scene is the living-room in the RADFERNS' house, 'Ferndale',
Laburnum Grove, Shooters Green – a suburb in North London. The
time is Sunday evening in late summer, still daylight at first. On the
back wall from right to left are a small window, then a door that can
lead directly into a greenhouse, then a larger window looking out on
to a back garden. In the right wall, downstage, is a door into a small
hall, leading to the front door of the house and the stairs. In the left
wall is a door leading into the kitchen. Against this wall, beyond the
door, is a small sideboard with whisky decanter, soda syphon, and
several bottles of beer on it. In the corner, between the left wall and
the large window, is an oval or round table, on easy castors, that is
laid for supper but is covered with two cloths. In the opposite corner
is a small table on which is a telephone, and near it a loud-speaker
and wireless set. There are one or two easy chairs and several dining-
room chairs in the room, which is brightly, comfortably furnished in
a suburban style. When the curtain rises MRS BAXLEY and ELSIE
are discovered seated at a small card table in the centre. MRS BAXLEY
is a woman in her forties, dressed in a smart-shabby style, a mixture
of silliness and calculating selfishness. ELSIE is a pretty but rather
petulant and discontented girl of twenty or so, the kind you see in the
High Street of every fairly prosperous suburb. ELSIE is shuffling a
pack of cards and when she has finished she cuts them into two,
towards MRS BAXLEY, who then proceeds to put them together and
deal them face downward on the table into six packs.

MRS BAXLEY: (*As she finishes dealing the cards.*) To
   yourself...your home...your wish. Have you wished,
   Elsie?

ELSIE: Yes, Auntie. Very definitely.

MRS BAXLEY: What you do expect – what you don't
   expect and what's sure to come true. Mind you, I'm not
   always in the mood, you know. Sometimes I can't see
   things at all, and then at other times, it's all as clear as
   anything, and everything I tell people comes true. It's a
   gift, you know. One can't control it.

23

ELSIE: (*With signs of excitement.*) Well, you must be in the mood tonight, Aunt Lucy.

MRS BAXLEY: Why? What's exciting you tonight? I know there's something.

ELSIE: I'll tell you afterwards. It would spoil it if I told you now. You must tell me things first.

MRS BAXLEY: All right, but I hope your mother won't come back in the middle of it, because she doesn't like me to read the cards for you – she told me so, the other day.

ELSIE: Mother won't be back from Mrs Repington's until after supper. That's why she got supper all ready (*Indicating table in corner.*) before she went. So you needn't worry about her.

MRS BAXLEY: All right then.

(*Picks up first lot of cards and examines them, and does the same with succeeding lots throughout the speeches that follow. She assumes the usual far-away mystical air of the clairvoyant, which is in sharp and comic contrast to her tone and manner when making remarks not directly concerned with the fortune-telling.*)

Um… Um… Well, the first thing I see, Elsie, is a great surprise. Yes, you're going to have a great surprise.

ELSIE: A surprise? When?

MRS BAXLEY: Very soon.

ELSIE: How soon? Next week?

MRS BAXLEY: Perhaps sooner.

ELSIE: Well, it can't be much sooner. It's Sunday night and nearly next week now.

MRS BAXLEY: Well, it's coming very soon. And it isn't a nice surprise. I don't think you'll like it.

ELSIE: (*Reproachfully.*) Oh – Aunt Lucy!

MRS BAXLEY: I can't help it. I'm only telling you what's here in the cards.

ELSIE: What's it about?

MRS BAXLEY: (*Brooding over more cards.*) I think it's something to do with a medium-coloured man.

ELSIE: (*Thinking hard.*) A medium-coloured man? Is he young?

MRS BAXLEY: No, I don't think he is. Your home comes into it.

ELSIE: (*Disappointed.*) Oh!

MRS BAXLEY: Yes, I think the medium-coloured man must be your father.

ELSIE: Is it – is it about an engagement?

MRS BAXLEY: No, I don't see an engagement connected with it. I think you're simply going to get a great surprise from your father.

ELSIE: (*Disgusted.*) That's just like the cards. They're always like that. A great surprise – from Dad – of all people! I suppose the great surprise will be that he's grown two tomatoes in his greenhouse. Or they're going to play Handel's Largo for him on the wireless. Or he can't find his pipe or one of his silly detective stories or something. Dad!

MRS BAXLEY: Well, it's all here – quite plain.

ELSIE: Perhaps you're not in the mood tonight, Auntie.

MRS BAXLEY: (*Coldly.*) As a matter of fact, I am seeing very clearly tonight. But it was you who asked me to read the cards, Elsie, and if you don't choose to accept what I see, I'll stop.

ELSIE: No. Sorry. Go on.

MRS BAXLEY: (*Examining more cards.*) Also a great surprise for two people staying in your house. And they're going to leave quite soon.

ELSIE: That must be you and Uncle Bernard. You're the only people staying in the house, besides Dad and Mother and me.

MRS BAXLEY: (*Not pleased at this.*) Humph! Very queer. I can't imagine what surprise we'll get and anyhow we hadn't thought of leaving you yet and nothing's been said about our going. Humph! Perhaps I'm not getting it right after all.

ELSIE: Go on. Tell me some more.

MRS BAXLEY: (*Examining last lots of cards.*) You're going to travel. And quite soon.

ELSIE: (*Excitedly.*) I'm not, am I?

MRS BAXLEY: You are. It's all here. A journey. Strange beds. Crossing water. And it'll come as a great surprise. This isn't the same surprise as the other, though. That's quite different. You're going on a long journey very soon, across water.

ELSIE: It sounds too good to be true. You're not just making this up to please me, are you?

MRS BAXLEY: (*On her dignity.*) Certainly not. I never make up anything to please anybody.

ELSIE: Then it's just the cards again. They call anything a long journey, just to make it exciting. They've had me before like that. They tell you about a journey and crossing water and a strange bed and a fair woman and a dark man until you think you're in for something marvelously exciting, and then it turns out you're going to spend the night at Aunt Florrie's at Sydenham. I'll believe in this long journey when I see it. I'll bet it turns out to be like that great surprise from the medium-coloured man – just something dull about Dad.

MRS BAXLEY: (*Putting the cards together.*) Next time you'd better tell your own fortune. I've told you all I could see.

ELSIE: But you've missed the really important thing. Wasn't there anything about an engagement for me?

MRS BAXLEY: Not a sign of one.

ELSIE: (*Triumphantly.*) Well, that's where they're wrong – and it just shows you – because I'm really engaged now, and I'll be properly engaged tonight.

MRS BAXLEY: Engaged! Well, I am surprised.

ELSIE: You don't sound very pleasantly surprised, Aunt Lucy.

MRS BAXLEY: If you must know, I'm not.

ELSIE: Why?

MRS BAXLEY: Because I think you're too young to be engaged.

ELSIE: I'm not too young. I'm twenty.

MRS BAXLEY: Well, what's twenty. You're not old enough to know your own mind.

ELSIE: Yes, I am. I don't see what age has got to do with knowing your own mind. I've always been old enough to know my own mind.

MRS BAXLEY: That's what you think. Is it that young man who was here the other night?

ELSIE: Yes, Harold Russ. And I'm bringing him here to supper tonight and he's going to ask Dad.

MRS BAXLEY: Funny time to come, isn't it, when he's had all day to do it in?

ELSIE: He couldn't help it. He's been helping a friend of his to sell second-hand cars, and he had to take a man out in one of them tonight. He wants to start in the second-hand car business for himself, when he gets some capital.

MRS BAXLEY: Well, I can tell you one thing, Elsie. Your Dad doesn't like him much.

ELSIE: I know that. But then Dad doesn't really know him. And you know what Dad is. If Harold was as dull as ditchwater and lived here in Laburnum Grove or somewhere in Shooters Green, and went into the City in the morning and came home at night and pottered about in a greenhouse, Dad would think he was marvellous. But just because Harold's smart and wants to get on and once laughed at Laburnum Grove and Shooters Green – (*Enter BERNARD BAXLEY, a rather glossy, shifty fellow in his forties, always either over-confident or uneasy.*)

MRS BAXLEY: Well, I don't see anything to laugh at.

BAXLEY: Who's laughing at what?

ELSIE: I'm talking about Harold Russ, Uncle.

BAXLEY: Oh – your boy friend who was here the other night.

ELSIE: Yes. Dad doesn't like him because he once made fun of Laburnum Grove here and Shooters Green.

MRS BAXLEY: And I see nothing to laugh at. It's a very nice, respectable, refined neighbourhood.

ELSIE: That's just it. It's all so deadly dull, all slippers and greenhouses. Nothing ever happens except that the

people at Ben Machree have bought a new car or the
woman at Heather Brow is going to have a baby.

MRS BAXLEY: Well, wait until you're going to have a
baby, you'll find it exciting enough.

BAXLEY: Ah – Elsie's like me. She doesn't care for this
ultra-respectable, humdrum, suburban sort of existence.
I don't mind paying it a visit – like this – just while I'm
wondering what to do next, but I couldn't live in it.
I want life. There's no life here. What is there here for a
man who's been out East?

MRS BAXLEY: (*Emphatically.*) I can tell you what there is
for a *woman* who's been out East – three decent meals a
day and a good night's sleep.

BAXLEY: Yes, but Lucy, you never got into the life out
there.

MRS BAXLEY: Well, you didn't seem sorry to get out of it.

ELSIE: Well, I agree with Uncle Bernard. And I know
Harold does too. Oh – what time is it?

BAXLEY: Just after nine.

ELSIE: I promised to meet him at the Tube station in ten
minutes. I must fly. (*Hurries out.*)

BAXLEY: What's on?

MRS BAXLEY: She's got herself engaged to that chap, and
she's bringing him here so that he can ask George's
permission.

BAXLEY: Oh – that's it, is it?

MRS BAXLEY: Yes, and another thing. What he's after is
borrowing some money from George to set him up in
the second-hand car business.

BAXLEY: How do you know?

MRS BAXLEY: I don't know. But it's a good guess – from
something that Elsie let drop. Besides, that chap wouldn't
bother asking her father's permission if he wasn't after
something.

BAXLEY: Well, how does that affect us?

MRS BAXLEY: Did you see that man – ?

BAXLEY: Simpson? Yes. And they won't look at me unless
I can put down four hundred and fifty pounds, and they
only give me until Wednesday.

MRS BAXLEY: Then the sooner we ask for that four hundred and fifty pounds the better.

BAXLEY: Shall I do it direct through him or had you better try and work it through Dorothy?

MRS BAXLEY: Not through Dorothy.

BAXLEY: Why not? After all, she's your sister.

MRS BAXLEY: Yes, but I think she's getting a bit fed-up with us. We've been here nearly a fortnight this time, and it's the third time we've stayed with them during this last year. And she knows you've been borrowing pretty freely from George. How much have you had out of him now?

BAXLEY: Well, you know.

MRS BAXLEY: (*Grimly.*) Oh no, I don't. I only know about the amounts you've mentioned to me, that's all.

BAXLEY: Well, that's all there's been.

MRS BAXLEY: And the rest!

BAXLEY: There might be – perhaps ten bob here and there – just something and nothing.

MRS BAXLEY: Too many somethings and nothings. Dorothy may be my sister and easy-going as a rule, but I think she's had about enough. She's been rather sharp with both of us, I've noticed, these last few days. So you try George himself. He's good-natured enough for anything.

BAXLEY: So he ought to be. Nothing to worry about. Just stuck in the one business and let it keep him. Money for nothing. You've only got to look at him to see that it must be money for nothing. He doesn't know he's born.

MRS BAXLEY: He ought to be married to you for a bit and then he would.

BAXLEY: All right, all right. The point is, are we going to try him tonight?

MRS BAXLEY: We'd better try him now, before Elsie's darling Harold begins borrowing.

BAXLEY: Is Dorothy in?

MRS BAXLEY: No, she's visiting a friend of hers, Mrs Repington, and she won't be back until after supper. So now's the time.

BAXLEY: He's out there in the greenhouse, I suppose?

MRS BAXLEY: Yes, call him in.

BAXLEY: Half a minute. I haven't worked out the tactics yet. Might be a good idea to sort of take a high hand with him. After all, I've seen the world, I've been somewhere, I've done something, and he hasn't. Now suppose I –

MRS BAXLEY: Suppose you just call him in and get done with it. And if you won't, I will. (*She goes towards door at back and calls.*) George, George.

RADFERN: (*Off, at back.*) All right. Just coming.

(*He enters through the door at the back. He is a man about fifty with nothing remarkable about his appearance, though even at the first there should be a certain quiet assurance and authority visible beneath his easy manner. At this hour, he is very much the suburban householder at ease, wearing slippers and an old coat, and smoking a pipe. He is carrying two small tomatoes in one hand, and he displays these with an air of humorous triumph.*)

(*Holding out tomatoes.*) Look at these. What more do you want? All fresh.

MRS BAXLEY: Charming. They look very nice, George. Won't you sit down?

RADFERN: Beautiful tomatoes. The Special Radfern brand. Apply Ferndale Nurseries, Laburnum Grove, Shooters Green. (*Looking round.*) But I thought supper was ready.

MRS BAXLEY: No. I called you in, George, because we just wanted to have a word with you while we're by ourselves.

RADFERN: Oh – I see. Well? (*Pause.*)

MRS BAXLEY: (*Impatiently.*) Go on, Bernard.

BAXLEY: It's like this, old man. I've just seen this chap Simpson I mentioned to you the other day. Only time I could see him, because he's out of London all the week. I think I told you the other day – it's a marvellous opportunity.

RADFERN: Doesn't sound like one to me. When there isn't much business, I don't see that you're going to sell a lot of business supplies.

BAXLEY: You are with these things. I've worked all that out, old man. Trust me. But the point is this, they say I can have that agency – exclusive agency – if I put down four hundred and fifty pounds.

RADFERN: Put it down?

BAXLEY: Just put it down, that's all, old man. These people don't need the money, but their agent has to put down four hundred and fifty pounds.

RADFERN: But you haven't got four hundred and fifty pounds, have you, Bernard?

BAXLEY: Of course I haven't. I haven't been as lucky as you have, old man.

RADFERN: How do you know I've been lucky?

MRS BAXLEY: He doesn't know. That's only his silly way of talking, George. We all know you've worked hard for your money.

BAXLEY: Certainly. I never suggested you hadn't. And I know you've lent me a bit already, George.

RADFERN: (*Good-humouredly.*) About two hundred and fifty pounds, I think, Bernard.

BAXLEY: Which you'll get back, of course.

MRS BAXLEY: Of course.

BAXLEY: But what we feel is that if you'd simply let me have this four hundred and fifty to put down –

MRS BAXLEY: You see, it's a wonderful chance for Bernard.

BAXLEY: And I thought I'd come straight to you instead of going to Dorothy, even if she *is* Lucy's sister.

RADFERN: Quite right. We can keep Dorothy out of this. As a matter of fact, she doesn't know you owe me two hundred and fifty already.

MRS BAXLEY: (*Bitterly.*) And she's not the only one.

BAXLEY: Well, I don't like dragging women into these things. And I know George doesn't. Well, what about it, old man?

RADFERN: (*Musingly.*) Four hundred and fifty. You know, it's quite a bit of money, Bernard. I'll have to think about it.

BAXLEY: There isn't much time, and I don't want to lose the chance.

RADFERN: I quite understand that, old man, but four hundred and fifty on top of the two hundred and fifty you've had already is quite a lot of money –
(*He has strolled towards the back; suddenly turning.*)
Look here, ask me again after supper, and I'll give you an answer.
(*He goes out. BAXLEY and MRS BAXLEY watch him go, then look at one another, raising their eyebrows.*)

MRS BAXLEY: What do you think?

BAXLEY: That'll be all right. After supper, over a drink or two, I'll be able to touch him.

MRS BAXLEY: Yes, but what about this chap of Elsie's?

BAXLEY: He'll have gone then.

MRS BAXLEY: Listen, if they want to be alone with him *before* supper, it's better for us than if they wait.

BAXLEY: That's right. Leave 'em to it, then. After all, I got in first.

MRS BAXLEY: This sounds like them.
(*Voices heard outside. Enter ELSIE, looking very bright. She is followed by HAROLD RUSS, not bad-looking and smartly dressed, but with nothing in him. In twenty years' time he will look and behave exactly like BAXLEY.*)

ELSIE: (*Happy and excited.*) Harold, this is my Aunt Lucy and my Uncle Bernard. But you've all met before, haven't you?

MRS BAXLEY: (*Smiling very falsely.*) Yes. Last Tuesday, I think it was. What a lovely day it's been, hasn't it?

HAROLD: Yes, hasn't it? I've seen a lot of it, too. Been taking a fellow round in a car, trying to sell it to him.

BAXLEY: Any luck?

HAROLD: Shouldn't be surprised.

BAXLEY: How *is* business?

HAROLD: Not too good. How are things with you?

BAXLEY: Well, just now – I'm – er – looking round.

HAROLD: Oh – yes. I remember you telling me, the other night. Been out East, haven't you?

BAXLEY: That's right. Malay States. Singapore chiefly. Wish I'd never come back. It's a man's life out there – even yet, a man's life. Isn't it, Lucy?

MRS BAXLEY: (*Tartly.*) I don't know about a man's life. I know it isn't a woman's life.

BAXLEY: She wanted to get back, you see. And I thought I'd give the Old Country another chance.

ELSIE: I'd love to travel. So would you, wouldn't you, Harold?

HAROLD: Wouldn't mind. I knock up and down a bit, you know.

BAXLEY: And now you're going to pop the question to Dad, eh?

HAROLD: Hello, who's been telling you?

BAXLEY: (*Fatuously.*) Never mind, but we know. (*To MRS BAXLEY.*) Don't we?

MRS BAXLEY: (*With ferocious parody of him.*) Yes, we know.

BAXLEY: And if you two want us to leave you to it, just say the word.

ELSIE: All right. Thanks. But I think we'll wait a bit.

MRS BAXLEY: (*With dignity.*) If a proper opportunity presents itself –

(*RADFERN appears in doorway at back, carrying another tomato.*)

HAROLD: Good evening, Mr Radfern.

RADFERN: Oh – good evening. And there's another one (*Indicating tomatoes.*) making three. Do for supper.

ELSIE: (*To MRS BAXLEY.*) You see, auntie. That's the surprise in the fortune. What did I tell you? Dad and his three tomatoes.

RADFERN: (*Pointing to cards on table.*) Oh – you've been telling fortunes again, have you? Don't you know it's unlucky to read the cards on Sunday?

MRS BAXLEY: That's just superstition.

RADFERN: Of course it is. But then it's all superstition, isn't it, and you might as well be thoroughly superstitious while you're at it. Well, what do the cards say tonight?

MRS BAXLEY: A great surprise for Elsie. And she's going on a long journey quite soon.

HAROLD: Oh?

ELSIE: (*Smiling at him.*) Well, I wouldn't mind.

RADFERN: Anywhere but Laburnum Grove and Shooters Green, eh?

ELSIE: No, not anywhere. But somewhere exciting.

BAXLEY: I know what you want. You go –

RADFERN: (*Chiming in hastily.*) Out East. And I said it first, Bernard.

ELSIE: Everybody's so smug and settled down and dull here, and so pleased with themselves.

RADFERN: Well, why shouldn't they be pleased with themselves? They've got nice peaceful homes –

ELSIE: (*Bitterly.*) Yes, and greenhouses and wireless sets.

RADFERN: (*Good-humouredly.*) Well, what do you want us to have – elephants and tigers and a scenic railway?

ELSIE: Yes – but it's all so – so –

HAROLD: (*Loftily.*) Suburban.

ELSIE: Yes – suburban.

RADFERN: That's all right to me. When your mother and I came here, we thought we'd got somewhere. That's why we were so pleased with ourselves and ready to live a nice quiet life.

BAXLEY: That's all right for you, George. You've always led that sort of life. But give me – adventure.

MRS BAXLEY: (*Bitterly.*) Oh – and since when?

HAROLD: I know what he means. I'm just the same.

ELSIE: I am too.

RADFERN: Well, I'm not. You know, you don't get this sort of life handed to you on a plate.

ELSIE: What do you mean, Dad?

RADFERN: I mean this. Though *you* get all this handed to you on a plate – given, free, gratis, and for nothing – *I* don't. And (*Pointing outside.*) he doesn't and he doesn't.

BAXLEY: (*Staring fatuously.*) Who doesn't?

ELSIE: I don't see what you're driving at.

RADFERN: Now listen. Here's Shooters Green, one of North London's newest suburbs. Very clean, very respectable, bright as a new pin. Nice little shops in the High Street. *Yes, Madam, shall I send it? Certainly, Madam.* Tea rooms. Picture palaces. *Good morning, Mrs Robinson. Good evening, Mr Johnson.* And here's Laburnum Grove, one of its best roads, very quiet, very select, best type of semi-detached villas. Ben Machree. Craig Y Don. Mon Repos. All nations, you see. Heather Brow – though there isn't any heather for miles around. And us – Ferndale. Nice little houses. Nice people. Quiet, respectable. No scandals. No brokers' men. No screams in the night. Morris Oxfords, little greenhouses, wireless sets.

ELSIE: (*Rather bitterly.*) That's it. You know it all right, Dad.

HAROLD: Gosh – yes!

RADFERN: (*Good-humouredly.*) Yes, I know it. But you don't. You're like somebody who thinks that buns grow on trees. You don't know the world. Because all this has been handed to you on a plate, you think it's been handed to everybody else –

BAXLEY: Well, hasn't it?

RADFERN: No. There are chaps who've sweated their guts out so they could settle down here. And God knows what they've risked – some of 'em. You don't know where they've been or what they've done.

BAXLEY: (*With suggestion of contempt.*) Well, George, I hope nobody shoots you tomorrow morning on your way to the City. I haven't noticed you running many risks.

RADFERN: Oh – me. Well, of course I'm different.

BAXLEY: You've been lucky.

MRS BAXLEY: I'm sure George has always worked hard, even if he has been safe and comfortable in his own business.

ELSIE: (*Looking at her.*) Er –

MRS BAXLEY: (*Taking the hint.*) Yes. Come on, Bernard.

BAXLEY: What for? (*As she glares at him.*) Oh – yes. Certainly.

(*They both go out.*)

RADFERN: (*Staring after them.*) What's the matter with those two?

ELSIE: They're leaving us alone because they know we want to talk to you.

RADFERN: I see.

HAROLD: It's like this, Mr Radfern – Elsie and I –

ELSIE: Dad, we're engaged.

HAROLD: Well, we want to be.

RADFERN: I see. (*To ELSIE.*) Have you told your mother yet?

ELSIE: No, I'll tell her when she comes in, after supper.

HAROLD: Naturally I wanted to talk to you about it.

RADFERN: Quite so.

HAROLD: We'd like to get married very soon.

RADFERN: What on?

HAROLD: Well, that's the point. Of course I'd like to get a bit more settled first.

RADFERN: Let me see, aren't you helping a friend of yours to sell second-hand cars just now?

HAROLD: (*Loftily.*) Yes. Of course that's just while I'm looking round.

RADFERN: Ah – you're looking round, are you? Like your Uncle Bernard, Elsie. He's great on looking round.

ELSIE: (*Impatiently.*) Oh, Harold, why don't you talk to him properly. The point is, Dad, we're engaged – and Harold knows of a second-hand car business he could buy if he only had some capital.

RADFERN: Not four hundred and fifty pounds, by any chance, is it?

HAROLD: Well, it could be more and it could be a bit less. I can give you the figures.

RADFERN: (*Stopping him.*) Not just now. I asked if it was four hundred and fifty pounds because that seems to be the popular amount tonight.

(*Front door bell rings loudly.*)

ELSIE: Oh – bother! Who can that be?

RADFERN: Probably Joe Fletten. I expected him to look in this evening.

ELSIE: (*Petulantly.*) Why does he want to come here at this time? He'll be coming in the middle of the night to ask about his greenhouse soon.

RADFERN: I shouldn't be surprised. Well, just let him in.
(*ELSIE goes out.*)
It looks as if we'll have to postpone this little talk.

HAROLD: That's all right. We could talk it over after supper perhaps.

RADFERN: Yes, perhaps we could. But it seems to me I'm going to be rather busy after supper tonight. By the way, you've never thought of becoming an agent for business supplies, have you?

HAROLD: Not my line. But I do know a car when I see one. And there's a business there just waiting to be picked up –

RADFERN: If only you can put some money down. Just put it down, eh?

HAROLD: That's all it amounts to. You see –

RADFERN: (*Stopping him.*) After supper.
(*Enter ELSIE, followed by FLETTEN, a rather loud, jovial, middle-aged man, somewhat lower in the social scale than anybody we have met here so far. He carries his hat.*)

FLETTEN: Good evening, Mr Radfern.

RADFERN: Good evening, Joe. Thought you might be looking in.

FLETTEN: (*To HAROLD.*) Good evening. Seen you before here, haven't I?

HAROLD: (*Rather sulkily.*) I believe so. Good evening.

FLETTEN: Sorry to be so late, Mr Radfern. But that greenhouse of mine's giving me a lot of trouble, and I just wanted a tip or two about –

RADFERN: (*Hastily.*) About your tomato plants. Come on then, I'll show you how I manage them. (*Moves towards door at back.*)

FLETTEN: (*As he follows.*) Shan't keep you a minute.
(*Jovially to ELSIE and HAROLD.*) This greenhouse business is a terrible hobby, I give you my word. Keeps you busy all the time, all the time. (*They go out.*)

HAROLD: (*Softly, grumbling.*) I hope that chap's not going to stay for hours.

ELSIE: (*Going over to him.*) No, he won't stay long. But he's an awful old nuisance, though. Comes here two or three

times a week now, to look at Dad's greenhouse. Oh –
Harold – I hope it'll be all right.

HAROLD: Well, it ought to be. Only – I don't think your
father likes me much.

ELSIE: He will when he gets to know you better. He's just a
bit stupid, that's all.

HAROLD: And I don't know that I'm very keen on *him.*

ELSIE: Oh – Dad's all right when you know him. He's dull,
but he's rather nice, and he'll always do anything for me.
It's mother I'm frightened of. Dad's easy.

(*Door into house opens and MRS BAXLEY peeps into the
room.*)

MRS BAXLEY: Oh – all alone?

ELSIE: (*Not too pleased.*) Yes, you can come in. (*As she comes
in, leaving the door open behind her.*) Mr Fletten called and
Dad's gone back into the greenhouse with him.

MRS BAXLEY: Can't imagine what your Dad sees in that
man. Common, I call him.

HAROLD: Yes, looks like a bookie's clerk.

MRS BAXLEY: (*With dignity.*) I've never seen a bookie's
clerk. (*BAXLEY looks in.*) All right, Bernard, you needn't
stand there looking so silly. You can come in. (*He does.*) I
wonder if we could get ready for supper now.

BAXLEY: That's a good idea!

ELSIE: Yes, why not?

MRS BAXLEY: I was only thinking that if supper was here,
all ready, your father might take it into his head to ask
that Mr Fletten to stay, and we don't want that, do we?

ELSIE: Good Lord, no!

HAROLD: No, don't let's have anybody else, if we can help
it.

BAXLEY: Hear, hear!

ELSIE: But he won't stay, he never does. We can risk it.

MRS BAXLEY: Come on then, Bernard. Don't just sit there.
(*He, MRS BAXLEY and ELSIE move the table forward,
removing the small table with the cards on it, and take off the
cloths. ELSIE can go into the kitchen for something, and
BAXLEY can be putting the beer or whisky from the sideboard*

on to the table. HAROLD should stand up looking on in a rather lofty fashion.)

Why your Dad won't have a servant in the house, I can't imagine. He can well afford it.

BAXLEY: Two or three, I should think.

ELSIE: It's one of his little fads. Mother doesn't mind. She and the char do it easily – with my help.

MRS BAXLEY: (*Sarcastically.*) I'm glad you said – *with your help.*

ELSIE: It's not my fault I'm kept at home, pretending to help mother, instead of going out to work. I'd much rather go out to work.

BAXLEY: They're coming in.

(Enter RADFERN and FLETTEN. The supper table, now in the centre of the room, is being laid for five people. The meal consists of slices of ham and tongue, cold potatoes, stewed fruit and custard, bread and butter. To drink – whisky, beer and a jug of lemonade. During this period of the action, the light can be going rapidly.)

FLETTEN: (*Jovially.*) Well, well, the feast is spread.

RADFERN: Have a bite with us, Joe?

FLETTEN: (*Moving towards door into house.*) No, thank you, Mr Radfern. Must be getting along. I'll look in tomorrow night, then.

RADFERN: (*Following him.*) Do. Any time after eight.

FLETTEN: (*Turning as he reaches door, to MRS BAXLEY.*) Nice weather we're having, isn't it? I should think it is. Good night, all. Good night.

(The others murmur 'good night'. RADFERN follows him out.)

MRS BAXLEY: (*Softly but with energy.*) He made me jump – with his *nice weather!* Common, I call him.

BAXLEY: (*Quoting.*) *The feast is spread.* That's a way to talk. Anyone would think he had never seen anybody laying a supper table before.

MRS BAXLEY: Perhaps he hasn't.

BAXLEY: Never seen the world, that's his trouble.

ELSIE: Oh, he's just one of Dad's silly old men. If it wasn't for the greenhouse he wouldn't come here.

MRS BAXLEY: Well, if he's what you get when you keep greenhouses I'm glad I don't keep one.

ELSIE: (*Softly.*) Harold – remember. You must get Dad's answer tonight.

HAROLD: Yes, I know, I know.

MRS BAXLEY: And Bernard, don't forget – after supper.

BAXLEY: Leave it to me.

(*Enter RADFERN, who switches on lights at door. It is essential that the supper table should be brilliantly lit.*)

RADFERN: (*Heartily.*) Let's have some light on the subject. And plenty of it. (*Comes forward.*) Supper ready? Good! Look at those tomatoes. Home grown on the premises. They absolutely light up the table.

MRS BAXLEY: If that's how you can go on about three tomatoes, I'm glad you don't grow pineapples. I don't know what would happen then.

RADFERN: (*Looks at supper table.*) Ham, tongue, salad. Beer. Everything in its place and just what I wanted. Let's get started. Come on, everybody.

(*They seat themselves in this order: RADFERN full facing the audience, ELSIE on one side of him, MRS BAXLEY on the other, then HAROLD next to ELSIE, and BAXLEY next to MRS BAXLEY. RADFERN helps them to meat, and they help themselves to salad and potatoes, making a few conventional remarks in the bustle. But when the dialogue begins, they are all quietly attentive.*)

BAXLEY: This ham looks good, George.

RADFERN: (*Heartily.*) I expect it *is* good, Bernard. You know, I don't think there's a meal in the week I enjoy more than Sunday night supper, and I couldn't tell you why. Unless it's all so nice and peaceful.

ELSIE: (*With a touch of contempt.*) You're all for it being nice and peaceful, aren't you, Dad?

RADFERN: (*With mock humility.*) I'm afraid I am. I'm not like you folks.

MRS BAXLEY: Don't count me with them. I don't want any adventures. I want to see a regular income arriving.

HAROLD: We'd all like that.

RADFERN: (*Faintly sardonic.*) Yes, I believe you would. But it's not so easy these days.

BAXLEY: (*With loud complacency.*) It's not so easy if you're straight. That's the point. I like money as much as the next man, but it's got to be clean money.

HAROLD: (*In the same strain.*) Of course. I'm just the same. Won't touch it if it isn't straight.

MRS BAXLEY: Good gracious! I should think not.

BAXLEY: I've had chances of the other kind – packets of it –

RADFERN: (*Ironically.*) No, Bernard, have you really?

BAXLEY: I have, George. But I've always turned it down. Tainted money. Wouldn't touch it.

HAROLD: Wouldn't touch it with a barge pole. I've had my chances too – you get them in our business – but I'm the same as you – wouldn't look at queer money.

ELSIE: And I hope you never will, Harold.

HAROLD: Of course I shan't.

BAXLEY: (*Sententiously.*) It's the only thing to do, whatever happens – keep straight.

RADFERN: Well, I'm glad to hear you fellows feel like that. I used to feel like it myself in the old days.

ELSIE: What do you mean, Dad – in the old days?

RADFERN: I mean, in the days when I used to be in the wholesale paper trade.

BAXLEY: But you're still in the wholesale paper trade.

RADFERN: How do you know I am?

BAXLEY: I've always understood you were.

RADFERN: Well, I'm not. Haven't been in it for several years.

BAXLEY: But the firm's there and the office – ?

RADFERN: Oh, I keep them going, but that's just a blind. Pass the mustard, will you, Elsie.

ELSIE: But I never knew you'd changed your business.

RADFERN: No? I don't think this ham's as nice as the last. I must tell your mother about it, Elsie.

ELSIE: But listen, Dad – does Mother know you're not in the paper business any more?

RADFERN: No, she doesn't. And I don't want a word of any of this repeated to her. She's a bit old-fashioned in

41

some ways and it might give her a shock. You can ask me any questions you like, and I'll answer 'em truthfully. But not a word to her. If you can't promise that, we'll change the subject.

HAROLD / ELSIE: (*Together.*) I promise.

MRS BAXLEY: So do I.

BAXLEY: All right to me.

RADFERN: Honest to God?

(*They murmur agreement.*)

That's settled then. Not a word to her. Now what is it you'd like to know?

ELSIE: Dad, when did you leave your old business?

RADFERN: Do you remember that about four or five years ago we were very hard up?

ELSIE: Was it the year when we didn't go away for the holidays?

RADFERN: It was. We were on enough rocks without going to the seaside. We might easily have been sold up. Well, that was when I finished with the wholesale paper trade.

HAROLD: What happened?

RADFERN: Oh, I'd struggled with the business ever since I came back from the war. Slaved at it. Then the slump came. More slavery. But we had a good little connection in the fine-quality trade. And somebody wanted that, a big firm. They made me an offer. I didn't like it or the chap who made it. I turned it down, so this big firm did me in – never mind how – but they did. They won all right. Clever chap that, he's been knighted since – the dirty swine.

BAXLEY: And then – what?

RADFERN: Well, having given honesty a fair chance, I thought I'd try the other thing.

MRS BAXLEY: The *other thing?*

RADFERN: Yes.

MRS BAXLEY: You don't mean – dishonesty?

RADFERN: I do.

BAXLEY: You're pulling our legs.

RADFERN: Certainly not.

MRS BAXLEY: Then you are going to tell me you're deliberately dishonest?

RADFERN: That's what I am telling you.

ELSIE: But Dad, it's ridiculous. You're talking as if you were a crook.

RADFERN: (*Nonchalantly.*) Well, I am a crook.

MRS BAXLEY: A crook!

RADFERN: Yes, a crook. A criminal. An enemy of society. (*They all stare at him open-mouthed. ELSIE recovers first.*)

ELSIE: (*Getting up.*) Dad, you're being funny.

BAXLEY: Course he is. That'll do now, George. We've bought it.

RADFERN: (*With quiet earnestness.*) I'm perfectly serious, Bernard. This isn't a joke. Have a little more salad, Elsie?

ELSIE: (*Staring at him, faltering.*) No thanks, Dad. I – don't feel very hungry.

RADFERN: Now come along, none of that. Never let anything put you off your food – that's one of my mottoes. What do you say, Harold?

HAROLD: (*Dazed.*) Yes – Mr Radfern – I should think – that's a good idea.

MRS BAXLEY: (*Solemnly.*) George Radfern, you don't look like a crook to me.

RADFERN: Yes, but you can't judge by appearances. Why do you think Joe Fletten comes here?

MRS BAXLEY: You mean that man who comes to talk to you about greenhouses?

RADFERN: You must be innocent if you think that Joe Fletten knows anything about greenhouses. You've only got to look at him to see he's no gardener.

MRS BAXLEY: I suppose he's a crook too?

RADFERN: Of course he is. Very old hand, Joe. He works under me in the same organisation. (*To MRS BAXLEY.*) Have a little more tongue?

MRS BAXLEY: (*Faintly.*) I can't eat what I've got.

ELSIE: Dad, do you really mean all this?

RADFERN: Of course I mean it. Every penny that's come into this house for the last few years has been dishonestly earned.

43

BAXLEY: My God!

RADFERN: (*Coolly.*) Tainted money. You've eaten it and drunk it and it's clothed you and housed you and taken you to the pictures and sent you to the seaside. If I'd gone on trying to make an honest living, I don't know where you'd have been now, Elsie. As it is, look at us. So nicely off that Harold here – and your Uncle Bernard here – are both hoping I'll lend them several hundred pounds each, on very doubtful security.

HAROLD: Here, I say –

ELSIE: But Dad, what do you do?

MRS BAXLEY: Do you *burgle* places?

RADFERN: Burgle places! Certainly not. Do I look as if I burgled places?

MRS BAXLEY: No, you don't. But then you don't look like a crook at all to me.

ELSIE: (*Appealingly.*) You're not. Are you, Dad?

RADFERN: I've told you – I am. And one slip – just one slip, that's all – and I'd be for it.

MRS BAXLEY: (*Awed.*) Prison!

RADFERN: Yes, and a good long spell of it too.

ELSIE: (*Looking at him in awe and terror.*) Dad!

BAXLEY: But look here, George, what do you do?

RADFERN: Well, you might describe it as a private policy of inflation.

ELSIE: I don't know what that means.

MRS BAXLEY: Neither do I.

ELSIE: Do you, Harold?

RADFERN: I'm ready for a little of that stewed fruit now, Elsie. Let's put these plates on the side. (*Makes a move.*)

ELSIE: (*Hastily.*) No, let me do it, Dad.

MRS BAXLEY: Stewed fruit!

RADFERN: That's it, stewed fruit. What about it?

MRS BAXLEY: This is no time for stewed fruit.

RADFERN: Yes, of course it is. When do you want it?

BAXLEY: She doesn't mean that, old man. As a matter of fact, she's very fond of stewed fruit.

RADFERN: Good, and mind you, this is real garden rhubarb.

MRS BAXLEY: I don't want garden rhubarb – I want the truth.

RADFERN: All right, Lucy, you shall have the truth, and garden rhubarb and custard too, if you like it.

MRS BAXLEY: Custard!

(*ELSIE puts the used plates on the sideboard and then begins serving the fruit and custard.*)

BAXLEY: But what about this inflation business?

RADFERN: Ah, that. Well, a lot of people think this depression in trade is chiefly due to the fact that there isn't enough money in circulation. Like playing a game with counters and finding you haven't got enough counters to go round. Our organisation – my associates and myself – have been quietly busy these last few years trying to remedy this unhappy state of things. It started in America – forging and counterfeiting bonds and notes – and then developed here, but just lately the American end has been doing badly, almost stopped. But we're doing quite nicely here, and sometimes I think that things in England would have been worse if it hadn't been for us. In fact you might say we've been doing our bit.

BAXLEY: (*Dazed.*) Forging and counterfeiting bonds and notes!

HAROLD: (*Awed.*) My hat!

RADFERN: (*Blandly.*) Very interesting work. It begins as an art and ends as a profitable business.

ELSIE: But is it – serious?

HAROLD: Is it *serious!*

RADFERN: One of the most serious crimes in the calendar, Elsie. You see, the banks don't like it, and what the banks don't like must be a serious crime nowadays, like blasphemy in the middle ages.

ELSIE: And you're mixed up in it?

RADFERN: I'm engaged in it, not mixed up in it. I was able to join the organisation at first because I happened to have a supply of the right sort of paper. Since then I've been on the staff. My job now is distribution. That's what takes me away, of course. I'm off to Birmingham early tomorrow morning.

MRS BAXLEY: What, you're going to Birmingham on this crooked work?

RADFERN: Why not? If I can do it in London, I can do it in Birmingham. There's nothing peculiarly sacred about Birmingham, is there?

ELSIE: But are the police really after you?

BAXLEY: Don't be silly, Elsie. They must be. It's a terribly serious crime, forging bonds and counterfeiting notes.

RADFERN: (*Calmly.*) I should think we've given Scotland Yard it's biggest and most worrying case for years. After us! They're after us. Detectives, police, bank officials, magistrates, judges, the Treasury, the Army, the Navy, the Air Force. We haven't even the League of Nations on our side.

BAXLEY: But I don't see how you've managed to go on so long without being found out.

RADFERN: Partly luck, partly good management. Of course you can't really tell what's happening on the other side. They may have got the net out, and it may be closing in on us now.

(*Telephone bell rings, very sharp and loud.*)

ELSIE: (*With a little scream.*) Oh – what's that?

(*She rises, MRS BAXLEY half rises, and HAROLD pushes his chair back.*)

RADFERN: (*Coolly.*) That's the telephone. I'll answer it. Have you got a bit of cheese there for me? (*Goes to telephone.*) Hello! No... I'm not... Well, I can't help it. You've got the wrong number. (*Comes back from telephone.*) Wants to know if I'm the North London Dogs Hospital.

ELSIE: Oh – it gave me such a fright.

RADFERN: Well, I'm sorry, but after all you wanted a bit of excitement, didn't you?

BAXLEY: (*Solemnly.*) George, that might have been somebody who was after you, tracking you down.

HAROLD: Yes, it might.

RADFERN: And then again, it might not. If tracking people down consists of ringing them up and asking if

they're the Dogs Hospital, we could all be Sherlock
Holmeses.

ELSIE: (*Eagerly.*) And after all, I don't suppose they'd think
of looking for crooks of any kind in a place like
Shooters Green.

RADFERN: Oh – yes, they would. They haven't your
ideas, Elsie. People who break the law have got to live
somewhere, and why not in Shooters Green and
Laburnum Grove? They took away that solicitor who
used to live at Stella Maris and gave him a couple of
years. That was a stan. Probably there are one or two
more of us in Laburnum Grove who'll have to go yet.
(*HAROLD pushes his chair well back and rises.*)
Hello, what's the matter?

HAROLD: (*Muttering.*) I must be going.

ELSIE: (*Disappointed.*) Harold!

HAROLD: I'm sorry but I must be going.

RADFERN: (*Smoothly.*) What about that little talk we were
going to have? Another time, eh?

ELSIE: (*Moving round to him.*) But, Harold, you can't go like
this.

HAROLD: (*Muttering.*) I'm sorry, but it's getting late and
I'm feeling very tired –
(*He moves towards the door. ELSIE intercepts him, and puts a
hand on his arm.*)

ELSIE: Oh – but Harold.

HAROLD: (*Releasing himself and suddenly raising his voice in a
rather hysterical manner.*) Leave me alone. I tell you I've
got to go. Goodnight.
(*He hurries out and she follows him. The other three watch
them, and then stare at the door. After a moment the outer
door is heard to bang. Then ELSIE, looking tearful, opens
the door and stands in the doorway.*)

MRS BAXLEY: Has he gone?

ELSIE: (*Tearfully.*) Yes. And I'm going to bed. Good night.

RADFERN: (*Gravely.*) Listen, Elsie –

ELSIE: (*Shaking her head.*) No, no more now. I can't, Dad.
Good night.
(*She closes the door and vanishes.*)

RADFERN: (*Looking after her, gravely.*) Poor kid, I'm afraid she's got more than she bargained for.

MRS BAXLEY: (*Tartly.*) We've all got more than we bargained for, if you ask me. Even the great adventurer, Bernard here.

BAXLEY: (*Dazed, staring at RADFERN.*) Look here, George, for God's sake tell us the truth now.

RADFERN: (*Impressively.*) I'm telling you the truth. I've not been in the wholesale paper trade for the last four years. All this (*Waves his hand.*) comes out of the proceeds of illegal and criminal actions. Tainted money, Bernard. And you've been enjoying it for some time, and I believe you'd like a good slice more of it, wouldn't you? Tainted money. Ill-gotten gains. And mind you're not an accessory.

BAXLEY: (*Frightened.*) I'll see to that.

MRS BAXLEY: This is upsetting my stomach. Why, every time I see a policeman now, I'll be frightened out of my life.

RADFERN: Oh – forget about it.

MRS BAXLEY: (*Scornfully.*) Forget about it!
(*There is a sharp ring at the front door bell.*)
What's that?

RADFERN: (*Coolly.*) I can tell you what that is. That's Dorothy and she's forgotten her front door key again. Now don't forget. Not a word to her.

BAXLEY: (*Moving towards door.*) Here, I'm off upstairs.

MRS BAXLEY: So am I. I couldn't face her tonight.

BAXLEY: Let's get out of the way first.

RADFERN: (*Almost pushing them in front of him.*) Go on then, hurry up.
(*They hurry out and he follows, stopping to light his pipe. Then he goes out and re-enters with MRS RADFERN, a pleasant-looking woman in her early forties.*)

MRS RADFERN: (*Staring.*) Hello, where is everybody?

RADFERN: I think Elsie had a bit of a tiff with that young man of hers, and went to bed early to have a little cry about it.

MISS RADFERN: Do you think I ought to go up?

RADFERN: No, leave her alone. She'll be all right.

MRS RADFERN: Well, where are Bernard and Lucy?

RADFERN: They've just gone to bed.

MRS RADFERN: They went early.

RADFERN: (*Very innocently.*) Yes, I think they must have wanted to have a talk about something.

MRS RADFERN: (*Taking her things off.*) Well, I must say, Dad – though Lucy is my own sister – I wouldn't be heart-broken if they'd gone upstairs to talk about leaving us. And I know you wouldn't be.

RADFERN: No, I'd get over it. (*Begins putting supper things together.*) Here, I'll give you a hand with these.

MRS RADFERN: No, you sit down and smoke your pipe in peace, Dad. You've got to get up early in the morning to get yourself off, haven't you?

RADFERN: Yes. Early train to Birmingham.

MRS RADFERN: Well, then. (*She begins bustling about with things, but stops to add affectionately.*) You know, Dad, I sometimes think you're a bit too quiet and easy-going, but – dear me ! – Mrs Repington's been letting drop one or two things about *her* husband – and I was thinking on the way back I ought to be thankful I've got a nice honest, sleepy old thing like you.

RADFERN: (*Giving her a pat on the shoulder.*) Ah – now you're talking!

The curtain falls on them as they clear the table.

End of Act One.

ACT TWO

Scene 1

Scene is the same as in Act One. Early next morning. The room has that very early morning look about it. ELSIE, not yet properly dressed, is discovered bringing in the milk. Then after a few moments BAXLEY enters. He is wearing an old dressing gown and looks dishevelled and still sleepy.

BAXLEY: (*Yawning.*) Morning.

ELSIE: Morning, uncle.

BAXLEY: Thought I heard somebody moving about down here.

ELSIE: It must have been me.

BAXLEY: Of course it was you. But you're usually the last downstairs and not the first. What made you get up so early?

ELSIE: I couldn't sleep. And why are you up, Uncle?

BAXLEY: Well, I couldn't sleep either. And I suddenly remembered your Dad was going to Birmingham early this morning.

ELSIE: I know. I thought I'd get up and make his breakfast.

BAXLEY: That's a new idea, isn't it?

ELSIE: Yes. But the woman we have is away – ill. So I thought I'd get up and do it.

BAXLEY: Quite right, quite right. But, you know, if he were out East, a man like your Dad could have twenty servants – thirty servants. Waited on hand and foot.

ELSIE: I know.

BAXLEY: Hand and foot.

ELSIE: He could be here, if he wanted to.

BAXLEY: I dare say, but you see now why he won't have a servant living in the house, don't you? You see?

ELSIE: Yes.

BAXLEY: He's too clever for that, much too clever. He knows what he's doing. Those his boots?

50

ELSIE: Yes.

BAXLEY: They could do with a bit of a rub.

ELSIE: I was going to do them.

BAXLEY: No, no, I'll give 'em a rub. It'll pass the time. Get me the polishing outfit, will you, Elsie.

(*Sits down with boots, yawning, while ELSIE brings him the polishing outfit.*)

Thanks. Now I'll make a good job of these. It'll amuse your Dad. What are you giving him for breakfast?

ELSIE: Boiled eggs. They're easiest.

BAXLEY: How does he like his eggs boiled?

ELSIE: I can't remember.

BAXLEY: (*Reproachfully.*) You ought to remember how your own Dad likes his eggs boiled.

ELSIE: Do you remember how *your* Dad liked his eggs boiled?

BAXLEY: Don't be silly, Elsie, that's quite different. You're a girl. And, besides, it's such a long time since I lived with my old governor.

ELSIE: What did your Dad do, Uncle?

BAXLEY: He used to travel the North Midlands – from Wolverhampton to Stockport – for the Wesleyan Methodist Publishing Company, selling hymn-books and Sunday school prizes. He had to look religious all the time, so he always dressed in black, and he wore a chin beard, like a Mormon. And he didn't smoke, and he didn't drink, so he used to eat a lot of cough candy. Bags of it. Absolutely stank of cough candy. I can smell it now. (*He sniffs.*) A sort of mixture of treacle and fire-lighters.

ELSIE: Was he nice?

BAXLEY: No, he was hellishly dull.

ELSIE: (*Plaintively.*) I thought my Dad was dull. And I wish he was now.

BAXLEY: Well, he isn't.

ELSIE: I know. Uncle, do you think it's really true – what Dad told us last night?

BAXLEY: Yes. Must be.

ELSIE: But Dad! Just think of it!

BAXLEY: (*Irritably.*) It's no good telling me to think of it, Elsie. I've been thinking about it – and talking about it – half the night.

ELSIE: I've hardly slept a wink.

BAXLEY: I'm not surprised.

ELSIE: I got so frightened in the middle of the night.

BAXLEY: Well, if you ask me, you've got something to be frightened about.

ELSIE: (*In tense whisper.*) Listen, Uncle – if they caught him, would he really be sent to prison?

BAXLEY: I should think he would. He'd get years and years. Penal servitude.

ELSIE: But he's never done anything before.

BAXLEY: What difference does that make, when he's been doing this all the time. This is a big job. They'd drop on him like a ton of bricks.

ELSIE: (*Awed.*) Would they?

BAXLEY: (*With gloomy pride.*) Go for him tooth and nail. Yes, tooth and nail. Like a ton of bricks. Penal servitude for years and years – and years.

ELSIE: But, Uncle – it's awful.

BAXLEY: (*Solemnly beginning on other boot.*) Well, speaking as a man of the world who's *seen* the world – I call that a well-polished boot! It's pretty serious – pretty serious.

ELSIE: And they've only got to catch him.

BAXLEY: Just got to lay their hands on him, once, that's all. (*ELSIE stares at him in horror. MRS BAXLEY enters, half dressed and looking very worn. ELSIE gives a tiny scream and whirls round.*)

ELSIE: Oh – Auntie – you made me jump.

MRS BAXLEY: I dare say. Anything's enough to make anybody jump, in this house. What are you up so early for?

ELSIE: I'm getting Dad's breakfast ready.

MRS BAXLEY: Well, I thought I'd just come down to see if I could do anything for him. And what are you doing, Bernard?

BAXLEY: (*Very off-handedly.*) Oh – just giving George's boots a bit of a rub.

MRS BAXLEY: Be careful – or you might be cleaning my boots next. Is the tea made yet? – Because I must say I could do with a cup. (*Sits down wearily.*) What a night!

BAXLEY: (*Irritably.*) We know, we know.

MRS BAXLEY: She doesn't know, does she? (*To ELSIE.*) I haven't had such a night for years. Talked and talked about it all, then thought and thought about it all, and then when I did get a bit of sleep, I had to dream about policemen, hundreds of policemen.

ELSIE: (*Distressed.*) Oh – don't!

BAXLEY: No. What do you want to start that for, first thing in the morning?

MRS BAXLEY: Start what?

BAXLEY: Talking about policemen.

MRS BAXLEY: Well, they still exist, don't they? And I know I shan't be able to look a policeman in the face.

BAXLEY: Well, why do you want to look a policeman in the face?

MRS BAXLEY: Oh – don't you begin again. You said enough last night.

BAXLEY: Yes, when I could get a word in edgewise.

MRS BAXLEY: It was two o'clock when I asked you to stop talking.

BAXLEY: Yes, and it was half-past two when you began again.

ELSIE: (*Who has gone to door into house and closed it.*) Now listen – you're not to tell anybody.

BAXLEY: Not likely!

MRS BAXLEY: (*Indignantly.*) As if we should! It's bad enough knowing about it without telling anybody.

ELSIE: But not even mother. Don't forget.

MRS BAXLEY: You're not going to tell me that all this has been going on all this time and your mother doesn't know anything about it?

ELSIE: I'm sure she doesn't know anything about it.

MRS BAXLEY: Well, I can't understand why. She's my own sister, and she never seemed to me to miss much. And if she doesn't know, she ought to. If your uncle here had been up to any queer game like that, I'd have known all about it.

BAXLEY: You might – and then again you might not.

MRS BAXLEY: What's that?

BAXLEY: I said you might – and then again you might not.

MRS BAXLEY: Oh – and what's your funny game been then?

BAXLEY: I didn't say there'd been any funny game. I only said – if there had been, you might know – and then again –

MRS BAXLEY: I might not. I heard you. Well, there isn't any might about it. I'd have known. And I don't see how George has kept it from Dorothy all this time.

BAXLEY: (*With gloomy pride.*) Ah – that's where he's been so clever, keeping it from her and from us and from everybody. That's where his cleverness comes in.

ELSIE: Yes, I suppose he must have been terribly clever all the time. And I never thought he was.

BAXLEY: Ah – I've always had my own ideas about him.

MRS BAXLEY: Well, his being clever was never one of them.

BAXLEY: Oh, yes, it was. I've had my suspicions for some time.

MRS BAXLEY: That's news to me.

ELSIE: The kettle! (*She hurries into the kitchen.*)

BAXLEY: He's got a lot of brains, George has.

MRS BAXLEY: Oh?

BAXLEY: Yes. Some of the things he's said to me showed that. He didn't bother saying them to you.

MRS BAXLEY: I see.

BAXLEY: Good.

MRS BAXLEY: Well, it isn't good. And let me tell you he never struck me as being clever.

BAXLEY: Yes, but what do you know about it?

MRS BAXLEY: I know this about it, that he'd have been cleverer if he'd kept all this to himself. It's bad enough telling us, but he went and told that young fellow of Elsie's. Is that clever?

BAXLEY: Yes, if he wanted to get rid of him. And I believe that's what he was after.

MRS BAXLEY: Yes, and where's that young fellow – Harold – now?

BAXLEY: In bed, if he's any sense.

MRS BAXLEY: You know what I mean. What's to prevent him going to the police and telling them?

BAXLEY: We had that out last night.

MRS BAXLEY: Well, let's have it out again this morning.

BAXLEY: I tell you, he's got no real evidence, and if he went to the police, they'd laugh at him. Besides, he wouldn't go. Would you?

MRS BAXLEY: Me! Don't be silly. I don't want to see a policeman for weeks.

(*ELSIE returns with the teapot, which she places on the table.*)

ELSIE: I know he likes his tea strong, anyhow.

MRS BAXLEY: (*Sniffing round the pot.*) That's a good thing, because by the time he comes down it'll have stewed itself as black as ink. I like my tea fresh.

ELSIE: You shall have a cup in a minute, Auntie. I expect Dad will be down soon. And now I know he's so clever, I wish I didn't. I wish now I hadn't said he was dull and stupid. I wish he *was* dull and stupid again.

BAXLEY: How could he be dull again if he never was?

ELSIE: (*Distressed.*) You know what I mean.

MRS BAXLEY: Oh, don't bother with your uncle. He doesn't know what anybody means this morning.

ELSIE: I believe I started it last night by saying this was a dull and stupid place where nothing happened.

MRS BAXLEY: I dare say you did – you and your young man between you.

BAXLEY: Don't be so silly. How could they start it when it's been going on for years?

MRS BAXLEY: It was all in the cards.

BAXLEY: If it was all in the cards, why didn't you tell us then?

MRS BAXLEY: Elsie, didn't I say your Dad was going to give us a big surprise?

BAXLEY: Well, what's the good of telling us we're going to get a big surprise, if you don't say what the surprise is?

MRS BAXLEY: If I knew what it was, it wouldn't be a surprise, would it – cleverhead?

ELSIE: The point is, if I hadn't started talking like that, last night, we shouldn't have known all about this, and it's knowing about it that's so awful. I can't help thinking about it all the time.

MRS BAXLEY: Same with me, just the same.

ELSIE: Besides, there's – Harold.

MRS BAXLEY: Ah, yes. How's he going to take it?

BAXLEY: You saw how he took it last night. (*In loud complacent tone.*) You've got to look at it this way.

ELSIE: He's coming down.

MRS BAXLEY: Shut up. He's here.

(*They all three of them are instantly expectant, rigid, like soldiers awaiting a general. RADFERN enters, a bustling genial figure, fully dressed except that he is wearing slippers.*)

RADFERN: Good morning. Hello, what's all this? Three of you up?

BAXLEY: (*Respectfully.*) Good morning, George.

RADFERN: (*Dryly.*) Good morning, Bernard. I trust I see you well. And you, Lucy. Morning, Elsie.

ELSIE: Good morning, Dad.

MRS BAXLEY: (*Gloomily.*) How did you sleep last night, George?

RADFERN: (*Heartily.*) How did I sleep? I slept like a top. I always do. Don't you?

MRS BAXLEY: (*Reproachfully.*) I didn't last night. None of us did.

RADFERN: Oh? Well, why have you all got up so early?

ELSIE: I thought I'd get your breakfast ready, Dad.

RADFERN: Very kind of you, Elsie, very kind of you. And – er – (*Looks quizzically at the other two.*) – ?

BAXLEY: Well, old man, I thought I'd just look down and see if there was anything I could do. Like to make myself useful at times, y'know. Knew you were going off early.

RADFERN: Aren't those my boots?

BAXLEY: (*Off-handedly.*) Yes. Matter of fact I've just been giving them a bit of a rub.

RADFERN: (*Looking at them.*) You've given them a very good rub, Bernard. Thank you. And what about you, Lucy?

MRS BAXLEY: (*Rather defiantly.*) Oh – you needn't thank me. I came down because I couldn't sleep and I wanted a cup of tea.

RADFERN: Quite right. And have you had a cup of tea?

MRS BAXLEY: No.

RADFERN: Then give your Aunt Lucy a cup of tea – quick, Elsie.
(*As ELSIE does this, RADFERN sits down and looks quizzically from one to the other of them.*)
Well, well, well. My boots. Tea all ready. I call this being waited on hand and foot. This is as good as being out East, Bernard.

BAXLEY: Oh no. I was just saying, George, that a man like you – out East – would have twenty or thirty servants.

RADFERN: I wouldn't know what to do with them.

ELSIE: Dad, how do you like your eggs boiling?

RADFERN: I haven't touched a boiled egg for the last two years, Elsie. Don't agree with me.

ELSIE: (*Self-reproachfully.*) Shows how much I've been noticing things, doesn't it?

RADFERN: (*Affectionately, embracing her.*) Never mind.

ELSIE: What will you have for breakfast then, Dad?

BAXLEY: Want a good breakfast if you're travelling, George.

RADFERN: Oh – I always breakfast on the train. Helps to pass the time.

ELSIE: Oh – but I've made the tea.

RADFERN: That's all right. I've time for a cup of tea. Very nice.

MRS BAXLEY: Where is it you're going, George?

RADFERN: (*Cheerfully.*) I'm going to Birmingham for the day – on business.

MRS BAXLEY: (*Bitterly.*) Business!

RADFERN: That's what I said – business. You don't think I'd go to Birmingham for pleasure, do you?

MRS BAXLEY: (*Still bitter.*) Yes – but there's business *and* business.

RADFERN: (*Genially, but with point.*) You mean – there's your own business – and other people's business?

MRS BAXLEY: No, I don't.

ELSIE: (*Reproachfully.*) You know what she means, Dad.

RADFERN: (*Echoing MRS BAXLEY.*) No, I don't.

BAXLEY: The queer work, that's what she means.

ELSIE: Yes – you know – crook stuff.

RADFERN: Crook stuff! Crook stuff! What a way to talk, especially early on Monday morning. Crook stuff.

MRS BAXLEY: Well, what do you call it then?

RADFERN: Business. Not crook stuff! This comes of going so often to the pictures. What would they think if they heard you at Ben Machree?

ELSIE: (*Earnestly.*) But, Dad, you told us last night.

RADFERN: Oh – so I told you last night, did I?

BAXLEY: You know very well you spilt it all last night, George. Can't get out of it now. We know.

ELSIE: And I was awake all night thinking about it. And so were Uncle Bernard and Aunt Lucy.

BAXLEY: No, not all night.

MRS BAXLEY: Well, you never stopped talking all night. I suppose you must have been talking in your sleep.

BAXLEY: And I suppose you must have been listening in your sleep.

RADFERN: Just a minute. Here's a very good rule, if you want to have a nice quiet comfortable existence.

MRS BAXLEY: (*Bitterly.*) Like you, I suppose, George?

RADFERN: Yes, like me. It's a rule I've just invented, but never mind about that. Somebody's got to invent the rules some time.

BAXLEY: Quite right, old man.

RADFERN: The rule's this. Never think or talk on Monday morning about something that's been said on Sunday night.

ELSIE: (*Half laughing, half tearful.*) Oh, Dad – that's silly.

RADFERN: No, it isn't. On Monday morning you must start with a clean slate, because you're beginning a new week.

MRS BAXLEY: (*Bitterly.*) Did you say – a clean slate?

RADFERN: That's what I said.

MRS BAXLEY: (*Angrily.*) Well, how you can talk like that, George Radfern, after all the things you told us last night and with the police perhaps ready to march in here any minute and take us all off –

(*A thundering knock outside. She stops and gives a little scream.*)

What's that?

RADFERN: (*Coolly.*) The postman.

ELSIE: (*Hastily.*) I'll go.

(*She hurries out. RADFERN lights his pipe.*)

RADFERN: (*Looking at watch.*) How's the time? Oh – I'm all right. (*Begins putting on his boots.*)

BAXLEY: Is there anything I can do for you, George?

RADFERN: (*Respectfully.*) No, I don't think so, thank you, Bernard. You've done enough. Look at these boots. You mustn't spoil me just because I don't make an honest living.

(*ELSIE returns with three letters, two of which she places on the table.*)

ELSIE: Two for you, Dad. This is mine.

BAXLEY: Nothing for us then?

MRS BAXLEY: Well, what should there be for us?

BAXLEY: Oh, I dunno. I thought one of the chaps might have written.

MRS BAXLEY: What chaps?

BAXLEY: Well – the chaps.

MRS BAXLEY: I heard you.

BAXLEY: All right then, if you heard me, shut up.

(*ELSIE opens her letter and reads it eagerly, then gives a sharp cry of dismay.*)

RADFERN: What is it?

ELSIE: (*In distress.*) It's from Harold. He says he won't – oh, it's all over.

RADFERN: (*Going to her.*) Never mind, Elsie.

ELSIE: (*Tearful.*) Oh – but you don't understand –

RADFERN: (*Softly.*) Listen, Elsie. Honestly, he's not worth bothering about –

ELSIE: (*Tearful and angry, cutting in.*) It's all your fault. You've done it. Oh!

(*She bursts into tears, pushes RADFERN away and hurries towards door into house. Before she gets there MRS RADFERN appears in doorway.*)

MRS RADFERN: (*Astonished.*) What's the matter?

ELSIE: (*In tears.*) Everything.

(*ELSIE pushes past and goes out. MRS RADFERN stares after her for a moment, then stares at the other three.*)

MRS RADFERN: Now will anybody tell me what's happening in this house? Elsie up early. You two up. Elsie crying. What in the name of wonder is it all about?

RADFERN: Leave Elsie alone, Mother. It's that blathering, weak-kneed, spineless young man of hers, Harold.

MRS RADFERN: What's he done?

RADFERN: She's just had a letter from him. They've had some sort of quarrel. And he's just broken it off.

MRS RADFERN: So that's it. I'd like to say something to that young man. Doesn't know his own mind.

BAXLEY: Hasn't got one. Spotted it in a minute.

MRS RADFERN: What does he want to make her miserable like that for? Who's he – I'd like to know – to be going on shilly-shallying and quarrelling –

RADFERN: He's not worth it.

BAXLEY: Of course he isn't. I could have told you that.

MRS BAXLEY: Pity you don't tell us all the things you know.

RADFERN: Listen, Mother. Don't say anything to her. Leave her alone.

MRS RADFERN: Well, that's all right, but I don't want her crying her eyes out all day –

RADFERN: Couldn't you take her out, for the day. Down into town – shopping – or something – ?

MRS RADFERN: I don't see how I can today, Dad. I've a lot to do, and I promised Mrs Repington I'd go to the servants' registry for her this morning.

RADFERN: Well, you're not doing anything this morning, are you, Lucy?

MRS BAXLEY: (*Bitterly.*) No, just enjoying myself, that's all.

RADFERN: Well, enjoy yourself a bit more, and you and Bernard take Elsie into the West End. Look at the shops. Go to the pictures.

MRS BAXLEY: And see one of these crook films, I suppose?

RADFERN: (*Heartily.*) That's it. Find a good crook film. Be a nice change after this dull suburb. Here. (*Takes two pound notes out of his pocket book.*) Take these and help her to spend them.

MRS BAXLEY: (*Taking the notes but looking at them dubiously.*) All right – I suppose...?

RADFERN: Go on – they won't bite you.

MRS RADFERN: But it's too much, Dad.

RADFERN: Oh – let her spend it.

MRS BAXLEY: (*Bitterly.*) Plenty more where these come from, I expect.

MRS RADFERN: Well, that's a nice way to talk, Lucy.

MRS BAXLEY: (*Grimly.*) I beg your pardon.

MRS RADFERN: You'll go and make Elsie worse. I'm sure she doesn't know the value of money as it is. The way she talks sometimes, you'd think all you have to do is to pick money up in parcels.

MRS BAXLEY: (*Grimly.*) Indeed!

RADFERN: Good idea that. Money in parcels. What do you say, Bernard?

BAXLEY: (*Embarrassed.*) Er – yes – quite. (*Laughs falsely.*)

RADFERN: Better than looking round, eh? Wish I knew where to pick some up.

MRS BAXLEY: You ought to try Birmingham.

RADFERN: I think I will. Time to be off too. If anybody wants me, you can say I'll be back about eight. Joe Fletten may call round. If he does, ask him to wait.

MRS RADFERN: What, Joe Fletten again! He'll never be out of the house soon.

MRS BAXLEY: No, these greenhouses do seem to give a lot of trouble, don't they?

RADFERN: You're right, Lucy, they do. Well, have a good day. And keep Elsie quiet. Must go and earn an honest penny now.

MRS BAXLEY: (*In a deep disapproving tone.*) A what?

RADFERN: I said an honest penny. Bye-bye.
(*Gives BAXLEY and MRS BAXLEY a quizzical grin, kisses MRS RADFERN and then briskly departs.*)

MRS RADFERN: I don't know what brought you down so early this morning, Lucy, but you seem to have got out of the wrong side of the bed.

MRS BAXLEY: (*Bristling.*) Oh – and why?

BAXLEY: You know why, Lucy.

MRS BAXLEY: (*Severely.*) And you be quiet. (*To MRS RADFERN.*) May I ask what's the matter with you?

MRS RADFERN: Well, George gives you two pounds to take Elsie out with – and if you ask me, it's a lot too much – and then you go and stare at him and at the money, without a word of thanks, as if – as if –

MRS BAXLEY: As if what?

MRS RADFERN: I don't know. As if he'd stolen it or something instead of having worked hard for years for it.

MRS BAXLEY: I suppose he *has* worked hard for years for it?

MRS RADFERN: (*Indignantly.*) Of course he has. I've told you so many times.

MRS BAXLEY: Yes, but sometimes I think he looks a bit too pleased with himself to be a man who's worked hard for years.

MRS RADFERN: Indeed! But you see *some* men don't mind working hard.

MRS BAXLEY: That's one at you, Bernard. I'll leave you with it. (*She makes a move.*)

MRS RADFERN: You can first explain what's the matter with you.

MRS BAXLEY: (*With cold dignity.*) Perhaps I can get into the bathroom now. (*She stalks out.*)

MRS RADFERN: Now what is the matter with her? She's very queer this morning.

BAXLEY: (*Uneasily.*) Oh – she didn't sleep so well last night.

MRS RADFERN: (*Significantly.*) Perhaps she could do with a change.

BAXLEY: Oh – no. Bit too much noise perhaps and not enough air.

MRS RADFERN: (*With hostility.*) There's plenty of air in this house.

BAXLEY: (*Hastily.*) Yes, but it all depends on what you're used to. Now when we were out in Singapore –

MRS RADFERN: (*Coldly.*) Just a minute, Bernard. You had a great time in Singapore, didn't you?

BAXLEY: Oh – yes, a great time, a great time.

MRS RADFERN: Well, there's one thing you seem to forget about Singapore.

BAXLEY: Oh no, never forget anything about Singapore.

MRS RADFERN: No, there's one thing you forget about it.

BAXLEY: What's that?

MRS RADFERN: You forget that it's still there, waiting for you. (*She marches towards kitchen.*)

BAXLEY: (*Puzzled.*) Eh?

(*By the time it dawns on him, she has disappeared into the kitchen, and the curtain is rapidly falling.*)

Scene 2

Scene is the same as Act One. Late afternoon.

When the curtain rises, the room is empty. On the centre table there is a book, 'The Great Bank Mystery', and a work basket. MRS RADFERN enters and begins looking in the work basket for things, finally produces some work and sits down with it. The front door bell rings, and she goes out to open the door, and the sound of her voice and her visitor's can be heard a moment later. She returns, followed by INSPECTOR STACK, a plain-clothes officer, a smart-looking fellow about forty with an assured authoritative manner. MRS RADFERN likes the look of him.

STACK: Only for the day, eh?

MRS RADFERN: Yes. Won't you sit down?

STACK: Thank you.

(*They both sit.*)

MRS RADFERN: (*Chattily.*) Yes, he's gone to Birmingham on business, just for the day. He often goes there.

STACK: I see. Do you happen to know what time he'll be back tonight?

MRS RADFERN: He said about eight o'clock.

STACK: Then if I called some time after eight, I'd catch him in.

MRS RADFERN: Sure to. I don't think he'll be going out again. It'll be either the greenhouse or the wireless for him tonight.

STACK: (*Respectfully.*) Very wise of him too, Mrs Radfern. I wish they'd let me have more nice quiet evenings at home like that.

MRS RADFERN: (*Enjoying the little chat.*) Oh – my husband's always been quite a home bird, you know. His business takes him out, of course, and sometimes away too, but the minute he's back, all he wants are his slippers and his pipe, and a book or his greenhouse or the wireless.

STACK: Let me see, he's in the paper trade, isn't he?

MRS RADFERN: Yes, the wholesale paper trade, not newspapers, you know, but paper for printing and writing on, and chiefly very fine-quality papers.

STACK: (*Blandly.*) Good enough for – what shall we say? – bank notes, eh?

MRS RADFERN: I dare say, but I don't know exactly. But I do know it's wholesale paper he's in, and always has been.

STACK: Got an office and a warehouse somewhere in the city, I suppose?

MRS RADFERN: Oh yes. It's just off Cloth Fair, you know, by Smithfield, I remember the only time I went there, it was a very warm day and you could smell the meat in Smithfield Market – horrid it was.

STACK: I know. Never cared for that smell myself. Puts you off your beefsteaks. And he's been able to keep going all right, through all these bad times?

MRS RADFERN: Yes, I'm sure we can't grumble. He got a bit down four or five years ago – like a lot of other people, you know – no fault of theirs at all –

STACK: (*Sympathetically.*) Quite. Just the hard times.

MRS RADFERN: That's it. But, however, he's picked up again wonderfully since then. I'm sure we can't grumble at all.

STACK: And I'm sure you don't grumble, Mrs Radfern.

MRS RADFERN: Why do you say that?

STACK: (*Smiling politely.*) Well, you don't look the grumbling sort.

MRS RADFERN: (*Pleased.*) Oh, I've always believed in making the best of everything. We're only on this earth once, I always say, and so we'd better make the best of it. (*With more energy, though not at all rudely.*) Though why I'm talking like this to a complete stranger, I really don't know. Let me see, you didn't give me your name, did you?

STACK: No. I'm sorry. Here's my card. (*Hands it over.*)

MRS RADFERN: (*Reading.*) Detective Inspector Stack, Criminal Investigation Department, New Scotland Yard. Good gracious! Are you from Scotland Yard? A detective? (*Puts card down in prominent place on the table.*)

STACK: (*Smiling.*) I am. Do I look like one?

MRS RADFERN: I'm sure I don't know. I've never seen anybody from Scotland Yard before. You certainly don't look like a policeman.

STACK: Well, that's something to be thankful for.

MRS RADFERN: But what do you want with my husband?

STACK: (*Smoothly.*) I'm only making a few enquiries, and Mr Radfern's name was given to me as one of the people who might be able to give me a little information. I'm sorry to disappoint you, but it's nothing sensational. Nobody murdered. No jewels stolen. Just one of those dull routine commercial cases.

MRS RADFERN: Well, I'm sure if my husband can help you at all, he will. And it'll amuse him meeting somebody from Scotland Yard, because he's very fond of reading these detective stories. He's just made me read one with him.

STACK: Well, I understand Mr Radfern had some dealings with one of the firms in question, some years ago, so I thought he might be able to give me a little information. And then he gets up and down a good deal, I think, doesn't he?

MRS RADFERN: Yes, he has to get about.

STACK: Birmingham, for instance. Of course, that's not very far, is it?

MRS RADFERN: No, but that's about the nearest place. Sometimes he goes to Liverpool. And Newcastle.

STACK: And up into Scotland, I expect?

MRS RADFERN: Yes, he has to go to Glasgow quite a lot.

STACK: Has he really? Still that's not so troublesome as having to go abroad, after all.

MRS RADFERN: Oh – he has to do that sometimes, too.

STACK: Yes? Well, I'm not surprised. I used to have a friend in the same line of business and he used to have to go quite often to Amsterdam and Brussels.

MRS RADFERN: That's just where my husband has to go sometimes. Amsterdam and Brussels. He probably knows this friend of yours.

STACK: I wouldn't be surprised if he did.

MRS RADFERN: You must ask him, if you're calling in tonight.

STACK: I will. (*Rising.*) I won't detain you any longer, Mrs Radfern. I'll look in again tonight, if Mr Radfern won't mind having a private little chat with me.

MRS RADFERN: I'm sure he won't. (*Noise of people entering house.*) Just a minute, that's my daughter and my sister and her husband coming back. Do just let me introduce you because they'll be terribly interested in meeting a detective from Scotland Yard.

(*STACK nods, smiling, and stands half facing door. ELSIE, BAXLEY and MRS BAXLEY enter, carrying some small parcels. They stare at STACK but MRS RADFERN begins before they have a chance to speak.*)

(*Playfully.*) Now you three, I'll bet you anything you'll never guess who this is.

(*All three look enquiringly at STACK.*)

MRS BAXLEY: (*Gloomily.*) Nobody I know.

BAXLEY: (*Hopefully.*) The face is familiar.

ELSIE: No, I can't guess.

MRS RADFERN: (*Pleased with herself.*) Well, this is Detective Inspector Stack from Scotland Yard.

(*ELSIE, BAXLEY and MRS BAXLEY instantly look the picture of dismay, alarm and horror. ELSIE just stifles a little scream. BAXLEY's face drops. MRS BAXLEY's eyes nearly pop out of her head.*)

You needn't look like that. If he'd come to lock you all up, you couldn't look worse. (*To STACK.*) I'm sorry, if they've all been up to something, I don't know what it is.

STACK: Oh, that's nothing. We get used to people looking at us like that. Well, I'll call again tonight to see Mr Radfern. Good afternoon.

(*Moves to the door, and MRS RADFERN follows, to let him out. The other three, dumb with terror, simply stand watching them. MRS RADFERN returns at once.*)

MRS RADFERN: Well, I must say you're a fine lot. It's a wonder he didn't think you were a lot of crooks or something. Such a nice man, I thought, too. Superior, and very gentlemanly manners, I'm sure. What's the matter?

ELSIE: Mother, was he really from Scotland Yard and wanting to see Dad?

MRS RADFERN: Of course.

BAXLEY: My God! Here, Lucy, we're packing.

MRS RADFERN: What do you mean you're packing? What's the matter?

MRS BAILEY: Arresting and prison and penal servitude's the matter.

ELSIE: (*Ready to break down.*) Oh – Mother!

BAXLEY: (*Moving towards door.*) Come on, Lucy. We're getting out of this – sharp.

MRS RADFERN: (*Taking a place in front of door and blocking the way.*) Oh no, you're not, Bernard, not until you've told me what's wrong. What have you done?

BAXLEY: (*Indignantly.*) Me! I've done nothing.

MRS BAXLEY: No, don't start trying to blame it on to us now.

MRS RADFERN: Blame what on to you?

MRS BAXLEY: Better ask Elsie. This isn't any place for us.

MRS RADFERN: Well, it's going to be until you tell me what it is you're all frightened of.

ELSIE: Oh – Mother – it's Dad.

MRS RADFERN: Dad!

MRS BAXLEY: (*Bitterly.*) Yes, Dad, your precious quiet respectable George with his honest pennies.

ELSIE: It's true, Mother. He told us himself, last night.

MRS RADFERN: (*Exasperated.*) Told you *what*, you stupid – ?

MRS BAXLEY: Told us he was a crook.

BAXLEY: And been one for years.

MRS BAXLEY: Every penny dishonest.

BAXLEY: Working with a big gang, all the detectives after them.

MRS BAXLEY: And proud of it, glories in it.

BAXLEY: And he'll get years and years, penal servitude.

ELSIE: (*Tearfully.*) Oh – Mother, it's true.

MRS RADFERN: (*Loudly.*) Stop, stop!
(*They are quiet, so she continues quietly.*)
Now what is it you're all trying to tell me? What did Dad say to you last night?

BAXLEY: You'd better get Elsie to tell you. We're going to pack.

MRS RADFERN: No, you're not. Nobody's leaving this room until I understand exactly what all this is about. Now who's going to tell me?

MRS BAXLEY: Go on, Elsie. You tell her.

ELSIE: Last night, just before you came back, Dad told us that he hadn't been in the paper business for years, but that he'd been a crook.

MRS RADFERN: He told you and Lucy and Bernard here –

ELSIE: And Harold.

MRS RADFERN: Oh, he told Harold too, did he?

ELSIE: Yes. And he said he'd been a sort of crook for years, and that he worked for a big international gang –

BAXLEY: That started in America.

MRS RADFERN: I see. That started in America. Go on.

ELSIE: And that they swindled banks, in America, and here and in France and all over.

BAXLEY: Counterfeiting notes and forging bonds.

MRS BAXLEY: All sorts of dangerous dirty tricks.

ELSIE: And that the detectives had been trying for years to track down this gang but they couldn't manage it, but if he was caught, he'd get years and years of prison.

BAXLEY: And so he would too.

MRS RADFERN: And that's what he told all the four of you, is it?

ELSIE: Yes – and mother, it's true. And that's why he has to keep going to various places, up and down the country, and abroad. And that's why Mr Fletten comes here such a lot, because he's working for this gang too, and he doesn't really know anything about greenhouses – that's –

BAXLEY: Just a blind, just a blind. He's taken everybody in up to now, but this time he's for it.

MRS RADFERN: And he asked you not to tell me?

MRS BAXLEY: Yes. Said you didn't know, and weren't to know, though I must say how he's kept it from you all this time beats me.

MRS RADFERN: Oh – that's quite simple.

MRS BAXLEY: Is it?

MRS RADFERN: Certainly it is. I can explain in three seconds why he's never told me and yet told you all about it last night.

BAXLEY: Why?

MRS RADFERN: Because he knew very well that you were four silly fools who'd believe any nonsense he told them, and he knew very well he couldn't come out with that silly stuff in front of me. Can't you see he was simply having a game with you? And serve you right too. Just because he likes to be quiet when he's at home, you've got it into your heads that he's a dull old stick. I've heard you say as much, Elsie. And you two are as bad. And as for your Harold, I know what Dad was trying to do to him – just scaring him away. (*To ELSIE.*) And is that why you had that letter from him this morning, breaking it off, and why you cried your eyes out?

ELSIE: Yes of course.

MRS RADFERN: And why you were all so queer and said you hadn't slept last night?

MRS BAXLEY: (*With dignity.*) Naturally.

MRS RADFERN: And why you all got up so early this morning?

BAXLEY: That's it.

MRS RADFERN: Then you're all sillier than I ever thought you were.

ELSIE: But mother, it's true.

MRS RADFERN: Of course it isn't true. Not a word of truth in it. Do you think I wouldn't have known? How you could ever have thought it was true, I can't imagine.

BAXLEY: It's all right talking like that –

MRS RADFERN: And now I suppose you thought that Inspector had come to arrest him. If you want to know, that Inspector was only making some enquiries about a commercial case –

BAXLEY: That's what *he* says.

MRS RADFERN: Oh – have some sense, Bernard, even if you have been to Singapore. Do you think I'd be calmly talking about it like this if I thought for a minute Dad had ever done anything wrong?

MRS BAXLEY: Well, you don't know he hasn't.

BAXLEY: *We* heard him last night, remember – not you.

MRS RADFERN: I know that story he told you last night was all nonsense, just made up to tease you and frighten you.

ELSIE: (*Hopefully.*) Oh Mother, do you think it was?

MRS RADFERN: I tell you, I *know* it was.

BAXLEY: But you can't prove it.

MRS RADFERN: (*Triumphantly.*) I can. (*She goes to table and picks up the book there.*) You see this book. It's called 'The Great Bank Mystery'. I've just read it, and Dad's just read it. And if you want to know all the rest of that story about the international gang of bank swindlers and bond forgers that started in America, you'll find it in this book.

BAXLEY: (*Sitting down and mopping forehead.*) Well, I'll be damned!

ELSIE: (*Joyfully.*) Mother! (*Hugs her.*)

MRS BAXLEY: (*Grumbling.*) Well, that's a nice trick, frightening people with a lot of silly stuff out of a detective tale!

BAXLEY: Yes, it's a bit thick.

MRS BAXLEY: (*Indignantly.*) It's a lot thick.

MRS RADFERN: (*Suddenly beginning to laugh.*) Dad's a monkey –

MRS BAXLEY: And I call it a foul monkey trick, too. I've had an awful day. Every time I've set eyes on a policeman I've shivered, and when I found that detective here my heart stopped and my blood went cold. I might easily be ill after this.

BAXLEY: Well, I must say it's not my idea of a joke.

MRS RADFERN: (*Still laughing.*) Evidently not, Bernard. But it seems to be George's. And very well he did it too, though he'll hear something from me about it when he comes back.

ELSIE: (*Happily.*) Oh, I don't care now. Everything's different. It's been awful. I'll never say anybody's dull again – never, never, never. I don't care how dull they are. It's all nice and safe and sensible again now. Lovely. (*She hurries out.*)

MRS RADFERN: Well, she's feeling a lot better already. It was silly of George to frighten her like that. Poor Elsie!

MRS BAXLEY: And what about us, Dorothy? Weren't we frightened, too?

BAXLEY: I've been worried to death about George ever since he told us that story.

MRS BAXLEY: So have I. And I do think, Dorothy, that George owes us some consideration after this silly trick he's played on us.

MRS RADFERN: You do, eh?

MRS BAXLEY: Yes, I do. He's not been as pleasant as he might have been these last few days, and I hope he'll

realise now that the least thing he can do is to help
Bernard to buy that little business we've talked about.

BAXLEY: Well, seeing you've mentioned it, Lucy, I might
as well say that's what I feel too. He's had his fun –

MRS RADFERN: (*Very quietly.*) And now he must pay for it.
Is that it?

BAXLEY: Oh – you can't put it like that. But you know our
position, Dorothy. If George can let me have a
temporary loan of a few hundreds and we can stay on
here until the deal goes through –

MRS BAXLEY: I don't think you can object to that,
Dorothy. And you can tell him how much he's upset me
with that silly joke of his –

MRS RADFERN: (*Quietly, but decisively.*) Just a minute. I
want to understand you properly. You both feel that, after
this, I ought to persuade George to let you have the
money and I also ought to ask you to stay on until
you've bought the business you're after. Is that it?

BAXLEY: Yes, that's it.

MRS RADFERN: Well, Lucy – and Bernard – I'm going to
tell you straight what I think about it. I think – you're
both the limit. And I see now that Dad was right about
you and I was wrong.

MRS BAXLEY: What do you mean?

MRS RADFERN: I mean that he was right in not wanting
to put up with you any longer. You're my relations, not
his. You've taken advantage of his good nature, and so
have I, through you. You've stayed here and borrowed
money from him too often. He'd had enough of it when
he told you that story last night. And now I've had
enough of it too.

BAXLEY: But here, half a minute, what have we done?

MRS RADFERN: You've shown me quite plainly you don't
really care tuppence about him, and that you're only
here to get what you can out of him. Only a few minutes
ago, when you thought he was in trouble and might be
arrested, what did you do? All you thought about was
yourselves. You wanted to pack up and go at once. I had

to stop you going out of that door. Well, now I'm not stopping you. You can pack and go as soon as you like. (*MRS BAXLEY and BAXLEY look at one another. ELSIE enters, and looks enquiringly from one to the other of them.*)

MRS BAXLEY: That's a nice thing to say to a sister, isn't it?

MRS RADFERN: No, it isn't, but that's how I feel, Lucy.

BAXLEY: More shame to you. Come on, Lucy. We'll pack. I'm not staying where I'm not wanted. (*Goes to door, MRS BAXLEY following. Then, turning at door.*) I'd laugh now if the old boy really was a wrong 'un all the time.

MRS RADFERN: Well, you'll have to find something else to laugh at, Bernard.

MRS BAXLEY: (*Bitterly, at door.*) That oughtn't to be difficult − here.

(*They go out.*)

ELSIE: Are they going?

MRS RADFERN: Yes. I told them to. They've been sponging on Dad long enough and they're not going to get anything else out of him. Wanted to bolt as soon as they thought he was in trouble. (*As ELSIE goes to telephone.*) What are you going to do?

ELSIE: I'm going to tell Harold it was all Dad's nonsense. At least I'm going to ask him to come here, so that I can tell him.

MRS RADFERN: He broke it off, didn't he, after what he heard last night?

ELSIE: Yes.

MRS RADFERN: Another one that was found out.

ELSIE: Well, Mother, you can't blame him for not wanting to be engaged to the daughter of a crook.

MRS RADFERN: (*Sharply, derisively.*) Can't you?

ELSIE: (*Doing her best.*) No, of course you can't.

MRS RADFERN: *Can't you?*

ELSIE: (*Confusedly.*) No. Yes − I suppose you can.

MRS RADFERN: Of course you can blame him. He ought to have been ready to stick to you, whatever your father turned out to be. And you know it. I can see Dad's right

about your Harold. He's a weak-kneed, shuffling boy –
just out for what he can safely get.

ELSIE: You've no right to say that, Mother. I don't blame
Harold really for breaking it off. And anyhow he
deserves another chance. I'll tell him it was all a joke.

MRS RADFERN: If you do, I'll be ashamed of you.

ELSIE: What for?

MRS RADFERN: Well, where's your pride?

ELSIE: I don't see where my pride comes in. After all, it
was a joke.

MRS RADFERN: This is where your pride comes in, or
ought to come in. He's proved already that he's not
sufficiently fond of you to marry you whatever your
father is.

ELSIE: (*Hurt by this.*) Don't – Mother.

MRS RADFERN: And now you want to tell him it's all
right. If it was me, I wouldn't have him on those terms.
You get him up here – give him a last chance if you like
– but don't tell him that last night was a joke. Let him
think it's still serious and then ask him if he still wants to
break off the engagement finally. That'll be a fair test.

ELSIE: All right, Mother, I'll do that. (*Begins dialling at
telephone.*) I'll simply ask him to come and see me, and
then when he comes, I won't say a word about last
night's business not being true. Hello, I want Mr Harold
Russ.

MRS RADFERN: (*Moving to kitchen.*) And I want a cup of tea.

Quick Curtain.

End of Act Two.

ACT THREE

Scene is the same as Act Two.

The book and the INSPECTOR's card are still prominent on the table in centre. In front not far from the door into the house is a fairly large suitcase, with a hat and raincoat on top of it. BAXLEY is discovered poking about the room, looking for something. He is out of temper, though not furiously angry.

BAXLEY: (*Going to door into house and calling.*) I say, Lucy. Lucy. Is my cigarette case up there? (*Pauses, listening to reply.*) It isn't. I've just looked for it. Oh, all right. (*Gives a final glance round the room, but can't see it. Then goes over to his raincoat and carefully searches pockets. He finds the case in one of them, opens it and discovers that it is empty. He goes to the sideboard, finds a box of cigarettes there and – after one glance over his shoulder – fills his case from the box, finally lighting one. Then he puts the case in his pocket, and replaces the raincoat on the suitcase. As he does this, the front door bell rings. He hesitates a moment, then goes out, re-entering a moment later, followed by HAROLD.*)

HAROLD: Isn't Elsie in?

BAXLEY: Yes, she'll be down in a minute. She's helping my wife to finish her packing.

HAROLD: What? You off?

BAXLEY: Yes. Night train to Scotland – Dundee. Got a brother there. Nothing for me down here, you know.

HAROLD: (*Sceptically.*) No?

BAXLEY: Oh no. Not the right sort of opening. They tried to persuade me to take an agency for business supplies – exclusive agency too – chap called Simpson – I said 'What's the good of business supplies, when business itself is so bad?' That stumped him. Mind you, there's an opening there – in a small way. Might suit a youngster like yourself. But no good to me. So I'm on the move. I like to be on the move, always did. Bit of a roamer, you know, old man, bit of a roamer.

HAROLD: (*Sceptical.*) Sez you.

BAXLEY: What's the *sez you* about. We're not doing a talkie.

HAROLD: No, but you're not going to tell me that you're clearing out so suddenly just because you like travelling.

BAXLEY: Oh?

HAROLD: No, I know why you're going, and I don't blame you.

BAXLEY: Very good of you, old man, but still I don't know what you're talking about.

HAROLD: And I think if I'd any sense, I wouldn't be here either.

BAXLEY: Of course you wouldn't. Marriage is a mug's game, you can take it from me.

HAROLD: I'm not talking about marriage.

BAXLEY: Then why shouldn't you be here? – Oh – you mean because of what he told us last night?

HAROLD: Yes, of course.

BAXLEY: And you still believe that?

HAROLD: Yes, don't you?

BAXLEY: Of course not. All a joke. Bit of leg-pulling, that's all. We're always pulling one another's legs here, you know. Sometimes I pull his leg, sometimes he pulls mine. Last night it was his turn.

HAROLD: It was his turn all right.

BAXLEY: And he's taken you in all this time. Well, you surprise me. I thought you were smart. In the second-hand car trade, too.

HAROLD: Was it a joke?

BAXLEY: Yes. All rot. Out of a book. There's the book.

HAROLD: Look here, are you sure?

BAXLEY: Well, I know a book when I see one.

HAROLD: Yes, but I mean – are you sure it did come from that book and it was a joke?

BAXLEY: I keep telling you, don't I? If you don't want to believe me, don't. It doesn't matter to me.

HAROLD: Oh well, I do believe you. Does Elsie know?

BAXLEY: Yes. She knows.

HAROLD: I suppose she's asked me to come so that she can tell me, though she could have done that on the telephone.

BAXLEY: (*Looking cunning.*) Perhaps she isn't going to tell you.

HAROLD: Of course she's going to tell me. Why shouldn't she?

BAXLEY: She might be going to try you out.

HAROLD: Try me out? Oh – I see, pretend it wasn't a joke. Keep the old man's game up for him, eh?

BAXLEY: It's a possibility, isn't it?

HAROLD: Yes. Look here, don't tell her you've told me that it was all a joke.

BAXLEY: I won't tell her. I hope it works – with her and her father too. Serve 'em right.

HAROLD: What do you mean – serve them right? Do you mean I'd serve them right, because if you do, you're being very insulting.

BAXLEY: Then that isn't what I mean. (*Looks at his watch.*) Time's going on. (*Goes to door and shouts outside.*) I say, it's time we were off... Well, come on, then. Oh, all right. (*He goes out, and after a moment, ELSIE enters.*)

ELSIE: Hello, Harold.

HAROLD: Hello, Elsie. You see, I came as soon as I could. (*He tries to kiss her, but she fends him off.*)

ELSIE: No, I want to talk first.

HAROLD: Oh, all right. Well, let's talk then.

ELSIE: Wait a minute. My uncle and aunt are just going. (*Enter MRS BAXLEY, dressed for travelling and carrying a small case.*)

MRS BAXLEY: Oh – you're here again, are you?

HAROLD: Yes – do you mind?

MRS BAXLEY: It doesn't matter to me who's here, though I know one who won't be here again for a long time – not if some people beg on their bended knees – and that's me.

ELSIE: Must you go now, Aunt Lucy?

MRS BAXLEY: Your Uncle Bernard says so, if we're going to get that train.

ELSIE: You won't wait to say good-bye to mother? She'll be back in a minute.

MRS BAXLEY: No, thank you. If I could wait, I wouldn't. But you can give her one message from me.

ELSIE: What's that?

MRS BAXLEY: Just remind her, from me, that there's no smoke without fire. That's all. No smoke without fire.
(*Enter BAXLEY, carrying another bag.*)

MRS BAXLEY: Here you are then. I'm all ready.

BAXLEY: What about a taxi?

MRS BAXLEY: We're not having any taxis. We can go to the station by Tube, can't we?

BAXLEY: Yes, but what about from here to the Tube?

MRS BAXLEY: We can walk that.

BAXLEY: Yes, but what about these bags?

HAROLD: (*Maliciously.*) It's ten minutes' walk.

MRS BAXLEY: Ten minutes' walk won't kill us.

BAXLEY: It won't kill you but it will kill me, carrying these bags. (*Tries them.*) This comes of giving the old country a chance. Carrying bags. It's a good job some of the chaps I knew out East can't see me now.

MRS BAXLEY: (*Coldly.*) What chaps?

BAXLEY: Well – the chaps – you know – out East.

MRS BAXLEY: Anybody would think you'd been Emperor of China to hear you talk. What chaps?

BAXLEY: (*Shouting.*) Never mind what chaps. I don't like carrying these damned bags. So there.

MRS BAXLEY: Well, you'll have to put up with it for once. Good-bye, Elsie. (*Kisses her perfunctorily.*) And just try and be sensible, though that won't always be easy in *this* house. (*To HAROLD.*) Good-bye.

HAROLD: Good-bye.

MRS BAXLEY: (*Very grimly.*) Pleased to have met you. Come on, Bernard.
(*She stalks out.*)

BAXLEY: (*Grappling with bags.*) Ten minutes' walk! It's murder. I've known stronger chaps than me strain their hearts doing silly things like this.

ELSIE: Never mind, Uncle, you'll be able to have a good rest in the train.

BAXLEY: (*Grumbling.*) Good rest! It's a stopping train to Dundee. I'll be able to take root. Well, good-bye.

HAROLD: Good-bye.

ELSIE: Good-bye, Uncle.

BAXLEY: Good-bye, Elsie. (*Groans.*) Good-bye.
>   (*Goes out, followed by ELSIE, with HAROLD going as far as the door. You hear the outer door banged to, then ELSIE returns.*)

HAROLD: They're clearing off suddenly, aren't they?

ELSIE: Yes, as soon as they thought we were in trouble, they wanted to pack up and go, and that made mother angry –

HAROLD: (*Puzzled.*) In trouble? You mean, because of what your father told us last night?

ELSIE: Oh – it went further than that, because they thought somebody was coming here to arrest Dad. So they wanted to go at once. So then mother told them to go. She doesn't like people who leave you in the lurch, and (*Meaningly.*) I don't either.

HAROLD: But wait a minute. There isn't anybody coming here to arrest your father?

ELSIE: (*Watching him.*) Perhaps.

HAROLD: (*Watching her, with faint smile.*) Well – I don't care.

ELSIE: (*Eagerly.*) Harold – do you mean that?

HAROLD: (*Whose tone must suggest insincerity.*) Yes, I do. I really came to tell you how sorry I was – and am – about the way I went off last night and the letter I wrote to you. You see – I hadn't time to think. The whole thing completely took me by surprise.

ELSIE: You hadn't time to think about – what?

HAROLD: About you. And me. When all that stuff came out, last night, all I felt – as any honest man would – was that I must keep out of this. And for the moment – well – I suppose I mixed you up in it. I realise now that's where I was wrong. It's got nothing to do with us what your father is and does.

ELSIE: Do you really mean that, Harold?

HAROLD: (*Uneasily.*) Yes, Elsie.

ELSIE: (*Gravely.*) Are you sure?

HAROLD: (*Still uneasy.*) Well – yes.

ELSIE: Think of the disgrace, though, if Dad is found out.

HAROLD: (*With mock nobility.*) Never mind. We'll stick it. (*Then hesitating.*) And, after all, your father was exaggerating it, wasn't he?

ELSIE: Was he?

HAROLD: You know he was. I should think he's rather a leg-puller, anyhow, isn't he?

ELSIE: (*Solemnly.*) Oh no. Dad isn't. That's not like him at all. Now, Uncle Bernard – you know, the one who was here just now – he'd say anything for tuppence. You can't believe a word he says.

HAROLD: (*Uneasily.*) Can't you?

ELSIE: Good Lord, no! He's an awful mischief-maker and a liar. I hope he hasn't said anything to you.

HAROLD: Er – no – of course not.

ELSIE: (*Watching him.*) That's all right then, because you simply can't believe him. Dad's quite different.

HAROLD: Look here – I don't quite understand this.

ELSIE: (*Who is now standing in front of the centre table.*) Well, it doesn't matter, does it? After all, the important thing is – us.

HAROLD: Oh yes – of course.

ELSIE: That's all that matters, isn't it?

HAROLD: (*Approaching her.*) Yes.

ELSIE: (*Edging away.*) No, I'm not going to kiss you – just yet.

HAROLD: (*Moving.*) Oh – come on, Elsie.

ELSIE: You must remember, Harold, you upset me terribly – running away like that last night and then writing me that letter. I haven't got over it yet.

HAROLD: Well, I've told you it's all right now.

ELSIE: Yes, it may be for you, but it isn't for me. I'd given you up, you see. And it'll take me a very long time to get very fond of you all over again.

HAROLD: No, it won't.

ELSIE: (*Who now puts the table between them.*) Yes, it will. Besides, I want to talk. And if you're kissing, you can't talk seriously.

HAROLD: Well, we don't need to talk seriously.

(*They are now standing, looking at each other across the table.*)

I've told you, I want you and I don't care now what your father is and does. (*He catches sight of the card on the table and stares at it.*)

ELSIE: What's the matter?

HAROLD: (*Uneasily.*) I suppose this is part of the joke, too?

ELSIE: (*Coolly.*) Oh – the card. No, the man left it when he came here this afternoon.

HAROLD: An Inspector from Scotland Yard?

ELSIE: Yes, he came here this afternoon, to see Dad. And he's coming again tonight.

HAROLD: My God!

ELSIE: (*Watching him.*) Oh – I was terribly upset at first, but I've got over it now.

HAROLD: (*Angrily.*) Look here, what's going on here? First, your father tells us all that stuff about being a crook, and then your uncle tells me it's all a joke, and now you say there's somebody coming from Scotland Yard.

ELSIE: So Uncle told you it was all a joke?

HAROLD: (*Sulkily.*) If you must know – yes.

ELSIE: And you didn't tell me he told you. You let me think you didn't know.

HAROLD: Well, what does that matter?

ELSIE: It matters a lot.

HAROLD: (*Flinging away, then turning on her.*) I'm fed up with this. Is it a joke or isn't it? And if it is a joke, why did this chap from Scotland Yard come here?

ELSIE: You'd better wait and ask him. He'll be here soon.

HAROLD: (*Nervously.*) I'm not going to wait for him, I can tell you that. It's no business of mine.
(*Noise outside.*)

ELSIE: (*Scornfully.*) There's somebody there now. Hadn't you better go while there's time?
(*Enter RADFERN and FLETTEN.*)

RADFERN: (*Heartily.*) Hello, Elsie. I found Joe Fletten here waiting on the doorstep. Hello, what's the matter?

ELSIE: I think you'd better go now, Harold.

RADFERN: (*To HAROLD, rather grimly.*) I thought you had gone – for good.

ELSIE: So did I, this morning. But I thought I'd give him another chance. And now you can tell him, Dad.

RADFERN: Tell him what?

ELSIE: You can tell him what we found out from mother this afternoon, that what you said last night was all a joke and that Harold ran away for nothing.

RADFERN: Oh – you've found that out, have you?

ELSIE: Yes, Mother showed us the book – it's this one, isn't it? – you got all that stuff out of.

FLETTEN: What stuff? Or is this private and confidential?

ELSIE: No, it isn't. Dad, last night, pretended he was a crook –

FLETTEN: (*Humorously shocked.*) Mr Radfern, how could you!

ELSIE: And told us a lot of stuff he got out of this book. We all believed him at the time, and Harold here still thinks it's true and wants to run away.

FLETTEN: (*Severely to HAROLD.*) Do you mean to say you could believe for one minute that my friend, Mr Radfern, was a crook? Mr Radfern of all people!

RADFERN: Oh, he swallowed it all right.

HAROLD: (*Sulkily.*) And so did everybody else.

FLETTEN: Where's your intelligence, young man? Where's your what's it? – you know – sense of character. Mr Radfern a crook! You'll be thinking I'm a crook next.

ELSIE: (*Demurely.*) We all did.

FLETTEN: What me! Poor old Joe Fletten, who never did anybody any harm. And is this your idea of a joke, Mr Radfern?

RADFERN: Sorry, Joe. Just a bit of fun on my part. But I thought it might catch one or two people.

FLETTEN: (*Severely, looking at HAROLD.*) And it seems to have done.

RADFERN: Have your Aunt Lucy and Uncle Bernard gone?

ELSIE: Yes, but that was because Mother told them to go.

RADFERN: That's all right, as long as they've gone.

FLETTEN: (*To HAROLD.*) Don't you think you might apologise to one or two of us?

HAROLD: No, I don't. (*To ELSIE.*) Look here, I've had enough of this.

ELSIE: (*Sadly.*) All right, Harold. I gave you a chance, you know. Dad was right after all. Good-bye.

HAROLD: (*As if about to break out angrily.*) Oh – good night. (*Swings away and goes out quickly with RADFERN following him to the door. ELSIE remains quite still. FLETTEN looks at her, clears his throat as if to speak, thinks better of it and coughs instead, then hums a little. When RADFERN returns, MRS RADFERN, dressed in her outdoor things, follows him in.*)

MRS RADFERN: Good evening, Mr Fletten. (*To ELSIE.*) So Lucy and Bernard have gone?

ELSIE: Yes, quarter of an hour ago. And so has Harold.

MRS RADFERN: I know that. I nearly bumped into him at the front gate. Has he – gone for good?

ELSIE: (*Rather unhappily.*) Yes. Tried and tested – and found wanting.

RADFERN: Never mind, Elsie. I'll think of something very nice to make up for it.

FLETTEN: Young man actually thought your husband and me was a pair of crooks or something. The cheek of it!

MRS RADFERN: Oh – that was only George's nonsense, last night. And a very silly thing to do, too, Dad.

FLETTEN: I can't understand how anybody believed it for a minute.

MRS RADFERN: Well, I must say, I'm surprised, too.

RADFERN: I did it very well.

FLETTEN: (*Sententiously.*) Well, I wouldn't have thought you had it in you, Mr Radfern, to play a part like that well – even for a bit of a joke. And I doubt if it's anything to joke about.

MRS RADFERN: I rather agree with you there, Mr Fletten.

FLETTEN: (*As before.*) We oughtn't to trifle with our good names – even in fun. That's what I feel.

RADFERN: (*Dryly.*) And it does you credit.

ELSIE: (*As she begins moving towards door.*) As a matter of fact, it wasn't anything Dad had said, but that card that caught Harold out tonight.

RADFERN: What card?

ELSIE: (*Turning in doorway.*) That one on the table.
(*Goes out.*)

MRS RADFERN: (*Amused.*) Oh – how absurd! She means
the one left by the man from Scotland Yard.

FLETTEN: (*Alarmed.*) From where?

RADFERN: (*Quietly.*) What's this about, then, Mother?

MRS RADFERN: Well, it's all rather amusing. It happened
that a Detective Inspector from Scotland Yard called to
see you this afternoon – a very nice man indeed, and we
had quite a nice little chat –

FLETTEN: (*With glances of despair at RADFERN.*) Did you
now?

MRS RADFERN: And he left his card. But what was so
amusing was that Elsie and her aunt and uncle arrived
before he'd gone and you ought to have seen their faces
when I told them he was from Scotland Yard. You'd have
screamed.

FLETTEN: (*Who is wearing the same sort of face they had.*)
I know I should. Oh – very amusing.

RADFERN: (*Putting up a good show.*) Oh – yes, that's good.
Ha, ha, ha!

FLETTEN: (*Not so good.*) Isn't it? Ha, ha, ha!

RADFERN: Did he say what he'd come for?

MRS RADFERN: Yes. Of course it was something and
nothing. Just some enquiries he was making in
connection with a commercial case. I told him to come
back tonight. He'll be here any minute now, I expect.
You ought to have a good chat.

RADFERN: I'm sure we shall.

MRS RADFERN: Well, I'll go and take my things off and
see what sort of mess Lucy and Bernard have made of
their room upstairs.
(*Goes out.*)

FLETTEN: Look here, what's the idea?

RADFERN: I don't know.

FLETTEN: I don't believe in that commercial case he's
come to make a few enquiries about.

RADFERN: Neither do I.

FLETTEN: Look here, I don't like this –

RADFERN: Now don't get into a panic. Take it easy, but keep on your toes. Listen, you've got to stay here. I can't risk letting you go now. Besides, there may be a lot to do. Now the minute we hear him, I want you to go out through the greenhouse and sit on the grass on the other side, so you can't be seen.

FLETTEN: Well, somebody'll see me.

RADFERN: Yes, but this chap won't or anybody he's got with him. Doesn't matter about the neighbours. Look as if you're studying botany.

FLETTEN: I can't look as if I'm studying botany.

RADFERN: Well, look as if you're half tight and are falling asleep.

FLETTEN: I can do that all right.

(*Front door bell rings.*)

RADFERN: And don't come out until you hear me calling you, but when you do hear me calling you, don't lose a second. Understand? Outside, quick. And keep down.

(*FLETTEN goes out through door at back, closing it behind him. RADFERN goes through door into house, and then re-enters, followed by STACK.*)

Take a seat, Inspector.

STACK: Thanks.

RADFERN: Have a drink?

STACK: No, thanks.

(*They both sit down, preferably near the table.*)

RADFERN: This is very interesting. I've never had the pleasure of talking to anybody from Scotland Yard before.

STACK: No, I don't suppose you have, Mr Radfern.

RADFERN: Must have a very exciting life, you chaps. Different from some of us.

STACK: It's not as exciting as people seem to think. Most of it's dull routine, and very long hours at that. Not many quiet evenings at home.

RADFERN: Ah – that's a pity.

STACK: Yes, Mrs Radfern was telling me this afternoon that you liked to be quiet at home, with your greenhouse and so forth.

RADFERN: Yes. My wife and daughter often laugh at me. They think I'm a very dull old stick.

STACK: Still, I've known wives and children go sadly wrong about men, and think they were leading one sort of life when all the time they were leading a very different sort of life.

RADFERN: Is that so? I've never struck that myself.

STACK: (*Meaningly.*) Really? Are you sure?

RADFERN: Well, I can't recall a case at the moment.

STACK: (*Meaningly.*) You surprise me.

RADFERN: But if there's anything I can tell you, I'll be only too pleased, though I can't imagine why you've taken the trouble to come and see me.

STACK: Trouble's nothing to us, Mr Radfern, if the case is big enough. (*He idly reaches out for book and looks at title.*)

RADFERN: I can well believe that.

STACK: (*Holding up book.*) Have you read this?

RADFERN: What is it? Oh – 'The Great Bank Mystery'. Yes, I finished it yesterday.

STACK: What do you think of it?

RADFERN: Oh – very entertaining. But like most of these things, very far-fetched. Have you read it?

STACK: Yes, I have.

RADFERN: What do you think of it?

STACK: Well, as you say, it's rather far-fetched. The swindlers work on far too big a scale, to start with.

RADFERN: Yes, I should think so.

STACK: All the same, though, it reminds me of a case we've been working at now – one or other of us – for over three years.

RADFERN: Really! Now I call that interesting. And over three years, you say.

STACK: Yes, over three years. And no trouble and reasonable expense spared. Mind you, we'll win in the end. We can't lose.

RADFERN: Well, Inspector, I should hope not. We taxpayers want to see something for our money.

STACK: We're sometimes very slow –

RADFERN: But you're sure. Isn't that it?

STACK: That's it, Mr Radfern. You see, for the last four years, at least, there's been a gang – a very clever, well-organised gang – who've been engaged in counterfeiting bank notes and Treasury notes.

RADFERN: No? I shouldn't have thought it could be done, these days.

STACK: This gang operates here in England and also abroad, chiefly from Amsterdam and Brussels. Some of the notes are printed there, some of them here. Here's one of their notes. Perhaps you'd like to see it. (*Brings out pocket-book and produces pound note.*)

RADFERN: I would. (*He brings out handkerchief and takes up note by one corner with a bit of handkerchief between his fingers and the note.*)

STACK: You needn't handle it as carefully as all that, Mr Radfern.

RADFERN: Well, I thought one couldn't be too careful.

STACK: (*Softly.*) If I wanted your fingerprints, you know, I could think of better ways of getting them.

RADFERN: (*Examining note, laughs.*) Never occurred to me. I always thought this fingerprint business chiefly belonged to these detective yarns. Well, y'know, if this is a fake, it would take me in. I'm no expert, of course, but I'm in the paper trade, you know.

STACK: (*Significantly.*) So I understand, Mr Radfern.

RADFERN: I wouldn't have hesitated a minute giving anybody eight half-crowns for this chap. Isn't it marvellous what they can do. Never would have thought it!

STACK: Surprising, isn't it? Oh – they're a clever lot.

RADFERN: They must be.

STACK: Humph!

RADFERN: Humph!

STACK: They've been clever at getting the right sort of paper, and with their engraving and printing, and with the way they've distributed the slush.

RADFERN: Slush?

STACK: Slush. And the Treasury and the banks haven't given us a minute's peace about this case. But at last we're getting results.

RADFERN: Splendid!

STACK: Yes, hundreds of little details that haven't meant anything much for months are now beginning to look like something.

RADFERN: Just like a jigsaw puzzle, eh?

STACK: That's it. Of course there are still a few pieces missing, but not many – not many. It's only a matter of time now.

RADFERN: That's good, isn't it? You must be feeling very pleased with yourselves, eh?

STACK: We'd feel better still if we could just mop it all up now.

RADFERN: (*Sympathetically.*) Of course you would.

STACK: You see – this is how it often works in these cases – I hope I'm not boring you, Mr Radfern.

RADFERN: Not at all, Inspector. Very interesting.

STACK: It works like this. We come across a nice little nest of clues in – say – Birmingham –

RADFERN: Birmingham will do. I was there only today.

STACK: And among these clues is a name, just one of several names in a notebook. And that name may turn up somewhere else – perhaps in Glasgow – perhaps in Amsterdam. Well, the owner of that name is perhaps passing himself off as an ordinary respectable citizen and business man. And he thinks he's safe. Do you follow me?

RADFERN: (*Beaming, but with sardonic emphasis.*) Yes, I should think I do. Poor devil. I can see it all. This chap imagines he's safe. And of course he isn't because you've got a lot of evidence against him.

STACK: Yes, a lot of evidence.

RADFERN: (*As before, but with more emphasis.*) And of course it's solid evidence, cast-iron solid evidence that wouldn't make you look silly if you took such a quiet respectable chap into a police court.

STACK: (*Now taking up the challenge.*) No, that's not quite it, because in this instance, we haven't bothered to pile up the solid evidence yet. But we've got one or two interesting little bits. Would you like to hear them?

RADFERN: I would, Inspector.

STACK: Well – for example – we know that a member of this counterfeiting ring arrived in Glasgow from the continent on the twenty-third of last month and was met by one of his confederates here. And we're pretty sure we can prove that this quiet respectable citizen we're talking about was also there, in Glasgow, on the twenty-third of last month.

RADFERN: In Glasgow on the twenty-third of last month? You know, that reminds me of something. The twenty-third? (*He takes out pocket diary and consults it.*) Not that I was in Glasgow. As a matter of fact I was in –

STACK: (*Quickly, triumphantly, standing.*) Newcastle. And so was this man who came from the continent. Not in Glasgow at all. That was a little trap and you walked straight into it.

RADFERN: (*Very calmly.*) Did I? I'm afraid I don't quite follow you there, Inspector. Bit too sharp for me, I expect.

STACK: (*Grimly.*) I shouldn't be surprised.

RADFERN: But what I was going to say was that I remember the twenty-third of last month because the Bowling Club here had an outing that day – up the river first and then finished off at the Palladium – and I was with them. About twenty of us, there were.

STACK: (*Disappointed.*) Humph!

RADFERN: (*Quietly, but forcibly.*) Now that's what I was meaning, you know, Inspector. Isn't that what they call an alibi? Well, you know, if I was that man and you were silly enough to rush me into court, that's the sort of thing – an alibi like that – which would make you all look very foolish, I imagine. Mind you, I know nothing about it – but I've read some of these detective tales.

STACK: (*Walks away, then suddenly swings round.*) If you were that man we're talking about, do you know what I'd say to you?

RADFERN: I can't imagine.

STACK: I'd say to you straight out, look here, we *know* you've been in this, but as yet we can't prove it, though sooner or later we'll be able to prove it. But as the case has dragged on long enough and we want quick results, don't wait like a fool until we can put you in the dock, where nobody's going to have any mercy on you, but tell us all you know *now* – help us to clean the whole thing up – and we won't even *try* to prove anything against you.

RADFERN: Well, of course, I can't answer for this man –

STACK: (*Sardonically.*) Never mind. Make an effort and try.

RADFERN: I fancy the first thing he'd say is that you're bluffing.

STACK: And do you know what I'd reply to that, just to show him we weren't bluffing? First, I'd simply give him two addresses: 59, Pool Road, Glasgow. And, 17, Bellingham Street, Newcastle.

RADFERN: (*Admiringly.*) Just two addresses, like that. Isn't that interesting, now?

STACK: (*Grimly.*) Oh – he'd find it interesting all right. Then I'd give him two names. Peter Korderman and William Frazerly. No bluffing there, you see. We know about Korderman and Frazerly.

RADFERN: (*Keeping it up.*) You know, Inspector, this is as good as any of the films and detective tales to me. Better. It's a treat. Go on.

STACK: All right. Seeing that I'm putting some of my cards on the table, I might as well put this one. (*He produces half a playing card, the Knave of Diamonds.*) What do you think of that?

RADFERN: (*Examining the card.*) Half a Jack of Diamonds. That's grand. But you're not going to tell me these chaps you're after use a thing like this?

STACK: (*Ironically.*) We've got an idea they do. Sort of visiting card, you know, Mr Radfern. Quite romantic, isn't it?

RADFERN: (*Shaking his head.*) That's the trouble. It seems a bit too romantic to me.

STACK: What do you mean?

RADFERN: (*Apologetically.*) Well, of course, I don't know anything about these things.

STACK: (*Grimly.*) No, no. We know all about that.

RADFERN: But I'd say offhand that this torn card business looks like a bit of leg-pulling. Too much in the story-book style, you know. Sherlock Holmes. Edgar Wallace. I can imagine some chaps – you know, chaps who like a bit of fun – just planting something like this card on you, to keep you guessing and to amuse you. (*Gives the card back.*) And that Carl Korderman you mentioned –

STACK: Peter Korderman.

RADFERN: Peter Korderman, then. Well (*Shaking his head.*) he doesn't sound quite real to me, you know, Inspector. Perhaps that's another bit of leg-pulling.

(*STACK stares at him speculatively, grunts, then walks away.*)

STACK: (*Suddenly turning.*) Now listen, Radfern. Let's drop this nonsense and talk straight.

RADFERN: Go on.

STACK: (*Accusingly.*) You're in this counterfeiting game. I know damned well you are, and you know I know. That's straight talking, isn't it?

RADFERN: I don't know whether it's straight or not, but it seems to be very offensive talking.

STACK: Well, here's some more. We want convictions, of course, but what we want even more than that is to break up the ring as soon as possible, because the Treasury and the banks are at us all the time. Tell us all you know *now*, put the game into our hands, and we'll forget about you. And you know what it means if we don't forget about you. There'll be none of this my-first-offence-and-I-didn't-know-any-better humbug for you if you do find yourself in court. You'll get as much as the judge can give you, and that's plenty. Now what do you say?

RADFERN: (*Impressively.*) This is what I say, Inspector Stack. My name is George Radfern, and I'm in the paper trade and can prove it. I live at Ferndale, Laburnum Grove, Shooters Green, where I'm well known as a decent respectable citizen and a householder. I've been swindled myself in my time, but if ever I've injured any

man, woman or child in this country, then it's news to
me. And you haven't enough evidence against me to take
me to that door. And you know it.

STACK: Give me a bit more time, and I'll take you a lot
further than that door.

(*There is a knock at the door. MRS RADFERN looks in,
smiling.*)

MRS RADFERN: Oh – good evening, Inspector.

STACK: Good evening, Mrs Radfern.

MRS RADFERN: Excuse me interrupting you for a minute,
but I've left my scissors down here. (*Comes in, looks for
them, and finds them.*) Here they are. Are you having an
interesting talk, Dad?

RADFERN: Very interesting.

MRS RADFERN: (*Returning to door.*) That's good. I won't
interrupt again.

RADFERN: Oh, Mother. You know all that stuff from the
shipping companies – all those little books – that Elsie
got to amuse herself with?

MRS RADFERN: Yes, a whole heap of them. She's still got
them in her bedroom.

RADFERN: Good. Well, tell her to bring them down with
her when she comes. Not just yet. Later on.

MRS RADFERN: All right. (*Nods and smiles at them both,
then goes out.*)

STACK: Well, what do you say?

RADFERN: You heard me ask for all those little books
from the shipping companies that my daughter's been
collecting. She's always worrying me to take her away
somewhere, and I think she could do with a change. So
could I, and business is slack now. I've a good mind to
go away on a nice long sea voyage.

STACK: Oh, you have, have you? Far?

RADFERN: Oh – I don't know. I should think so. Australia
perhaps. Or the Far East. Might find something new in
the way of business. And see the world, you know.

STACK: Always wanted to do it myself. I'd hate to have to
stop another man going.

RADFERN: I shouldn't like to see you even try, Inspector. Just for your own sake.

STACK: Awkward things, though, ships. You can't get off them when you like, that's the trouble. And now that we've got wireless, they can't get out of hearing.

RADFERN: Yes, that's true.

STACK: An English ship, you know, is as safe to us as an English police court.

RADFERN: No! An English ship as safe as an English police court – Then you'll know where to find me if you want me, won't you?

STACK: I think so. Well, that's that. (*Preparing to go.*)

RADFERN: And thank you very much for calling, Inspector. I've enjoyed this. A peep behind the scenes. Something to tell my friends about.

STACK: (*As he moves to door.*) Good. Any friend of yours, Mr Radfern, is interesting to me. You wouldn't like to take me round and introduce me, would you?

RADFERN: I shouldn't think that would be necessary, Inspector.

(*He goes out with him, leaving door behind him open. You hear them give one another ironically polite 'good nights', then you hear the sound of the front door being closed and locked. RADFERN returns hastily and closes the sitting-room door behind him. He is now a man of rapid decisive action. He goes quickly to door at back and calls JOE. JOE FLETTEN comes at once, brushing his trousers with his hands, his hat on the back of his head.*)

FLETTEN: (*Excitedly.*) What's happened? What does he know?

RADFERN: Quite enough. Now listen, Joe, and keep your head screwed on. It's up to you now. Go straight to Westerburg – and it doesn't matter where he is or what he's doing, you've got to see him –

FLETTEN: I know where Westerburg is. Always at the same place, Monday nights.

RADFERN: Tell him I've had a Scotland Yard man here. They've got the Glasgow and Newcastle addresses, and they know about Korderman and Frazerly –

FLETTEN: The hell they do! We're done then.

RADFERN: No, we're not. That's all they do know *yet*. And that's got to be all too. Tell Westerburg it's Plan B now or nothing.

FLETTEN: What! Sink the plates and presses, and scatter!

RADFERN: Yes, he knows what to do. And tell him that anyhow I'm working on Plan B from tonight, and he'd better wire Amsterdam for me. And I'll ring up Middleton myself now. Have you got that?

FLETTEN: Yes.

RADFERN: And you'd better put Plan B into action yourself, Joe, if you don't want to see Maidstone and Parkhurst again.

FLETTEN: You bet your life I will.

RADFERN: (*Pointing to back door.*) That way then, and as quick as you can. There's a narrow lane at the back. Turn to the right at the top and you're at the Tube station in three minutes. And for God's sake, make haste, but don't look as if you think the nearest bobby's going to put his hand on your shoulder. Good luck, Joe. Shan't see you for a long time – I hope.

FLETTEN: All the best, Mr Radfern.

(*He hurries out at the back. RADFERN goes to the telephone and begins dialling.*)

RADFERN: (*At telephone.*) I want to speak to Mr Middleton, please... Hello, is that you, Charlie? Yes, Radfern. Yes, everything all right at Birmingham... But, listen, Charlie...

(*MRS RADFERN and ELSIE enter. The latter is carrying a lot of shipping booklets, etc. She is listless and looks miserable.*)

I've just had an Inspector from Scotland Yard... Yes... And you know how these chaps get about a bit, and he was saying that he didn't think business would be very good these next few months... Yes, so I thought I'd take that holiday I've been promising myself for some time... Yes, what we used to call Plan B – you remember our little joke... Holland, of course... All right, Charlie... Good-bye.

(*Puts down telephone.*)

MRS RADFERN: (*Jovially.*) You didn't get arrested then, Dad?

RADFERN: (*In same tone.*) No, just managed to escape.

MRS RADFERN: What did the Inspector want?

RADFERN: What you said. Just making some enquiries about a commercial case he's on. Queer life they have, those chaps.

ELSIE: (*Joining in, but still listless.*) Wouldn't suit you, Dad. Too much excitement. Not enough peace and quietness.

RADFERN: That's it.

MRS RADFERN: (*Chaffing.*) You didn't tell him what a tough old crook you were yourself, did you?

RADFERN: No need to. He knew it already.

ELSIE: (*Still listless.*) What were you saying on the telephone about going away?

RADFERN: (*With affectionate concern.*) Look here, Elsie. You've got to brighten up, because there's a lot to do.

ELSIE: (*Indifferently.*) What is there to do?

RADFERN: Well, one of the things you've got to do is to take your mother to Brussels tomorrow.

ELSIE: (*A changed girl.*) Dad! You don't mean it!

RADFERN: I do. We're going to close this house and go on our travels.

MRS RADFERN: Good gracious me!

ELSIE: Dad!

RADFERN: Now, we've got passports.

ELSIE: Where are they marked for?

RADFERN: Everywhere. You see – we're going to close this house, pack up and go on a long sea voyage – East Indies, Far East, Australia – God knows where. Only we're starting on one of those Dutch boats.

MRS RADFERN: Dutch boats! Why not an English boat?

RADFERN: Oh, all the best boats that go out East are Dutch. They're much more comfortable. English boats are like police courts! You and your mother are going to Brussels first, and then you're going to meet me later, over there.

MRS RADFERN: But how are you going?

RADFERN: I'm going straight to Holland. Some business to attend to first. A friend of mine will take me.

ELSIE: But how?

RADFERN: By underground perhaps. Never mind about that.

ELSIE: Oh – I don't mind about anything. (*Embraces him.*) Mother, we're going to travel. (*Embraces her.*)

MRS RADFERN: I hope this isn't another of your jokes, Dad?

ELSIE: Oh, Dad, I'll never forgive you if it is.

RADFERN: It isn't. You've got twenty-four hours to pack up in and close this house and get off to Brussels.

ELSIE: (*Babbling happily.*) Then we won't go to bed at all. And let's look at these things (*Holding up shipping booklets.*) and then we'll have supper and begin packing. But we'll have to have some clothes, won't we, Mother, especially if we're going to hot countries, but I suppose we could get them in Brussels or wherever we're going – couldn't we go to Paris first and then we could buy some clothes there and it would be nearly as easy to get from Paris to Holland or wherever it is –

MRS RADFERN: (*Loudly.*) Oh, Elsie, stop it. My head's going round.

(*There is a ring at the front door, very loud and persistent. It startles them all.*)

ELSIE: I'll go. (*Runs off.*)

MRS RADFERN: That child's so excited she doesn't know what she's talking about.

RADFERN: Do her good.

MRS RADFERN: It won't if she's disappointed again.

RADFERN: I'll see to that.

MRS RADFERN: You're very masterful tonight, Dad, aren't you? What's the matter?

RADFERN: Have to assert myself sometimes, Mother.

(*ELSIE returns a moment later, looking frightened.*)

ELSIE: Dad, it's a police sergeant and he wants to see you.

RADFERN: (*Gravely, steadily.*) All right.

ELSIE: (*Going over to him, softly.*) Dad – it's not true – after all is it?

RADFERN: (*Cheerfully.*) That's all right, Elsie. Ask him to
come in.

(*ELSIE is clinging to his arm.*)

MRS RADFERN: Don't be ridiculous, Elsie.

(*She goes and admits the sergeant, a heavily built, middle-
aged man with a deep voice and a rather pompous manner.*)

SERGEANT MORRIS: Mr George Radfern.

RADFERN: (*Steadily.*) That's me, Sergeant.

SERGEANT MORRIS: I think you've seen me before. I'm
from the local station.

RADFERN: Know you well by sight.

SERGEANT MORRIS: I've just heard that you might be
going away soon.

RADFERN: That's right. I'm seriously thinking of it,
Sergeant.

SERGEANT MORRIS: Well, Mr Cross at the end house
said you'd like to be one of the patrons and vice
presidents of the new Shooters Green Football Club.

RADFERN: Oh – you've come round to make sure of my
subscription.

SERGEANT MORRIS: (*Relieved.*) That's it, Mr Radfern.
Three guineas – for a vice-president.

RADFERN: (*Producing money.*) Must be a vice-president.
There you are. There's a flyer for luck.

SERGEANT MORRIS: (*Who has been writing.*) That's the
official receipt. And thank you very much, Mr Radfern.
Good night, mum, good night, miss. Good night.

(*He goes out, and MRS RADFERN goes as far as the door
behind him. ELSIE gives an hysterical laugh, really of relief.*)

RADFERN: What are you laughing at?

ELSIE: I don't know. Everything. Oh – Dad – how long
shall we be away?

RADFERN: Don't know yet. Four months. Six months.

ELSIE: Oh – what about your greenhouse?

RADFERN: Where we're going it'll be all greenhouse.

(*Enter MRS RADFERN.*)

ELSIE: And what about Laburnum Grove?

MRS RADFERN: (*Briskly.*) It'll be still here when we come
back.

ELSIE: (*Excitedly.*) Let's look at all these things. (*Indicating shipping booklets.*)

MRS RADFERN: (*Firmly.*) It's my turn now. We don't look at anything until we've had some supper. And you can help me to get it ready for once.

ELSIE: (*Happily.*) All right, mother. (*Hurries into kitchen, where she can be heard singing happily.*)

MRS RADFERN: (*As she removes various things and cloth from table.*) And you needn't tell me you haven't been up to *something*, you know, Dad.

RADFERN: (*Grinning at her.*) All right, Mother. I needn't tell you.

(*MRS RADFERN is spreading a tablecloth and ELSIE entering with some supper things and RADFERN smiling at them both, as the curtain slowly descends.*)

The End.

WHEN WE ARE MARRIED

A Yorkshire Farcical Comedy

Characters

RUBY BIRTLE

GERALD FORBES

NANCY HOLMES

Alderman JOSEPH HELLIWELL

MARIA HELLIWELL

Councillor ALBERT PARKER

ANNIE PARKER

HERBERT SOPPITT

CLARA SOPPITT

MRS NORTHROP

FRED DYSON

HENRY ORMONROYD

LOTTIE GRADY

Rev CLEMENT MERCER

When We Are Married was first produced at St Martin's Theatre, London on 11 October 1938, with the following cast:

RUBY BIRTLE, Patricia Hayes

GERALD FORBES, Richard Warner

NANCY HOLMES, Betty Fleetwood

HELLIWELL, Lloyd Pearson

MARIA HELLIWELL, Muriel George

PARKER, Raymond Huntley

ANNIE PARKER, Helena Pickard

SOPPITT, Ernest Butcher

CLARA SOPPITT, Ethel Coleridge

MRS NORTHROP, Beatrice Varley

FRED DYSON, Alexander Grandison

HENRY ORMONROYD, Frank Pettingell

LOTTIE GRADY, Mai Bacon

Rev CLEMENT MERCER, Norman Wooland

Producer, Basil Dean

The sitting-room of Alderman Helliwell's house in Cleckleywyke, a town in the West Riding, on a September evening early in the twentieth century.

ACT ONE

The sitting-room in HELLIWELL's house, a solid detached late-Victorian house. On left (Actor's left) wall is a window. Left of centre in back wall is a door to rest of house, leading directly into the hall. On right wall is a small conservatory, with door leading into this, and then into garden. The room is furnished without taste in the style of about thirty years ago. There is an upright piano. Little cupboards, drawers, small tables, etc. At rise, evening sunlight coming through window. Nobody on stage.

We hear the front door bell ring. A moment later, RUBY BIRTLE ushers in GERALD FORBES. RUBY is a very young 'slavey' of the period, who looks as if her hair has just gone 'up'. FORBES is a pleasant young man, in the smart clothes of the period and, unlike RUBY and most of the other characters, does not talk with a marked West Riding accent.

RUBY: You'll have to wait 'cos they haven't finished their tea.

GERALD: Bit late, aren't they?

RUBY: (*Approaching, confidentially.*) It's a do.

GERALD: It's what?

RUBY: A do. Y'know, they've company.

GERALD: Oh – I see. It's a sort of party, and they're having high tea.

RUBY: (*Going closer still.*) Roast pork, stand pie, salmon and salad, trifle, two kinds o' jellies, lemon cheese tarts, jam tarts, swiss tarts, sponge cake, walnut cake, chocolate roll, and a pound cake kept from last Christmas.

GERALD: (*With irony.*) Is that all?

RUBY: (*Seriously.*) No, there's white bread, brown bread, currant teacake, one o' them big curd tarts from Gregory's, and a lot o' cheese.

GERALD: It *is* a do, isn't it?

RUBY: (*After nodding, then very confidentially.*) *And* a little brown jug.

GERALD: (*Astonished.*) A little brown jug?

103

RUBY: (*Still confidentially.*) You know what that is, don't you? Don't you? (*Laughs.*) Well, I never did! Little brown jug's a drop o' rum for your tea. They're getting right lively on it. (*Coolly.*) But you don't come from round here, do you?

GERALD: (*Not disposed for a chat.*) No.

(*A distant bell rings, not front door.*)

RUBY: I come from near Rotherham. Me father works in t'pit, and so does our Frank and our Wilfred.

(*Distant bell sounds again.*)

GERALD: There's a bell ringing somewhere.

RUBY: (*Coolly.*) I know. It's for me. Let her wait. She's run me off me legs today. And Mrs Northrop's in t'kitchen – she can do a bit for a change. There's seven of 'em at it in t'dining-room – Alderman Helliwell and missus, of course – then Councillor Albert Parker and Mrs Parker, and Mr Herbert Soppitt and Mrs Soppitt – and of course, Miss Holmes.

GERALD: Oh – Miss Holmes *is* there, is she?

RUBY: Yes, but she's stopped eating. (*Giggles. Coolly.*) You're courting her, aren't you?

GERALD: (*Astonished and alarmed.*) What!

RUBY: (*Coolly.*) Oh – I saw you both – the other night, near Cleckley Woods. I was out meself with our milkman's lad.

(*GERALD turns away.*)

Now don't look like that, I won't tell on you.

GERALD: (*Producing a shilling, then rather desperately.*) Now – look here! What's your name?

RUBY: Ruby Birtle.

GERALD: Well, Ruby, you wouldn't like Miss Holmes to get into a row here with her uncle and aunt, would you?

RUBY: No, I wouldn't like that. But I'd like that shilling.

GERALD: (*After giving it to her.*) You said Miss Holmes had finished eating.

RUBY: Yes. She can't put it away like some of 'em. I'd rather keep Councillor Albert Parker a week than a fortnight. D'you want to see her?

GERALD: Yes. Could you just give her the tip quietly that I'm here – if the rest of them aren't coming in here yet?

RUBY: Not them! You'd think they'd been pined for a month – way they're going at it! I'll tell her. She'd better come round that way – through t'greenhouse –
(*Before she can actually move, MRS NORTHROP, an aggressive but humorous working-woman of about fifty, puts her head in the door.*)

MRS NORTHROP: (*Aggressively.*) Oh – 'ere y'are!

RUBY: (*Coolly.*) That's right, Mrs Northrop.

MRS NORTHROP: (*Aggressively.*) I see nought right about it – you gassin in 'ere as if you owned t'place instead o' gettin' on wi' your work. She's rung for yer twice, an' I've just taken another lot o' hot water in. Nah, come on, yer little crackpot!
(*She holds the door open, and RUBY goes to it – turns and grins. Exit RUBY.*)

MRS NORTHROP: Aren't you t'organist at chapel?

GERALD: Yes.

MRS NORTHROP: (*Cheerfully.*) Ay, well, they've got it in for you.

GERALD: (*Astonished.*) How do you know?

MRS NORTHROP: 'Cos I 'eard 'em say so. (*Complacently.*) I don't miss much.

GERALD: So that's why Mr Helliwell asked me to come round and see him.

MRS NORTHROP: That's right. There's three of 'em 'ere tonight, d'you see – all big men at chapel. You've been enjoyin' yerself a bit too much, I fancy, lad.

GERALD: So that's it – is it?

MRS NORTHROP: (*With very confidential air.*) Ay – and d'you know what I say? I say – to 'ell with 'em!
(*She goes out, leaving GERALD looking a little worried. He moves about restlessly, takes cigarette-case out of his pocket mechanically, then puts it back again. He keeps an eye on the door into the conservatory. After a few moments, NANCY HOLMES, an attractive girl in her early twenties, hurries in through this door.*)

NANCY: (*In breathless whisper.*) Gerald!

GERALD: Nancy! (*Makes as if to kiss her.*)

NANCY: (*Breathlessly.*) No, you mustn't, not here – no, Gerald – please –

(*But he does kiss her and no harm has been done.*)

Now, listen, Gerald, and be sensible. This is serious. You know why Uncle Joe sent for you?

GERALD: (*With a slight grin.*) They've *got it in* for me. I've just been told.

NANCY: It's serious, Gerald. They've been grumbling about you some time, and now, as far as I can gather, one of these miserable old beasts saw you late one night – with *me* –

GERALD: (*Serious now.*) Oh – I say – you weren't recognised, were you?

NANCY: No. But *you* were.

GERALD: Well, that's not so bad, as long as they can't drag you into it. I know how strict your aunt is, and you can't afford to quarrel with them here until we're ready to be married –

NANCY: (*Earnestly.*) No, but you can't either, Gerald. And they're going to be very cross with you, and you'll have to be awfully careful what you say to them. And there's that beastly Councillor Parker here too, and you loathe him, don't you?

GERALD: Absolutely. And I'll loathe him more than ever now that he's full of roast pork and trifle. I think I'd better give them time to recover from that huge ghastly tuck-in they're having.

NANCY: I should. Though they've nearly finished now.

GERALD: If I clear out for half an hour or so, could you slip away too?

NANCY: I might. They don't really want me. I'm in the way. You see, it's an anniversary celebration, and I don't come into it at all.

GERALD: What are they celebrating?

(*Before she can reply, RUBY opens door, announcing.*)

RUBY: It's Yorkshire Argus – two of 'em.

(*GERALD rises, moves down right. NANCY rises up to door. Enter FRED DYSON, a cheerful, rather cheeky youngish reporter, and HENRY ORMONROYD, who carries a large and old-fashioned newspaperman's camera and a flashlight apparatus. ORMONROYD is a middle-aged man with an air of beery dignity and wears a large drooping moustache. DYSON walks down to NANCY.*)

RUBY: This is Miss Holmes, Alderman Helliwell's niece. T'others is still having their tea.

(*RUBY goes out.*)

DYSON: (*Cheerfully.*) 'Evening, Miss Holmes. (*To GERALD.*) How d'you do? This is Mr Henry Ormonroyd, our photographer.

ORMONROYD: (*Bowing.*) Pleased to meet you, I'm sure. Delightful weather we're having for the time of year.

GERALD: Isn't it?

ORMONROYD: (*Profoundly.*) It is.

DYSON: We seem to have come too early.

NANCY: I'm afraid you have –

ORMONROYD: (*With dignified reproach.*) What did I tell you, Fred? Always wanting to rush things. We could have had at least a couple more – with my friend at The Lion. He's a chap who used to have a very good little peppermint-rock business on the Central Pier, Blackpool at the time I had my studio – there. Old times, y'know, Mr – er, and happy days, happy days! (*Hums.*)

DYSON: (*Briskly.*) All right, Henry. I'm sorry we're early. Matter of fact, I don't know yet what this is about. I just got a message from the office to come up here and bring a photographer.

NANCY: You see, it's their Silver Wedding.

DYSON: Henry, it's Alderman Helliwell's *Silver Wedding.*

ORMONROYD: Very nice, I suppose.

NANCY: Yes, but not only my uncle and aunt's. There were three couples – my uncle and aunt, Mr and Mrs Soppitt, Mr and Mrs Parker.

DYSON: Is that Councillor Albert Parker?

NANCY: (*Pulling a little face.*) Yes. You know him?

DYSON: (*Gloomily.*) Yes, we know him.

ORMONROYD: Every time he opens his mouth at the Town Hall, he puts his foot in it, so they call him 'the foot and mouth disease'. Ha. Ha. Are all three happy couples here?

NANCY: Yes, because they were all married on the same morning at the same chapel. They have a photograph – a combined wedding group. (*She goes to find it – on top of the piano.*)

GERALD: You'll have to interview 'em, and they'll tell you how happy they've been –

DYSON: Oh – yes. I see the idea now.

NANCY: (*Returning with old photograph.*) Here you are. All six of them on their wedding morning. Don't they look absurd in those clothes?

ORMONROYD: (*Solemnly.*) To you – yes. To me – no. I was married myself about that time. (*Holding photograph at arm's length.*) Now, you see, Fred, what's wanted is another group in the very same positions. After twenty-five years' wear and tear. Very nice.

DYSON: You're holding it upside down.

ORMONROYD: I know, lad. I know, that's the way we always look at 'em professionally. Either flies 'ave been at this or somebody's touched up Albert Parker with a screwdriver. Well, if we're too early, we're too early. Might nip back to The Lion, Fred lad, eh?
(*ORMONROYD takes camera from top of settee left.*)

DYSON: We'll come back in about an hour.

ORMONROYD: They're keeping a very nice drop of beer down at The Lion now.
(*DYSON and ORMONROYD go out, NANCY going towards the door with them, and shutting it behind them. GERALD looks at the photograph, then at the back of it, and is obviously interested and amused.*)

GERALD: This was when they were all married then – September the fifth, 'Eighty-three?

NANCY: Yes – why? What's the matter, Gerald?
(*He has started laughing.*)

Gerald, what is it? Oh – don't be so mean. They'll be here in a minute.

(*As he shakes his head, still laughing softly, we hear voices behind door into hall.*)

GERALD: They're coming in. Nancy, let's dodge out that way.

(*He puts photograph on table behind settee right, picks up his straw hat, while she has gone to door into conservatory, and they hurry out that way, shutting door behind them.*

Voices outside door into hall are louder now, and after a moment the PARKERS, the SOPPITTS, the HELLIWELLS enter. They are dressed in their best, and obviously crammed with high tea. ALBERT PARKER is a tall, thin, conceited, sententious man; his wife ANNIE, a hopeful kind of woman. HERBERT SOPPITT is a smallish neat man, clearly dominated by his wife CLARA, a noisy woman. The HELLIWELLS are high-coloured, rather bouncing, rather pompous, very pleased with themselves. Their ages are all between forty-five and fifty-five. HERBERT SOPPITT and MRS PARKER talk a rather genteel ordinary English; the other four have pronounced north-country accents, with particularly broad 'a' sounds.)

HELLIWELL: (*Very much the host.*) Now what's wanted now's a good cigar, an' I've got the very thing. (*Goes to get box from drawer or table.*)

MARIA: (*Indignantly.*) That Mrs Northrop! When she's finished her washing-up tonight she goes – and goes for good.

CLARA: And quite right too! They're all the same. Answering back – if you say anything.

MARIA: Trouble with her is – she likes a drop. I've smelt it before today.

(*CLARA sits below sofa left. MARIA to corner. ANNIE drops down right to sofa down right.*)

HELLIWELL: (*Offering cigar-box to PARKER.*) Now then, Albert! You'll find that's a good cigar, La Corona.

PARKER: (*Taking one.*) Thanks, Joe. As you know, I don't smoke a lot, but when I do, I like a good cigar.

HELLIWELL: (*Offering to SOPPITT.*) Herbert?

SOPPITT: I don't think – er – I will – thanks, Joe.

MARIA: (*Expansively.*) Nay, Herbert, 'ave one o' Joe's cigars.

CLARA: If he'd had it to pay for himself, he'd have been wanting one.

SOPPITT: (*Rather nervously.*) I think – I'd rather not smoke just now – I believe I ate too much at tea.

ANNIE: (*To keep him company.*) I know I did.

PARKER: (*Severely.*) Yes, an' you'll be complaining before the night's out.

CLARA: An' so will Herbert.

PARKER: (*Complacently.*) Now that's something that never bothers me.

HELLIWELL: No, we've noticed that, Albert.

PARKER: (*Offended.*) How d'you mean?

MARIA: Go on, Albert, you know what Joe is – must 'ave his little joke.

ANNIE: I know *I* ought to have stopped long before I did – I mean, at tea – but, Maria, everything was *so* nice.

CLARA: 'Ear, 'ear.

MARIA: (*Complacently accepting this.*) Well, I said to Joe, 'Now, Joe,' I said, 'we'll only have just the six of us, but we'll make it an occasion an' do it well while we're at it,' I said. Didn't I, Joe?

HELLIWELL: (*Busy attending to his cigar, though he does not remove the band.*) Did you?

MARIA: (*Indignantly.*) You know very well I did.

HELLIWELL: (*Still not interested.*) All right, you did then.

MARIA: (*Same indignant tone.*) You know quite well I did, Joe Helliwell.

HELLIWELL: (*Suddenly annoyed himself.*) All right, all right, all right, you did then.

CLARA: (*Pats MARIA's hand.*) They're all alike. Wait till somebody else's with you, and then try to make you out a liar.

PARKER: (*Severely.*) Speak for yourself! I don't try to make my wife out a liar, do I, Annie?

ANNIE: (*Rather timidly, hesitantly.*) Well – no – Albert, not – really –

PARKER: (*Very severely.*) How d'you mean – *not really* –
I just don't, that's all. (*Changing the subject, in rather lordly
style.*) A good smoke, Joe, quite a good smoke. It
reminds me of that cigar Sir Harold Watson gave me not
so long since at the club. I was standing near the
fireplace, and Sir Harold came up –

ANNIE: (*Gathering courage to interrupt.*) Albert – you told
them before.

PARKER: (*Glaring.*) Well, I can tell 'em again, can't I?

SOPPITT: Maria, have you got a copy of that old
photograph we had taken? I couldn't find ours.

MARIA: Yes. Where is it, Joe? (*While he looks round.*) Aaa, I
laugh many a time when I think o' that morning – six of
us, all so nervous –

HELLIWELL: And the parson worse still. He was only like
two-pennorth o' copper, an' I could ha' given him a few
years myself.

CLARA: I think we were about first he'd ever married.

ANNIE: I'm sure we were. I didn't feel I'd been married
properly –

PARKER: (*Severely.*) Of course you'd been married properly.
If he'd been ninety and doing it all his life, you wouldn't
ha' been married any better, would you?

MARIA: I've forgotten his name now. He was only a
temporary, wasn't he?

SOPPITT: I remember! (*A pause.*) It was a tree. Beech.

HELLIWELL: That's right – Beech – an' he'd a funny
squint. (*Has found photograph.*) And here's the old photo.
(*He hands it to his wife and the ladies look at it, with
exclamations, while the men remain aloof.*)

PARKER: (*The businessman now.*) I see Crossbreds are down
again.

HELLIWELL: (*Another businessman.*) Ay – and they'll stay
down with Australian market as it is. If I've said it once,
I've said it a thousand times – if Merinos is down and
staying down, then your Crossbreds'll have to follow.
Now, look at Merinos –

MARIA: (*Looking up to expostulate.*) Here, Joe, we didn't
come here to talk about Merinos. This isn't Wool

111

Exchange. Take a look at yourselves and see what we took on.

(*He ignores her. She puts photograph on table back of settee.*)

HELLIWELL: Now wait a minute. 'Ealths!

MARIA: That's right, Joe. Ring!

(*HELLIWELL rings. MARIA turns to others.*)

We ought to do it in proper style, an' drink our healths before we go any further.

SOPPITT: (*Attempting a joke.*) Further – where?

CLARA: (*Severely.*) That'll do, Herbert. A bit o' fun's all right, but you go too far.

SOPPITT: I didn't mean –

CLARA: (*Cutting in.*) That'll do.

(*MRS NORTHROP looks in.*)

MRS NORTHROP: (*Aggressively.*) Well?

MARIA: (*Rather grandly.*) There's a tray with glasses on – just bring it in –

MRS NORTHROP: (*Indignantly.*) What – me? How many pairs of 'ands –

HELLIWELL: (*Peremptorily.*) *Now then* – just tell thingumptyite – Ruby – to bring in the port wine.

MRS NORTHROP: What – on top o' your tea? You'll be poorly.

(*She withdraws. HELLIWELL is furious.*)

HELLIWELL: (*Angrily.*) Now did you 'ear that –

MARIA: (*Hastily.*) All right, Joe, we don't want any trouble. She goes tonight, an' she doesn't come back.

CLARA: I don't know what things are coming to! All the same! Answering back!

PARKER: (*Sententiously.*) They're all alike, that class of people. We have the same trouble at mill. Don't know when they're well off. Idle, that's what they are – bone idle!

CLARA: And impudent! Back-answers!

ANNIE: (*Timidly.*) Yes – but I suppose they don't know any better –

PARKER: (*Severely.*) They know a lot better. And what you want to stick up for 'em for, I can't think.

HELLIWELL: (*Heartily.*) Now then, Albert, don't start
fratching, but try an' enjoy yourself for once. This is an
anniversary. Which reminds me, Charlie Pearson told
me, t'other day, they built a new Wesleyan Methodist
Chapel up at Thornton, and they opened with an
anniversary. Anyhow, this is ours, so let's have peace an'
goodwill all round. Now I thought we'd first drink a bit
of a toast to ourselves –

MARIA: That was *my* idea.

HELLIWELL: (*Ignoring this, but only just.*) Then I thought
we'd have a bit of a chat about old times, an' then we'd
settle down to a game o' Newmarket –

MARIA: That was my idea too.

HELLIWELL: (*Annoyed.*) What the hangment does it matter
whose idea it was, so long as we get on with it and enjoy
ourselves!

SOPPITT: That's the great thing. (*Controlled belch. Catches
his wife's eye and falters.*) Enjoy ourselves. (*Rises. Moves to
door. Looks miserable and a bit sick.*)

CLARA: (*Severely.*) I told you to leave that salmon alone.

HELLIWELL: Nay, Clara, why can't he have a bit o'
salmon if he fancies it?

CLARA: (*Sharply.*) 'Cos it doesn't fancy him, Joe Helliwell,
that's why. Look at that time we all went to Scarborough!

SOPPITT: (*Turns.*) It was Bridlington.

CLARA: It was both! And what did that doctor say? *You're
digging your grave with your teeth, Mr Soppitt.*

HELLIWELL: Hahaha!
(*Enter RUBY, carrying tray with six small glasses on it, and
three bottles of port.*)
Here, what did you want to bring 'em all for? One bottle
at a time's enough.

RUBY: (*Putting down tray.*) Mrs Northrop said you'd better
'ave t'lot while you was at it.

HELLIWELL: In future, just take your orders from me and
not from Mrs Northrop. Now just trot along – an' no lip.
(*Starts to take cork out of bottle.*)

RUBY: (*Turning at door.*) Mrs Northrop says she's not
coming 'ere again –

HELLIWELL: (*Heatedly.*) We know all about it. (*Moves after her, cigar in mouth, bottle in hand.*)

MARIA: (*Cutting in.*) Now let it be, Joe.

(*HELLIWELL stands, draws cork with an effort. RUBY has now gone and closed door. HELLIWELL begins pouring out the port.*)

D'you know what we ought to do for this? We ought to get just in the same places we were in that old photo. Where is it? (*Finds it and directs them from it.*) Now here we are. (*Uses a sofa.*) I was in the middle. You were here, Clara. You this side, Annie. Now come on, Albert – behind Annie. Herbert.

(*MARIA sits last. These five have now arranged themselves in grouping of old photograph. HELLIWELL hands them their glasses of port, then takes up a position himself.*)

HELLIWELL: (*Facetiously.*) Here's to me and my wife's husband!

MARIA: Let's have none o' that silly business, Joe!

PARKER: (*Solemnly.*) A few serious words is what's needed.

ANNIE: (*Rather plaintively.*) Oh – must you, Albert?

PARKER: How d'you mean – must I? What's wrong with a few serious words on an occasion like this? Marriage – is a serious business.

CLARA: That's right, Albert. Where'd we be without it?

SOPPITT: Single.

CLARA: That'll do, Herbert.

PARKER: (*Sententiously.*) Marriage – well – marriage – to begin with, it's an institution, isn't it?

MARIA: (*Solemnly.*) That is so. (*Sighs profoundly.*)

PARKER: (*Getting into his stride.*) One of the *oldest* institutions. It goes back – right back to – well, it goes right back. And it's still going strong today. Why?

HELLIWELL: (*Hastily.*) Well, because –

PARKER: (*Sharply cutting in.*) Let me finish, Joe, let me finish. Now why is it still going strong today? Because it's the backbone of a decent respectable life.

HELLIWELL: (*Solemnly.*) True, Albert, true.

PARKER: Where would women be without marriage?

CLARA: (*Sharply.*) And where'd some o' you men be?

PARKER: All right, I'm coming to that.

HELLIWELL: Well, don't be too long, Albert. I want to try this port.

PARKER: (*Solemnly.*) Marriage may be a bit more necessary to women than it is to men –

ANNIE: Why?

PARKER: (*Annoyed at this.*) *Why?*

HELLIWELL: Children, you see, Annie.

ANNIE: (*Abashed.*) Oh – yes – I'd forgotten. Still –

PARKER: I'm talking now, *if* you please. But if a woman wants a 'ome and security and a respectable life, *which* she gets from marriage, a man wants something to –

CLARA: (*Quickly.*) He wants all he can get.

PARKER: He wants a nice comfortable 'ome, somebody to tell his troubles to and so forth –

HELLIWELL: (*Facetiously.*) That's good, Albert, the 'and so forth'.

PARKER: Now, Joe –

HELLIWELL: Well, cut it short –

PARKER: (*Slowly and solemnly.*) So, as we're all gathered 'ere to celebrate the anniversary of our joint wedding day, friends, I give you – the toast of *Marriage!*

MARIA: Very nice, Albert.

(*They all drink.*)

ANNIE: (*Confidentially.*) It'll go straight to my head. D'you remember that time at Harrogate? I could have sunk through the floor when that waiter laughed.

HELLIWELL: (*Producing bottle again.*) Now wait a minute. That's all right as far as it goes – but – nay – damn it! –

MARIA: (*Reproachfully.*) Joe!

HELLIWELL: We must have another toast, just for ourselves. I bet it isn't often there's three couples can meet like this who were all wed on same morning together. Now then –

(*He insists on filling the glasses again as they still hold them in their hands.*)

MARIA: (*Confidentially.*) I don't act silly, but my face gets so red.

HELLIWELL: Now – here's to all of us – and the Reverend Mr What's his name – Beech – who tied us up – wherever he is –

THE OTHERS: Here's to us. Here's to him. (*Etc.*)

(*They drink. When they have finished, the front-door bell is heard.*)

MARIA: Front door! Who'll that be?

HELLIWELL: (*Rather importantly.*) Well, I told Yorkshire Argus to send somebody round to have a word with us.

CLARA: (*Delighted.*) What – are you going to have a piece in the papers?

PARKER: They don't want to catch us like this.

(*PARKER swallows rest of his port hastily. The others do the same. The group breaks up. RUBY looks in.*)

MARIA: Is it Yorkshire Argus?

RUBY: No, it's Mr Forbes, t'organist from t'chapel. He came afore, an' then went away again.

HELLIWELL: Tell him to wait.

(*RUBY goes. HELLIWELL turns to the others.*)

You know about this business, Albert. You too, Herbert.

SOPPITT: (*Hesitantly.*) Yes – but – (*Crosses to HELLIWELL.*)

HELLIWELL: (*Sharply.*) But, nothing. You're too soft, Herbert.

CLARA: I'm always telling him so.

HELLIWELL: He's chapel organist – he's paid for t'job – an' either he behaves himself properly or he goes.

PARKER: (*Severely.*) He'll go anyhow, if I've *my* say.

ANNIE: No, Albert, he's not a bad young fellow –

PARKER: Now you shut up, Annie. You don't know half of what we know. An' I'll bet we don't know half there is to know about that chap. Never should ha' been appointed. I said so then. I say so now. I know my own mind.

ANNIE: (*Rebelliously.*) I wish sometimes you'd keep a bit of it to yourself.

PARKER: What's that mean?

(*NANCY now appears at door from conservatory.*)

MARIA: Hallo, love, where've you been?

NANCY: (*Who seems a trifle giggly.*) Just out a minute. You
   don't want me, do you, Auntie? Because if you don't,
   I thought I'd put my hat and coat on and see if Muriel
   Spencer's in. (*Crosses up to door.*)

MARIA: (*Rises.*) All right. There's that Gerald Forbes
   waiting outside – your uncle has something to say to
   him – now don't go talking to him.

HELLIWELL: I should think not. Just say 'Hello' or 'Good
   evening' and leave it at that. The less you have to do
   with that chap the better, Nancy.
   (*NANCY suddenly explodes into giggles.*)
   Now what's funny about that?

NANCY: (*Still giggling.*) I'm sorry, Uncle. I just remembered
   – something that amused me –
   (*NANCY goes out, giggling.*)

HELLIWELL: Now what's got hold of her?

MARIA: Oh – she's at silly age. They don't know half the
   time whether to laugh or cry when they're that age. Now,
   Clara – Annie – we'll leave the men to it. I expect that's
   what they want –

PARKER: (*Solemnly.*) Certainly. After all, it's chapel
   business.

MARIA: Well, we want to go upstairs anyhow!

HELLIWELL: That's right.
   (*CLARA glares at him.*)

MARIA: You haven't seen what Joe bought me yet. But
   don't take too long over him.

PARKER: *Him!* It wouldn't take *me* long –

HELLIWELL: It'll take me less long, 'cos I don't make
   speeches. Here, we'll put these out o' t'way – (*At
   sideboard.*)
   (*The women go out, and HELLIWELL puts the glasses back
   on the tray. A certain primness now descends on them.*)

PARKER: I said from first – it's a bad appointment. To start
   with, he's too young.

SOPPITT: (*Rather timidly.*) I don't think that matters much.

PARKER: (*Severely.*) Trouble with you, Herbert, is you don't
   think anything matters much, and that's just where you're
   wrong.

HELLIWELL: Young Forbes is a southerner an' all.

PARKER: (*With grim triumph.*) Ah – I was coming to that.

SOPPITT: Oughtn't we to have him in?

HELLIWELL: No, let him wait a bit.

PARKER: Do him good. No, as soon as they told me he's a
southerner and his name's Gerald, I said, 'We don't want
him.' I said, 'La-di-dah. That's what you're going to get
from him,' I said. 'La-di-dah. What we want at Lane End
– biggest chapel for miles – wi' any amount o' money in
congregation – what we want is a bit o' good old
Yorkshire organ-playing and choir training,' I said. 'We
don't want la-di-dah.' (*With awful imitation of ultra-refined
accents.*) 'Heow d'yew dew. Sow chawmed to meek your
acquaintance. Eoh, dee-lateful wethah!' Grr. You know
what I call that stuff?

SOPPITT: (*Who has a sense of humour.*) Yes. (*Broadly.*) La-di-
dah.

HELLIWELL: Albert's right. We made a mistake. Mind
you, he'd good qualifications, an' he seemed a nice quiet
lad. But I must say, after old Sam Fawcett, chapel didn't
seem right with an organist who goes round wearing one
o' these pink shirts and knitted ties and creases in his
trousers –

PARKER: It's all –

(*Here SOPPITT joins in.*)

PARKER/SOPPITT: La-di-dah!

PARKER: (*In disgusted tone.*) Then look at his Messiah! We
warned him. I said to him myself, 'I know it's a
Christmas piece, but you've got to get in quick, afore the
others.'

HELLIWELL: Right, Albert. After t'end o' November,
there's been so many of 'em you might as well take your
Messiah an' throw it into t'canal.

PARKER: And look what happened. Hillroad Baptist gave
Messiah. Salem gave Messiah. Tong Congregational gave
Messiah. Picklebrook Wesleyans gave Messiah. And
where was Lane End?

SOPPITT: Well, when we did get it – it was a good one.

HELLIWELL: I'm not saying it wasn't, but by that time who cared? But anyhow all that's a detail. Point is, we can't have any carrying on, can we?

SOPPITT: (*Gravely.*) Ah – there I agree, Joe.

PARKER: (*Indignantly.*) An' I should think so. Organist at Lane End Chapel *carrying on!* That sort o' game may do down south, but it won't do up 'ere.

HELLIWELL: We're all agreed on that.

(*SOPPITT and PARKER nod.*)

Right then! We'll have 'im in.

(*HELLIWELL goes to the door, the other two sitting up stiffly and looking official and important.*)

(*Rather grimly through open door.*) All right, come in.

(*GERALD FORBES follows him in, closing but not latching the door behind him. GERALD looks cool and self-possessed, with a twinkle in his eye. HELLIWELL sits down and looks as official and important as the other two. All three stare severely at GERALD, as he sits down. GERALD pulls out a cigarette-case, but no sooner has he taken a cigarette from it than ALBERT PARKER remonstrates with him.*)

PARKER: (*Severely.*) I wouldn't do that.

GERALD: (*Rather startled.*) Do what?

PARKER: (*Severely.*) Well, what 'ave you got in your 'and?

GERALD: (*Still surprised.*) This? Cigarette. Why?

PARKER: Under the circumstances, young man, don't you think it might be better – more – more suitable – more fitting – if you didn't smoke that just now?

(*The three men look at each other.*)

GERALD: (*With a shrug.*) Oh – all right, if that's how you feel about it. (*Puts case away. A pause.*) Well? You wanted to talk about something, didn't you?

HELLIWELL: (*Firmly.*) We did. We do.

PARKER: And if I'd 'ad *my* way, we'd have been talking to you long since.

GERALD: Well, not very long since, because I haven't been up here very long.

PARKER: No, you haven't been up here very long, and I don't think you'll be up here much longer.

HELLIWELL: Here, Albert, let *me* get a word in. Mr
Forbes, you're organist of our Lane End Chapel, and
that's the biggest place o' worship round here, and this is
a very respectable neighbourhood, with a lot o' money
behind it. You have a paid appointment as organist and
choir-master.

GERALD: Yes, though it doesn't keep me, y'know, Mr
Helliwell.

HELLIWELL: No, but because you *are* our organist, you're
able to get pupils and various extra jobs, so you don't do
so bad out of it, eh?

GERALD: (*A trifle dubiously.*) No, I'm quite satisfied – for
the time being.

PARKER: (*Annoyed.*) *You're* satisfied! For the time being!
You're satisfied!

GERALD: (*Quietly.*) That's what I said, Mr Parker.

PARKER: (*With dignity.*) Councillor Parker. (*Pointing.*)
Alderman Helliwell. Councillor Parker. *Mr* Soppitt.

GERALD: (*Indicating himself.*) Plain mud!

PARKER: (*Explosively.*) Now listen –

HELLIWELL: (*Cutting in noisily.*) Nay, let me finish, Albert.
We want to keep calm about this – just keep calm.

GERALD: I'm quite calm.

HELLIWELL: (*Explosively.*) You're a damn sight too calm
for my liking, young man. You ought to be sitting there
looking right ashamed of yourself, instead of looking –
looking – well, as you do look.

GERALD: But you haven't told me what's wrong yet.

PARKER: (*Angrily.*) Wrong? You're wrong. And carrying
on's wrong.

HELLIWELL: (*Loftily.*) In some chapels they mightn't care
what you did – I don't know – but Lane End's got a
position to keep up. We're respectable folk, and naturally
we expect our organist to behave respectably.

SOPPITT: (*Apologetically.*) I think you have been very
careless, Mr Forbes, and there really has been a lot of
grumbling.

PARKER: For one thing – you've been seen out – late at
night – wi' girls.

GERALD: Girls?

HELLIWELL: It may be t'same lass each time, for all I know, but if what I hear is true, whoever she is, she ought to be ashamed of herself. My word, if she'd owt to do wi' me, I'd teach her a sharp lesson.

PARKER: Somebody saw you once gallivanting away late at night, at Morecambe. And it gets round, y'know – oh – yes – it gets round.

GERALD: (*Beginning to lose his temper.*) Yes, so it seems. But I didn't think you'd find it worth while to listen to a lot of silly gossip –

PARKER: (*Sharply.*) Now don't start taking that tone –

GERALD: What tone can I take? I say, a lot of silly gossip –

SOPPITT: Now, steady, steady.

GERALD: Silly gossip. Old women's twaddle –

HELLIWELL: (*Heavily.*) That'll do. Just remember, you're not much more than a lad yet. We're nearly twice your age, and we know what's what –

GERALD: (*Angrily.*) Well, what is what then?

HELLIWELL: (*Angrily.*) This is what. We're not going to have any more of this. Either behave yourself or get back to where you came from. You're not going to make us a laughing-stock and a byword in t'neighbourhood. Now this is a fair warning –

GERALD: (*Steadily.*) I haven't done anything I'm ashamed of.

PARKER: What's that prove? If a chap's got cheek of a brass monkey, he never need do aught he's ashamed of.

SOPPITT: Careful, Albert.

PARKER: Why should I be careful? I'll tell him to his face what I've said behind his back. He never ought to have been appointed, and now he's been carrying on and not caring tuppence what respectable folk might think, he oughtn't to be given any warnings but told to get back to where he came from, and then he can carry on as much as he likes.

(*Both GERALD and HERBERT SOPPITT start to protest, but HELLIWELL loudly stops them.*)

HELLIWELL: Now, Albert, we mustn't be too hard. We must give young men just another chance. (*Severely and patronisingly to GERALD.*) I'm not sure I should if this were any other time. But nay – damn it this is a festive occasion an' we must take it easy a bit. So I'm giving you a last chance to mend yourself. And you can think yourself lucky catching me i' this humour. Just happens we're all celebrating anniversary of our wedding day – all three of us – ay, we've all been married twenty-five years today. (*Blows nose.*)

(*GERALD shakes his head rather sadly.*)

What're you shaking your head about?

GERALD: (*Quietly, gently.*) Well, you see, Mr Helliwell – I beg your pardon, Alderman Helliwell – I'm rather afraid you haven't been married twenty-five years.

HELLIWELL: (*Roaring.*) Do you think we can't count, lad?

GERALD: (*Same quiet tone.*) No, I don't mean that. But I'm afraid you've only been living together all this time.

HELLIWELL: (*Jumping up angrily.*) *Living together!* I'll knock your head right off your shoulders, lad, if you start talking like that to me.

GERALD: (*Also standing up.*) No, no, no. I'm not trying to insult you. I mean what I say.

PARKER: (*Rises, angrily.*) Mean what you say! You're wrong in your damned 'ead.

SOPPITT: (*Authoritative, for him.*) Wait a minute – Albert, Joe. We must listen. He means it.

HELLIWELL: (*Angrily.*) Means it! Means what?

GERALD: (*Impressively.*) If you'll just be quiet a minute I'll explain.

PARKER: (*Explosively.*) I don't want to –

GERALD: (*Sharply.*) I said – *quiet.*

HELLIWELL: Leave him be, Albert.

GERALD: (*Sits.*) Thanks. Mind if I smoke now?

(*All sit. With maddening slowness, GERALD takes out and lights cigarette. HELLIWELL and ALBERT PARKER watch him with impatience and look as if about to explode.*)

I went to North Wales for my holiday this summer –

HELLIWELL: (*Impatiently.*) Is this part of it, 'cos *I* don't care *where* you went for your holidays!

GERALD: (*Calmly.*) I went to North Wales, and only came back about a fortnight ago. While I was there I made the acquaintance of a parson, who'd been in Africa for the last twenty years. When he learnt that I was the organist of Lane End Chapel, Cleckleywyke, he became very excited, and then it turned out that he'd been at Lane End himself for a short time. About twenty-five years ago.

SOPPITT: What was his name?

GERALD: Beech. Francis Edwin Beech.

HELLIWELL: (*Boisterously.*) Oh – yes – Beech! We were only talking about him tonight. We remember Mr Beech. He married us, y'know. Yes, he married us, five-and-twenty years ago – all three couples. That's what we're celebrating –

(*His voice suddenly dies away because he realises what the other two have realised for the last minute, that there might be something wrong. So as he mutters the end of his sentence now, he glances unhappily at the others.*)

Y'know – being – married – twenty-five years –

(*GERALD looks at them over his cigarette.*)

PARKER: (*Swallowing.*) Go on. Go on.

GERALD: I could see that something he remembered about Cleckleywyke and Lane End worried him. (*With obvious relish.*) You might say, gentlemen, it was *preying* on his mind, it was *gnawing* at his conscience, it was *haunting* him, it was –

HELLIWELL: (*Angrily.*) What is this – a recitation?

GERALD: I must apologise if I'm boring you, gentlemen –

PARKER: (*In sudden passion, jumps up.*) La-di-dah! La-di-dah! (*As GERALD stares at him in astonishment.*) Now if you've anything to tell us, for God's sake tell us – and don't la-di-dah!

HELLIWELL: Quite right, Albert. (*To GERALD, impatiently.*) Well, what did Mr Beech say?

GERALD: He didn't say anything.

(*HELLIWELL and PARKER are at once relieved and annoyed. They breathe more freely, but then feel they have been needlessly alarmed. HERBERT SOPPITT waits to learn more and looks steadily at GERALD.*)

HELLIWELL: Well, what are you nattering on about him for – ?

SOPPITT: Just a minute, Joe. (*To GERALD.*) That's not all, is it?

GERALD: All? I should think not! Only you won't give me a chance. I said he didn't *say* anything, but he *wrote* something. The letter only came two days ago. I have it here. (*Produces one rather small sheet of notepaper, written on both sides. He now reads it impressively.*) From the Reverend Francis Edwin Beech. 'Dear Mr Forbes, Before returning to Africa I feel I owe it both to you and to myself to explain what you must have found puzzling in my many references to Cleckleywyke and Lane End Chapel. Although I was only temporarily at Lane End, I could not forget it for there I was guilty of the most culpable negligence.'

(*The three men look at each other.*)

'I went to Cleckleywyke straight from college, and during those first few months I did not realise that there were various forms I ought to have signed, and had witnessed by church officers, so that one may be recorded as an authorised person to perform the ceremony of marriage –'

HELLIWELL: (*Rises, shouting.*) What? (*Grabs the letter from GERALD, stares at it, then reads himself, slowly.*) '…the ceremony of marriage. The result was, I was not then an authorised person. Fortunately during that short period I was only called upon twice to marry people, but the first time there were no less than three hopeful young couples who imagined – poor souls – that I was joining them in holy wedlock – when – I – was completely – unauthorised – to – do – so –'

PARKER: (*Yelling and snatching the letter.*) Let's have a look. (*He looks and HERBERT SOPPITT joins him.*) It's signed all right too – Francis Edwin Beech.

GERALD: And if you compare that signature with the one in the chapel register, you'll see it's the same man. No deception.

HELLIWELL: (*Dazed and bitter.*) Why – the bloody donkey! (*HELLIWELL, PARKER and SOPPITT look at each other in silent consternation.*)

SOPPITT: (*Slowly, thoughtfully.*) Why, if we've never been married at all, then –

HELLIWELL: Don't start working it out in detail, Herbert, 'cos it gets very ugly – very ugly. There's that lad o' yours at grammar school, for instance – I wouldn't like to have to give him a name now –

SOPPITT: (*Indignantly.*) Here, steady, Joe –

HELLIWELL: Well, you see, it gets very ugly. Keep your mind off t'details.

PARKER: (*Bitterly.*) Silver wedding!

HELLIWELL: Now don't you start neither, Albert.

PARKER: (*Solemnly.*) Joe, Herbert, when them three poor women upstairs gets to know what they really are –

HELLIWELL: (*Grimly.*) Then t'balloon goes up properly. Talk about a rumpus. You'll 'ear 'em from 'ere to Leeds.

PARKER: (*Gravely.*) Joe, Herbert, they mustn't know. Nobody must know. Why – we'd be laughed right out o' town. What – Alderman Helliwell – Councillor Albert Parker – Herbert Soppitt – all big men at chapel too! I tell you, if this leaks out – we're done!

HELLIWELL: We are, Albert.

SOPPITT: (*Horrified.*) If once it got into the papers!

HELLIWELL: (*Even more horrified.*) *Papers!* Oh – Christmas! – it's got to be kept from t'papers. (*GERALD, who has been leaving them to themselves to digest this news, now turns to them again.*)

GERALD: (*Holding out his hand.*) You'd better give me that letter, hadn't you?

PARKER / HELLIWELL: (*Rising.*) Oh no! (*They stand together as if protecting it.*)

PARKER: (*Holding it out.*) This letter –

HELLIWELL: (*Snatching it.*) Here –

PARKER: (*Angrily.*) Nay, Joe – give it back –

HELLIWELL: I'm sorry, Albert, but I don't trust nobody wi' this letter but meself. Why – it's – it's dynamite!

GERALD: Yes, but it's addressed to me, and so it happens to be my property, you know.

SOPPITT: I'm afraid he's right there!

HELLIWELL: (*Turning on him, annoyed.*) You would have to put that in, wouldn't you? Dang me, you're in this mess just as we are, aren't you?

PARKER: (*Severely.*) Anyhow, *we've* a position to keep up even if you haven't, Herbert.

SOPPITT: (*Apologetically.*) I was only saying he's right when he says it's his property. We had a case –

HELLIWELL: (*Aggressively.*) Never mind about that case. Think about this case. It's a whole truckload o' cases, this is.

GERALD: My letter, please.

HELLIWELL: (*Ingratiatingly.*) Now listen, lad. I know you only want to do what's right. And we happened to be a bit 'asty with you, when you first came in. We didn't mean it. Just – a way o' talking. When Herbert Soppitt there gets started –

SOPPITT: (*Indignantly.*) What – me!

PARKER: (*Severely.*) You were 'asty, y'know, Herbert, you can't deny it. (*To GERALD.*) Mind you, I'll say now to your face what I've often said behind your back. You gave us best Messiah and best Elijah we've ever had at Lane End.

HELLIWELL: Easy, easy! Best i' Cleckleywyke! And why? I've told 'em when they've asked me. 'That young feller of ours is clever,' I said. 'I knew he had it in him,' I said.

SOPPITT: (*Hopefully.*) Yes, you did, Joe. (*To GERALD.*) And so did I. I've always been on your side.

GERALD: I believe you have, Mr. Soppitt. (*To all three of them.*) You can keep that letter tonight – on one condition. That Mr Soppitt has it.

SOPPITT: (*Eagerly, holding out his hand.*) Thank you, Joe.

HELLIWELL: (*Uneasily.*) What's the idea o' this?

GERALD: That happens to be the way I feel about it. Now either give it back to me at once – or hand it over to Mr Soppitt, who'll be answerable to me for it.

SOPPITT: (*Eagerly.*) Certainly, certainly.

(*HELLIWELL silently and grudgingly hands it over. SOPPITT puts it carefully in his inside pocket. The others watch him like hawks. There is a pause, then we hear a knocking from upstairs.*)

HELLIWELL: Knocking.

PARKER: (*Grimly.*) I 'eard.

HELLIWELL: That means she's getting impatient.

PARKER: I expect Clara's been ready to come down for some time.

HELLIWELL: (*Bitterly.*) They want to get on with the celebration.

PARKER: (*Bitterly.*) Chat about old times.

HELLIWELL: (*Bitterly.*) Nice game o' cards.

GERALD: (*After a pause.*) I'd better be going.

HELLIWELL: (*Hastily.*) No, no, no. Take it easy.

PARKER: No 'urry, no 'urry at all. I expect Joe has a nice cigar for you somewhere.

HELLIWELL: (*With forced joviality.*) Certainly I have. And a drink of anything you fancy.

GERALD: No, thanks. And I must be going.

HELLIWELL: Now listen, lad. We've admitted we were 'asty with you, so just forget about it, will you? Now you see the mess we're in, through no fault of ours – (*Goes up to get cigars.*)

GERALD: I do. And it *is* a mess, isn't it? Especially when you begin to think –

PARKER: (*Hastily.*) Yes, quite so, but don't you bother thinking. Just – (*Rather desperately.*) – try an' forget you ever saw that letter.

HELLIWELL: (*Who now comes with the cigars.*) We're all friends, the best of friends. Now you've got to have a cigar or two, lad – I insist – (*He sticks several cigars into GERALD's outside pocket as he talks.*) – and you're going to promise us – on your word of honour – not to tell anybody anything about this nasty business, aren't you?

(All three look at him anxiously. He keeps them waiting a moment or two.)

GERALD: All right.

(They breathe again. HELLIWELL shakes his hand.)

HELLIWELL: And you won't regret it, lad.

(The knocking from upstairs is heard again.)

PARKER: *(Miserably.)* 'Ear that?

HELLIWELL: It's wife again.

SOPPITT: *(Thoughtfully.)* Curious thing about wives. They're always telling you what poor company you are for them, yet they're always wanting to get back to you.

HELLIWELL: *(Darkly.)* That isn't 'cos they enjoy your company. It's so they can see what you're doing.

PARKER: Well, what are we doing?

HELLIWELL: *(Sharply now.)* Wasting time. *(To them.)* Now listen, chaps, we're in no proper shape yet to face t'wives. They'd have it all out of us in ten minutes, and then fat'll be in t'fire.

PARKER: I know. We've got to put our thinking caps on.

SOPPITT: I suppose Mr Beech couldn't have been mistaken, could he?

PARKER: We might take that letter and get expert advice –

HELLIWELL: *(Hastily.)* What! An' 'ave it all over the town?

PARKER: *(Quickly.)* We might put a case – without mentioning names.

HELLIWELL: *(With decision.)* I know what we'll do. We'll nip down to t'club, 'cos we can talk it over there in peace an' quiet. Come on, chaps. Just as we are, straight down t'club. *(To GERALD.)* Now, young man, you promised. You won't go back on your word?

GERALD: No. You're safe with me.

HELLIWELL: *(Urgently.)* Good lad! Now, wait till we've got off, then go out front way. Come on, Albert, Herbert, we've no time to lose an' we go this way – *(Bustling them towards exit through conservatory.)* – straight to t'club.

(They go out. GERALD looks at his watch, smiles, lights a cigarette, then makes for door, which has never been quite closed. When he opens it suddenly, MRS NORTHROP, still

holding a towel and a large glass dish, which she is wiping perfunctorily, is discovered just behind door. She is in high glee and not at all abashed at being found there.)

GERALD: (*With mock sternness.*) Have you been listening?

MRS NORTHROP: (*Who may have had a drink or two.*) Listening! I should think I have been listening! I wouldn't have missed this lot even if it means 'aving earache for a week. None of 'em rightly married at all! Not one of 'em properly tied up!

(*She begins laughing quite suddenly, and then goes off into peals of laughter, rolling against the door. The dish she holds seems to be in danger.*)

GERALD: (*Amused as he goes past her, out.*) Look out – or you may break that dish.

MRS NORTHROP: (*Calling to him.*) Brek a dish! If I want to, I'll brek a dozen now.

GERALD: (*Just off, challengingly.*) Not you! I dare you!

MRS NORTHROP: (*Coolly.*) Well, here's a start, any road. (*She tosses the dish down and it smashes noisily in hall. We hear GERALD give a laughing shout, then bang the front door. MRS NORTHROP now starts laughing helplessly again, still leaning against the door.*)

Nay – dammit! (*Laughing.*) Oh dear – oh dear – oh dear – (*She is still roaring with laughter as the curtain briskly descends.*)

End of Act One.

ACT TWO

About half an hour later. The lights are on. MARIA is drawing curtains, ANNIE and CLARA are laying out the cards and counters for Newmarket on a card-table, and they continue doing this throughout the scene that follows, chiefly counting the coloured counters and putting them into piles.

CLARA: (*With much discontent.*) Well, I must say – this is a queer way o' going on.

MARIA: They'll have just gone outside to finish their smokes.

CLARA: (*Grimly.*) When Herbert takes me out to enjoy myself, I don't expect him to be outside finishing any smokes.

ANNIE: (*At table.*) Perhaps they'd something they wanted to talk over.

CLARA: Well they can talk it over here, can't they?

(*RUBY enters from conservatory.*)

MARIA: Well, Ruby, are they out there?

RUBY: No, they aren't.

MARIA: (*Sharply.*) Have you looked properly?

RUBY: Well I couldn't miss three grown men in a garden that size.

MARIA: Did you look up and down the road like I told you?

RUBY: Yes, but they aren't there.

(*The three wives look at each other, puzzled.*)

CLARA: Didn't you hear them go?

RUBY: No. I was back in t'kitchen all time, doing t'washing up. That Mrs Northrop left me to it.

MARIA: Where was she then?

RUBY: Out 'ere somewhere, I fancy. I know she's gone like a dafthead, ever since she come back. Laughin' to herself – like a proper barnpot.

MARIA: Well, ask Mrs Northrop if she knows where they went.

(*RUBY goes.*)

That noise you heard upstairs was a bit o' this Mrs
Northrop's work – one o' my best dishes gone. An' Ruby
says she just laughed.

CLARA: Stop it out of her wages and see if she can get a
good laugh out o' that. I've no patience with 'em.

ANNIE: I thought she didn't look a nice woman.

CLARA: One o' them idle drinking pieces o' nothing from
back o' t'mill.

MARIA: Well, I was in a hurry and had to have somebody.
But she goes – for good – tonight.
(*RUBY appears.*)

RUBY: Mrs Northrop says they wanted to have a nice quiet
talk so they went down to their club.
(*RUBY disappears.*)

CLARA: (*Angrily.*) Club! *Club!*

ANNIE: And tonight of all nights – I do think it's a shame.

MARIA: (*Indignantly.*) I never 'eard o' such a thing in me
life.

CLARA: (*Furiously.*) *Club!* I'll club him.

ANNIE: Nay, I don't know what's come over 'em.

CLARA: (*Angrily.*) I know what'll come over one of 'em.

MARIA: Perhaps there's something up.

CLARA: Something down, you mean – ale, stout, an'
whisky. Drinks all round! Money no object!

MARIA: They're 'ere.
(*The three of them immediately sit bolt upright and look very
frosty. The men file in from the conservatory, looking very
sheepish.*)

HELLIWELL: (*Nervously.*) Ay – well –

MARIA: (*Grimly.*) Well what?

HELLIWELL: Well – nowt – really.

SOPPITT: (*Nervously.*) We didn't – er – think you'd be down
yet. Did we, Joe? Did we, Albert?

HELLIWELL: No, we didn't, Herbert.

ALBERT: That's right, we didn't.

CLARA: (*Cuttingly.*) Herbert Soppitt, you must be wrong in
your head. *Club!*

ANNIE: And tonight of all nights!

HELLIWELL: Well, you see, we thought we'd just nip down for a few minutes while you were talking upstairs.

MARIA: What for?

PARKER: Oh – just to talk over one or two things.

CLARA: What things?

SOPPITT: Oh – just – things, y'know – things in general.

PARKER: (*Coming forward, rubbing his hands.*) Well – I see the table's all ready – so what about that nice little game o' Newmarket?

CLARA: You'll get no Newmarket out o' me tonight.

ANNIE: You're – you're – selfish.

CLARA: Have you just found that out? Never think about anything but their own comfort and convenience.

MARIA: I'm surprised at you, Joe Helliwell – and after I'd planned to make everything so nice.

CLARA: Lot o' thanks you get from them! Club! (*Looking hard at SOPPITT.*) Well, go on – say something.
(*The men look at each other uneasily. Then the women look indignantly.*)

ANNIE: Just think what day it is!

CLARA: And after giving you best years of our life – without a word o' thanks.

MARIA: An' just remember, Joe Helliwell, there were plenty of other fellows I could have had besides you.

ANNIE: You seem to think – once you've married us you can take us for granted.

PARKER: (*Uneasily.*) Nay, I don't.

CLARA: (*Very sharply.*) Yes, you do – all alike!

MARIA: If some of you woke up tomorrow to find you weren't married to us, you'd be in for a few big surprises.

HELLIWELL: (*Uneasily.*) Yes – I dare say – you're right.

MARIA: (*Staring at him.*) Joe Helliwell, what's matter with you tonight?

HELLIWELL: (*Uneasily.*) Nowt – nowt's wrong wi' me, love.

CLARA: (*Looking hard at SOPPITT.*) You'll hear more about this when I get you 'ome.

SOPPITT: (*Mildly.*) Yes, Clara.
(*The women look at the men again, then at each other. Now they turn away from the men, ignoring them.*)

MARIA: What were you saying about your cousin, Clara?

CLARA: (*Ignoring the men.*) Oh – well, the doctor said, 'You're all acid, Mrs Foster, that's your trouble. You're making acid as fast as you can go.'

ANNIE: Oh – poor thing!

CLARA: Yes, but it didn't surprise me, way she'd eat. I once saw her eat nine oyster patties, finishing 'em up after their Ethel got married. I said, 'Nay, Edith, have a bit o' mercy on your inside,' but of course she just laughed. (*The men have been cautiously moving to the back towards the door. As HELLIWELL has his hand on the handle, MARIA turns on him.*)

MARIA: And where're you going now?

HELLIWELL: (*Uneasily.*) Into t'dining-room.

MARIA: What for?

HELLIWELL: Well – because – well – (*Gathers boldness.*) We've summat to talk over. Albert, 'Erbert, quick! (*They file out smartly, without looking behind them. The women stare at them in amazement. The door shuts. The women look at each other.*)

MARIA: Now what's come over 'em?

ANNIE: There's something up.

CLARA: What can be up? They're just acting stupid, that's all. But wait till I get his lordship 'ome.

ANNIE: Suppose we went home now?

CLARA: No fear! That's just what they'd like. Back to t'club!

MARIA: I'd go up to bed now and lock me door, if I didn't think I'd be missing something.

ANNIE: It's a pity we can't go off just by ourselves – for a day or two.

CLARA: And what sort o' game are they going to get up to while we're gone? But I've a good mind to go in and tell mine, 'Look, I've been married to you for five-and-twenty years and it's about time I had a rest.'

MARIA: And for two pins I'll say to Joe, 'If you got down on your bended knees and begged me to, I wouldn't stay married to you if I didn't have to.'

(*Door opens slowly, and MRS NORTHROP comes just inside, carrying large string bag, with clothes, two stout bottles in, etc. She is dressed to go home now.*)

MRS NORTHROP: I've done.

MARIA: (*Suspiciously.*) It hasn't taken you very long.

MRS NORTHROP: (*Modestly.*) No – but then I'm a rare worker. Many a one's said to me, 'Mrs Northrop, I can't believe you've just that pair of 'ands – you're a wonder.'

MARIA: (*Acidly.*) Well, I don't think I want a wonder here, Mrs Northrop. I'll pay you what I owe you tonight, and then you needn't come again.

MRS NORTHROP: (*Bridling.*) Ho, I see – that's it, is it?

MARIA: Yes, it is. I don't consider you satisfactory.

CLARA: I should think not!

MRS NORTHROP: (*Annoyed.*) Who's asking you to pass remarks? (*To MARIA.*) And don't think I want to come 'ere again. Me 'usband wouldn't let me, anyhow, when he 'ears what I 'ave to tell him. We've always kept ourselves respectable.

MARIA: And what does that mean?

CLARA: Don't encourage her impudence.

MRS NORTHROP: An' *you* mind your own interference. (*To MARIA.*) I was beginnin' to feel sorry for you – but now –

MARIA: (*Coldly.*) I don't know what you're talking about.

CLARA: What's she got in that bag –

MRS NORTHROP: (*Angrily.*) I've got me old boots an' apron an' cleanin' stuff in this bag –

MARIA: I can see two bottles there –

MRS NORTHROP: (*Angrily.*) Well, what if you can? D'you think you're the only folk i' Cleckleywyke who can buy summat to sup? If you must know, these is two stout empties I'm taking away 'cos they belong to me – bought an' paid for by me at Jackson's off-licence an' if you don't believe me go an' ask 'em.

MARIA: (*Stopping CLARA from bursting in.*) No, Clara, let her alone – we've had enough. (*To MRS NORTHROP, rather haughtily.*) It's twenty-four shillings altogether, isn't it?

MRS NORTHROP: (*Aggressively.*) No, it isn't. It's twenty-five and six – if I never speak another word.

MARIA: (*Going for her purse on side-table.*) All right then, twenty-five and six, but I'm going to take something off for that dish you broke.

MRS NORTHROP: (*Angrily.*) You won't take a damned ha'penny off!

CLARA: Language now as well as back-answers!

MARIA: (*Giving MRS NORTHROP a sovereign.*) Here's a pound and that's all you'll get.

MRS NORTHROP: (*Angrily.*) I won't 'ave it. I won't 'ave it.

MARIA: (*Leaving it on nearest table to MRS NORTHROP.*) There it is, Mrs Northrop, and it's all you'll get. (*Sitting down in stately fashion and turning to CLARA.*) Let's see, Clara, what were you saying?
(*All three women now ignore MRS NORTHROP, which makes her angrier than ever.*)

MRS NORTHROP: (*Drowning any possible conversation.*) An' don't sit there tryin' to look like duchesses, 'cos I've lived round 'ere too long an' I know too much about yer. Tryin' to swank! Why – (*Pointing to MARIA.*) I remember you when you were Maria Fawcett an' you were nobbut a burler and mender at Barkinson's afore you took up wi' Joe Helliwell an' he were nobbut a woolsorter i' them days. And as for you – (*Pointing to CLARA.*) I remember time when you were weighin' out apples an' potatoes in your father's greengrocer's shop, corner o' Park Road, an' a mucky little shop it wor an' all –

MARIA: (*Rising, angrily.*) I'll fetch my husband.

MRS NORTHROP: He isn't your husband. I was goin' to say I'm as good as you, but fact is I'm a damn sight better, 'cos I'm a respectable married woman an' that's more than any o' you can say –

CLARA: (*Angrily.*) Get a policeman.

MRS NORTHROP: (*Derisively.*) Get a policeman! Get a dozen, an' they'll all 'ave a good laugh when they 'ear what I 'ave to tell 'em. Not one o' you properly married at all. I 'eard that organist o' yours tellin' your 'usbands

– if I can call 'em your 'usbands. I wor just be'ind t'door – an' this lot wor too good to miss – better than a turn at t'Empire.

CLARA: (*Angrily.*) I don't believe a word of it.

MRS NORTHROP: Please yourself. But 'e give 'em a letter, an' that's why they went down to t'club to talk it over – an' I can't say I blame 'em 'cos they've plenty to talk over. An' by gow, so 'ave you three. It's about time yer thought o' getting wed, isn't it?

(*They stare in silence. She gives them a triumphant look, then picks up her sovereign.*)

And now you owe me another five an' six at least – an' if you've any sense you'll see I get it – but I can't stop no longer 'cos I've said I meet me 'usband down at 'Are an' 'Ounds, 'cos they're 'aving a draw for a goose for Cleckleywyke Tide an' we've three tickets – so I'll say *good night.*

(*She bangs the door. The three women stare at each other in consternation.*)

MARIA: That's why they were so queer. I knew there was something.

CLARA: (*Bitterly.*) The daft blockheads!

(*ANNIE suddenly begins laughing.*)

Oh – for goodness' sake, Annie Parker!

ANNIE: (*Still laughing.*) I'm not Annie Parker. And it all sounds so silly.

MARIA: (*Indignantly.*) Silly! What's silly about it?

CLARA: (*Bitterly.*) Serves me right for ever bothering with anybody so gormless. Isn't this Herbert Soppitt all over! Couldn't even get us married right!

MARIA: (*Looking distressed.*) But – Clara, Annie – this is *awful!* What are we going to do?

CLARA: I know what we're *not* going to do – and that's play *Newmarket.* (*Begins putting things away, helped by other two.*)

ANNIE: Eee – we'll look awfully silly lining up at Lane End Chapel again to get married, won't we?

CLARA: (*Angrily.*) Oh – for goodness' sake – !

MARIA: (*Bitterly.*) Better tell them three daftheads in t'dining-room to come in now.

CLARA: No, just a minute.

MARIA: What for?

CLARA: 'Cos I want to think, an' very sight of Herbert'll make me that mad I won't be able to think. (*Ponders a moment.*) Now if nobody knew but us, it wouldn't matter so much.

MARIA: But that fool of a parson knows –

CLARA: And the organist knows –

ANNIE: And your Mrs Northrop knows – don't forget that – and you wouldn't pay her that five-and-six –

MARIA: Here, one o' them men must fetch her back.

CLARA: I should think so. Why, if people get to know about this – we're – we're –

RUBY: (*Looking in, announcing loudly.*) Yorkshire Argus.

CLARA: (*In a panic.*) We don't want any Yorkshire Argus here – or God knows where we'll be –

(*She is interrupted by the entrance of FRED DYSON, who has had some drinks and is pleased with himself.*)

DYSON: (*Very heartily.*) Well, here we are again. At least I am. Fred Dyson – Yorkshire Argus. Mrs Helliwell?

MARIA: (*Rather faintly.*) Yes.

DYSON: (*Same tone.*) And Mrs Albert Parker and Mrs Soppitt – three lucky ladies, eh?

(*They are looking anything but fortunate.*)

Now, you'd never guess my trouble.

ANNIE: (*Who can't resist it.*) You'd never guess ours, either.

MARIA: (*Hastily.*) Shut up, Annie. What were you saying, Mr Dyson?

DYSON: I've gone and lost our photographer – Henry Ormonroyd. Brought him with me here earlier on, then we went back to The Lion, where he'd met an old pal. I left 'em singing 'Larboard Watch' in the taproom, not twenty minutes since, went into the private bar five minutes afterwards, couldn't find old Henry anywhere, so thought he must have come up here. By the way, where's the party?

ANNIE: This is it.

MARIA: (*Hastily.*) Shut up, Annie. (*Rather desperately, to DYSON.*) You see, my husband – Alderman Helliwell – you know him of course?

DYSON: (*Heartily.*) Certainly. He's quite a public figure, these days. That's why the Argus sent me up here tonight – when he told 'em you were all celebrating your silver wedding.

CLARA: (*Unpleasantly.*) Oh – he suggested your coming here, did he?

DYSON: He did.

CLARA: (*Unpleasantly.*) He would!

MARIA: Well, he didn't know then – what – I mean – (*Her voice alters and dies away.*)

DYSON: Our readers 'ud like to know all about this affair.

CLARA: (*Grimly.*) An' I'll bet they would!

MARIA: Now 'ave a bit o' sense, Clara.

CLARA: (*Quickly.*) Why, you nearly gave it away –

ANNIE: (*Coming in.*) What on earth are you saying, you two?

(*Smiles at DYSON, who is looking rather mystified.*)

It's all right, Mr Dyson. What Mrs Helliwell was going to say was that there was only just us six, y'know. It wasn't a real party. Just a little – er – private – er – sort of – you know.

DYSON: (*Looking about him, thirstily.*) I know. Just a cosy little do – with – er – a few drinks.

MARIA: That's it.

DYSON: A few drinks – and – er – cigars – and – er – so on. (*But they do not take the hint, so now he pulls out pencil and bit of paper.*)

Now, Mrs Helliwell, wouldn't you like to tell our readers just what your feelings are now that you're celebrating twenty-five years of happy marriage?

MARIA: (*Her face working.*) I – er – I – er –

DYSON: You needn't be shy, Mrs Helliwell. Now, come on. (*To his astonishment, MARIA suddenly bursts into tears, and then hurries out of the room.*)

CLARA: (*Reproachfully.*) Now, look what you've done, young man.

DYSON: (*Astonished.*) Nay, dash it – what have I done? I only asked her –

ANNIE: (*Hastily.*) She's a bit upset tonight – you know, what with all the excitement. It's no use your staying now – you'd better go and find your photographer.

CLARA: (*Angrily.*) Now, Annie, for goodness' sake! We want no photographers here.

ANNIE: (*To DYSON.*) That's all right. She's upset too. Now you just pop off.

(*ANNIE almost marches DYSON to the door and sees him through it. We hear him go out. CLARA sits breathing very hard. ANNIE returns, leaving door open behind her.*)

Well, we're rid of him.

CLARA: For how long?

ANNIE: (*Annoyed.*) You can't sit there, Clara, just saying 'For how long?' as if you're paying me to manage this business. If we want it kept quiet, we'll have to stir ourselves and not sit about shouting and nearly giving it all away as you and Maria did when that chap was here.

CLARA: (*Bitterly.*) If we hadn't said we'd marry a set o' numskulls, this would never 'ave happened. If my poor mother was alive to see this day –

(*MARIA returns, blowing her nose and sits down miserably.*)

MARIA: (*Unhappily.*) I'm sorry – Clara, Annie – but I just couldn't help it. When he asked me that question, something turned right over inside – an' next minute I was crying.

CLARA: (*Severely.*) Well, crying's not going to get us out of this mess.

ANNIE: (*Sharply.*) You're never satisfied, Clara. First you go on at me for laughing and now you blame poor Maria for crying.

CLARA: (*Loudly, sharply.*) Well, what do you want to go laughing an' crying for? What do you think this is? Uncle Tom's Cabin?

MARIA: They're coming in.

(*The women sit back, grimly waiting. HELLIWELL, PARKER, SOPPITT enter, and the women look at them.*)

PARKER: (*Uneasily.*) Who was that?

(*No reply. He exchanges a glance with SOPPITT and HELLIWELL.*)

I said, who was it came just then?

CLARA: (*Suddenly, fiercely.*) Yorkshire Argus!

PARKER: (*Resigned tone.*) They know.

ANNIE: (*Sharply.*) Course we know.

(*HELLIWELL looks at them, then makes for the door again.*)

MARIA: And where are you going?

HELLIWELL: To fetch t'whisky.

MARIA: And is whisky going to 'elp us?

HELLIWELL: I don't know about you, but it'll help me.

(*Goes out.*)

MARIA: (*Hopefully.*) It's not all a tale, is it?

PARKER: No, it's right enough. We put case to a chap at club – no names, of course – and he said it 'ad 'appened a few times – when a young parson thought he was qualified to marry folk – an' it turned out he wasn't. But of course it 'asn't happened often.

CLARA: No, but it has to 'appen to *us.* (*Fiercely to SOPPITT.*) I blame you for this.

SOPPITT: (*Unhappily, to PARKER.*) Didn't I tell you she would?

CLARA: (*Sharply.*) She! Who's *she?* The cat? Just remember you're talking about your own wife.

PARKER: Ah – but you see, he isn't – not now.

CLARA: (*Angrily.*) Now, stop that, Albert Parker.

(*HELLIWELL returns with large tray, with whisky, soda and glasses.*)

HELLIWELL: Any lady like a drop?

MARIA: State I'm in now, it 'ud choke me.

(*The other women shake their heads scornfully.*)

HELLIWELL: Albert?

PARKER: Thanks, I think I will, Joe. (*Goes to him.*)

HELLIWELL: (*Busy with drinks.*) 'Erbert?

CLARA: (*Quickly.*) He mustn't 'ave any.

HELLIWELL: *'Erbert?*

CLARA: (*Confidently.*) You 'eard what I said, Herbert. You're not to 'ave any.

SOPPITT: (*The rebel now.*) Thanks, Joe, just a drop.
(*He goes up, looks at his wife as he takes his glass and drinks, then comes away, still looking at her, while she glares at him.*)

HELLIWELL: 'Ere, but I'd never ha' thought young Forbes ud' have gone back on his word like that, when he promised solemnly not to tell another soul.

MARIA: But he didn't tell us.

HELLIWELL: (*Staggered.*) Eh? (*Exchanges alarmed glance with other men.*) Who did then?

MARIA: Charwoman – Mrs Northrop. She 'eard you, behind that door.

HELLIWELL: (*Alarmed.*) 'Ere, where is she?

MARIA: Gone.

ANNIE: (*With some malice.*) Maria's just given her the push.

PARKER: (*Angrily.*) If she's gone off with this news you just might as well play it on Town Hall chimes.

HELLIWELL: (*Angrily.*) Why didn't you say so at first? If this woman gets round wi' this tale about us, we'll never live it down. Did she go 'ome?

ANNIE: No, to the Hare and Hounds.

HELLIWELL: (*Masterfully.*) Herbert, swallow that whisky quick – an' nip down to t'Hare an' Hounds as fast as you can go, an' bring her back.

SOPPITT: But I don't know her.

HELLIWELL: Nay, damn it, you saw her in here, not an hour since.

SOPPITT: An' she doesn't know me.

HELLIWELL: Now, don't make difficulties, Herbert. Off you go. (*Moves him towards conservatory.*) And bring her back as fast as you can and promise her owt she asks so long as you get back. (*He is now outside, shouting.*) An' make haste. We're depending on you.
(*HELLIWELL returns, blowing, carrying SOPPITT's glass. He is about to drink out of this when he remembers, so takes and drinks from his own, then breathes noisily and mops his brow. They are all quiet for a moment.*)
You know, Albert lad, it feels quite peculiar to me.

PARKER: What does?

HELLIWELL: This – not being married.

MARIA: (*Rising, solemn.*) Joe Helliwell, 'ow can you stand there an' say a thing like that?

CLARA: (*Simultaneous with ANNIE.*) He ought to be ashamed of himself.

ANNIE: (*Simultaneous with CLARA.*) I'm surprised at you, Joe.

HELLIWELL: (*Bewildered.*) What – what are you talking about?

MARIA: (*Solemnly.*) After twenty-five years together. Haven't I been a good wife to you, Joe Helliwell?

HELLIWELL: Well, I'm not complaining, am I?

PARKER: (*Tactlessly.*) You've been the *same* as a good wife to him, Maria.

MARIA: (*Furiously.*) The *same!* I haven't been the same as a good wife, I've been a good wife, let me tell you, Albert Parker.

ANNIE: (*Simultaneous with CLARA.*) Nay, Albert!

CLARA: (*Simultaneous with ANNIE; angrily to PARKER.*) I never 'eard such silly talk.

PARKER: (*Aggressively.*) Oh – an' what's silly about it, eh?

CLARA: Everything.

HELLIWELL: (*Tactlessly.*) Nay, but when you come to think of it – Albert's right.

PARKER: (*Solemn and fatuous.*) We must face facts. Now, Maria, you might feel married to him –

MARIA: (*Scornfully.*) *I might feel married to him!* If you'd had twenty-five years of him, you wouldn't talk about *might*. Haven't I –

HELLIWELL: (*Cutting in noisily.*) 'Ere, steady on, steady on – with your *twenty-five years of 'im.* Talking about me as if I were a dose o' typhoid fever.

MARIA: (*Loudly.*) I'm not, Joe. All I'm saying is –

PARKER: (*Still louder.*) Now let me finish what I started to say. I said – you might feel married to him – but strictly speaking – and in the eyes of the law – the fact is, you're *not* married to him. We're none of us married.

CLARA: (*Bitterly.*) Some o' t'neighbours ha' missed it, couldn't you shout it louder?

PARKER: I wasn't that loud.

HELLIWELL: (*Reproachfully.*) You were bawling your 'ead off.

ANNIE: Yes, you were.

MARIA: (*Reproachfully.*) You don't know who's listening. I'm surprised you haven't more sense, Albert.

PARKER: (*Irritably.*) All right, all right, all right. But we shan't get anywhere til we face facts. It's not our fault, but our misfortune.

MARIA: I don't know so much about that either.

HELLIWELL: Oh? (*To ALBERT.*) Goin' to blame us now.

MARIA: Well, an' why not?

HELLIWELL: (*Irritably.*) Nay, damn it – it wasn't *our* fault.

MARIA: If a chap asks me to marry him and then he takes me to chapel and puts me in front of a parson, I expect parson to be a real one an' not just somebody dressed up.

HELLIWELL: Well, don't I?

MARIA: You should ha' found out.

HELLIWELL: Talk sense! 'Ow could I know he wasn't properly qualified?

MARIA: (*Sneering.*) Well, it's funny it's got to 'appen to us, isn't it?

PARKER: But that's what I say – it's not our fault, it's our misfortune. It's no use blaming anybody. Just couldn't be 'elped. But fact remains – we're –

CLARA: (*Interrupting angrily.*) If you say it again, Albert Parker, I'll throw something at yer. You needn't go on and on about it.

MARIA: (*Bitterly.*) Mostly at top o' your voice.

PARKER: (*With air of wounded dignity.*) Say no more. I've finished. (*Turns his back on them.*)
(*All three women look at him disgustedly. MARIA now turns to JOE.*)

MARIA: But, Joe, you're not going to tell me you feel different – just because of this – this accident?

HELLIWELL: (*Solemnly.*) I won't tell you a lie, love. I can't help it, but ever since I've known I'm not married I've felt *most peculiar.*

143

MARIA: (*Rising, sudden temper.*) Oo, I could knock your fat head off.

(*MARIA goes hurriedly to the door, making sobbing noises on the way, and hurries out.*)

ANNIE: (*Following her.*) Oh – poor Maria!

(*ANNIE goes out, closing door.*)

CLARA: Well, I 'ope you're pleased with yourself now.

HELLIWELL: (*Sententiously.*) Never interfere between 'usband and wife.

CLARA: You just said you weren't 'usband an' wife.

HELLIWELL: (*Angrily.*) 'Ere, if I'm going to argue with a woman it might as well be the one I live with.

(*HELLIWELL hurries out. A silence. PARKER remains sulky and detached.*)

CLARA: (*After pause.*) Well, after all these ructions, another glass o' port wouldn't do me any 'arm.

(*Waits, then as there is no move from PARKER.*)

Thank you very much. (*Rises, with dignity, to help herself.*) Nice manners we're being shown, I must say. (*Fills her glass.*) I said nice manners, Councillor Albert Parker!

PARKER: (*Turning, angrily.*) Now if I were poor Herbert Soppitt, I'd think twice before I asked you to marry me again.

CLARA: (*Just going to drink.*) Ask me again! There'll be no asking. Herbert Soppitt's my husband – an' he stays my husband.

PARKER: In the eyes of the law.

CLARA: (*Cutting in ruthlessly.*) You said that before. But let me tell you, in the sight of Heaven Herbert and me's been married for twenty-five years.

PARKER: (*Triumphantly.*) And there you're wrong again, because in the sight of Heaven nobody's married at all –

(*HELLIWELL pops his head in, looking worried.*)

HELLIWELL: Just come in the dining-room a minute, Albert. We're having a bit of an argument.

PARKER: Yes, Joe.

(*HELLIWELL disappears. PARKER goes out, leaving door a little open. CLARA, left alone, finishes her port, then picks*

up the old photograph and glares with contempt at the figures
on it. A house bell can be heard ringing distantly now.)

CLARA: (*Muttering her profound contempt at the figures in the
photograph.*) Yer silly young softheads! (*Bangs it down in
some prominent place, face up.*)

(*RUBY now looks in.*)

RUBY: Mrs Soppitt –

CLARA: (*Rather eagerly.*) Yes?

RUBY: Mrs Helliwell says will you go into t'dining-room.
(*As CLARA moves quickly towards door, RUBY adds coolly.*)
Aaa – they're fratchin' like mad.

(*CLARA goes out quickly, followed by RUBY. We hear in
distance sound of door opening, the voices of the three in the
dining-room noisily raised in argument, the shutting of the
door, then a moment's silence. Then several sharp rings at the
front door. After a moment, RUBY's voice off but coming
nearer.*)

(*Off.*) Yes, I know... All right... 'Ere, mind them things...
This way...

(*RUBY ushers in ORMONROYD, who is carrying his camera,
etc., and is now very ripe.*)

ORMONROYD: (*Advances into room and looks about him with
great care, then returns to RUBY.*) Nobody here. (*Gives
another glance to make sure.*) Nobody at all.

RUBY: They'll all be back again soon. They're mostly in
dining-room – fratchin'.

ORMONROYD: What – on a festive occasion like this?

RUBY: That's right.

ORMONROYD: Well, it just shows you what human nature
is. Human nature! T-t-t-t-t. I'll bet if it had been a
funeral – they'd have all been in here, laughing their
heads off. (*He goes over and looks closely at the cigars.*) There
isn't such a thing as a cigar here, is there?

RUBY: Yes, yer looking at 'em. D'you want one? 'Ere. (*As he
lights it.*) Me mother says if God had intended men to
smoke He'd have put chimneys in their heads.

ORMONROYD: Tell your mother from me that if God had
intended men to wear collars He'd have put collar studs

at back of their necks. (*Stares at her.*) What are you bobbing up an' down like that for?

RUBY: I'm not bobbing up an' down. It's you. (*Laughs and regards him critically.*) You're a bit tiddly, aren't yer?

ORMONROYD: (*Horror-struck.*) Tidd-ldly?

RUBY: Yes. Squiffy.

ORMONROYD: (*Surveying her mistily.*) What an ex't'rornry idea! You seem to me a mos' ex't'rornry sort of – little – well, I dunno, really – what's your name?

RUBY: Ruby Birtle.

ORMONROYD: (*Tasting it.*) Umm – Ruby –

RUBY: All right, I know it's a silly daft name, you can't tell me nowt about Ruby I 'aven't been told already – so don't try.

ORMONROYD: (*Solemnly.*) Ruby, I think you're quite ex't'rornry. How old are you?

RUBY: (*Quickly.*) Fifteen – how old are you?

ORMONROYD: (*Waving a hand, vaguely.*) Thousands of years, thousands and thousands of years.

RUBY: (*Coolly.*) You look to me about seventy.

ORMONROYD: (*Horrified.*) *Seventy*! I'm fifty-four.

RUBY: (*Severely.*) Then you've been neglectin' yerself. (*ORMONROYD looks at her, breathing hard and noisily.*) Too much liftin' o' t'elbow.

ORMONROYD: (*After indignant pause.*) Do you ever read the Police News?

RUBY: Yes. I like it. All 'orrible murders.

ORMONROYD: Then you must have seen them pictures of women who've been chopped up by their husbands –

RUBY: (*With gusto.*) Yes – with bloody 'atchets.

ORMONROYD: (*Impressively.*) Well, if you don't look out, Ruby, you'll grow up to be one of them women. (*Wanders away and then notices and takes up old photograph.*)

RUBY: (*Looking at it.*) Aaaaa! – don't they look soft? (*Looks suspiciously at him, dubiously.*) How d'you mean – one o' them women?

ORMONROYD: Don't you bother about that, Ruby, you've plenty of time yet.

RUBY: (*Puzzled.*) Time for what?

ORMONROYD: (*Intent on his art now.*) Now what I'm going to do – is to take a flashlight group of the three couples – just as they were in the old photograph. Now – let me see. (*Very solemnly and elaborately he sets up his camera.*)

RUBY: (*Who has been thinking.*) 'Ere, d'you mean I've plenty of time yet to grow up an' then be chopped up?

ORMONROYD: (*Absently.*) Yes.

RUBY: (*Persistently.*) But what would 'e want to chop me up for?

ORMONROYD: Now you sit there a minute.

RUBY: I said, what would 'e want to chop me up for?

ORMONROYD: (*Putting her into a chair and patting her shoulder.*) Perhaps you might find one who wouldn't, but you'll have to be careful. Now you stay there, Ruby.

RUBY: (*Hopefully.*) Are yer goin' to take my photo?

ORMONROYD: (*Grimly.*) Not for a few years – yet. (*Is now fiddling with his camera.*)

RUBY: (*After thoughtful pause.*) D'you mean you're waiting for me to be chopped up? (*Cheerfully, not reproachfully.*) Eeeee ! – you've got a right nasty mind, 'aven't you? (*A pause.*)

Are *you* married?

ORMONROYD: Yes.

RUBY: Yer wife doesn't seem to take much interest in yer.

ORMONROYD: How do you know?

RUBY: Well, I'll bet yer clothes hasn't been brushed for a month. (*Going on cheerfully.*) Yer could almost make a meal off yer waistcoat – there's so much egg on it. (*After pause.*) Why doesn't she tidy you up a bit?

ORMONROYD: (*Busy with his preparations.*) Because she's not here to do it.

RUBY: Doesn't she live with yer?

ORMONROYD: (*Stopping to stare at her, with dignity.*) Is it – er – essential – you should know all about my – er – private affairs?

RUBY: Go on, yer might as well tell me. Where is she?

ORMONROYD: Mrs Ormonroyd at present is – er – helping her sister to run a boarding-house called Palm

View – though the only palm you see there is the one my sister-in-law holds out.

RUBY: Where? Blackpool?

ORMONROYD: Not likely. There's a place you go to live in – not to die in. No, they're at Torquay. (*With profound scorn.*) *Torquay!*

RUBY: (*Impressed.*) That's right down south, isn't it?

ORMONROYD: (*With mock pompousness.*) Yes, my girl, Torquay is on the South Coast of Devonshire. It is sheltered from the northerly and easterly winds, is open to the warm sea breezes from the South, and so is a favourite all-year-round resort of many delicate and refined persons of genteel society. In other words, it's a damned miserable hole. (*Surveys his arrangements with satisfaction.*) There we are, all ready for the three happy couples.

RUBY: (*Sceptically.*) Did yer say 'appy?

ORMONROYD: Why not?

RUBY: Well, for a start, go an' listen to them four in t'dining-room.

ORMONROYD: (*Beginning solemnly.*) Believe me, Rosie –

RUBY: (*Sharply.*) Ruby.

ORMONROYD: Ruby. Believe me, you're still too young to understand.

RUBY: I've 'eard that afore, but nobody ever tells what it is I'm too young to understand. An' for years me brother kept rabbits.

ORMONROYD: (*Solemnly but vaguely.*) It's not a question of rabbits – thank God! But marriage – marriage – well, it's a very peculiar thing. There's parts of it I never much cared about myself.

RUBY: Which parts?

ORMONROYD: Well – now I'm a man who likes a bit o' company. An' I like an occasional friendly glass. I'll admit it – I like an occasional friendly glass.

RUBY: It 'ud be all t'same if you didn't admit it. We could tell. (*Sniffs.*)

ORMONROYD: If these three couples here have been married for twenty-five years and – er – they're still

sticking it, well, then I call 'em three happy couples, an'
I won't listen to you or anybody else saying they're not.
No, I won't have it. And if you or anybody else says,
'Drink their health,' I say, 'Certainly, certainly, with
pleasure.' (*Gives himself a whisky with remarkable speed.*)
Wouldn't dare to refuse, 'cos it would be dead against my
principles. Their very good health. (*Takes an enormous
drink.*)

RUBY: Eeee! – you are goin' to be tiddly.

ORMONROYD: (*Ignoring this, if he heard it, and very mellow
and sentimental now.*) Ah – yes. To be together – side-by-
side – through all life's sunshine and storms – hand-in-
hand – in good times and bad ones – with always a
loving smile – (*Waving hand with cigar in.*)

RUBY: (*Coldly.*) Mind yer cigar!

ORMONROYD: In sickness and in health – rich or poor –
still together – side-by-side – hand-in-hand – through all
life's sunshine and storms –

RUBY: (*Quickly.*) You said that once.

ORMONROYD: Oh – yes – it's a wonderful – it's a bee-
yutiful thing –

RUBY: What is?

ORMONROYD: *What is!* Lord help us – it's like talking to
a little crocodile! I say – that it's a wonderful and bee-
yutiful thing to go through good times and bad ones –
always together – always with a loving smile –

RUBY: Side-by-side – an' 'and-in-'and –

ORMONROYD: Yes, and that's what I say.

RUBY: Then there must be summat wrong wi' me 'cos when
I've tried goin' side-by-side an' 'and-in-'and even for
twenty minutes I've 'ad more than I want.

ORMONROYD: (*Staring at her.*) Extr'ord'n'ry! What's your
name?

RUBY: It's still Ruby Birtle.

ORMONROYD: Well, haven't you had a home?

RUBY: Course I've 'ad a home. Why?

ORMONROYD: You talk as if you'd been brought up in a
tramshed. No sentiment. No tender feeling. No – no –
poetry –

RUBY: (*Indignantly.*) Go on. I know poetry. We learnt it at school. 'Ere –

(*RUBY recites, as ORMONROYD sits.*)
They grew in beauty side by side,
They filled one home with glee;
Their graves are severed, far an' wide,
By mount and stream and sea.

The same fond mother bent at night
O'er each fair sleeping brow;
She 'ad each folder flower in sight –
Where are those dreamers now?

One 'midst the forest of the west,
By a dark stream is laid –
The Indian knows his place of rest
Far –

(*RUBY hesitates. CLARA enters quietly and stares at her in astonishment. RUBY gives her one startled look, then concludes hurriedly.*)

– Far in the cedar shade.

(*RUBY hurries out. CLARA stands in RUBY's place. ORMONROYD, who has turned away and closed his eyes, now turns and opens them, astonished to see CLARA there.*)

ORMONROYD: (*Bewildered.*) Now I call that most peculiar, *most* peculiar. I don't think I'm very well tonight.

CLARA: (*Same tone as RUBY used.*) You're a bit tiddly, aren't you?

ORMONROYD: Things aren't rightly in their place, if you know what I mean. But I'll get it.

CLARA: Who are you, and what are you doing here?

ORMONROYD: (*Still dazed.*) Henry Ormonroyd –
Yorkshire Argus – take picture – silver wedding group –

CLARA: (*Firmly.*) There's no silver wedding group'll be taken *here* tonight.

ORMONROYD: Have I come to t'wrong house?

CLARA: (*Firmly.*) Yes.

ORMONROYD: Excuse me. (*Moving to door, which opens to admit ANNIE.*)

ANNIE: Who's this?

ORMONROYD: (*Hastily confused.*) Nobody, nobody – I'll
  get it all straightened out in a minute – now give me
  time –
  (*ORMONROYD goes out.*)
ANNIE: Isn't he the photographer?
CLARA: (*Bitterly.*) Yes, an' he's drunk, an' when I come in,
  Maria's servant's reciting poetry to him, an' God knows
  what's become of Herbert an' Albert an' that Mrs
  Northrop an' (*Angrily.*) I'm fast losing my patience, I'm
  fast losing my patience –
ANNIE: Now, Clara –
  (*MARIA enters, rather wearily.*)
MARIA: I can't knock any sense at all into Joe. Where's
  Herbert?
CLARA: (*Grimly.*) Still looking for that Mrs Northrop.
  (*Front door bell rings.*)
  Somebody else here now.
MARIA: Well, don't carry on like that, Clara. I didn't ask
  'em to come, whoever it is.
CLARA: If you didn't, I'll bet Joe did. With his Yorkshire
  Argus!
  (*RUBY enters, rather mysteriously.*)
MARIA: Well, Ruby, who is it?
RUBY: (*Lowering voice.*) It's a woman.
CLARA: (*Hastily.*) What woman?
MARIA: Now, Clara! (*To RUBY.*) What sort of woman? Who
  is it?
RUBY: (*Coming in, confidentially.*) I don't know. But she
  doesn't look up to much to me. Paint on her face. An' I
  believe her 'air's dyed.
  (*The three women look at each other.*)
CLARA: (*Primly.*) We don't want that sort o' woman here,
  Maria.
MARIA: Course we don't – but – (*Hesitates.*)
ANNIE: You'll have to see what she wants, Maria. It might
  be something to do with – y'know – this business.
CLARA: (*Angrily.*) How could it be?
ANNIE: Well, you never know, do yer?

CLARA: Let Joe see what she wants.

MARIA: Oh – no – state of mind Joe's in, *I'd* better see her. Ask her to come in, Ruby – and – er – you needn't bother Mr Helliwell just now.

(*RUBY goes out. The three women settle themselves, rather anxiously. RUBY ushers in LOTTIE, who enters smiling broadly. MARIA rises, the other two remaining seated.*)

(*Nervously.*) Good evening.

LOTTIE: Good evening.

MARIA: (*Step down.*) Did you want to see me?

LOTTIE: (*Coolly.*) No, not particularly.

(*She sits down, calmly, and looks about her. The other three women exchange puzzled glances.*)

MARIA: Er – I don't think I got your name.

LOTTIE: No. You didn't get it because I didn't give it. But I'm Miss Lottie Grady.

MARIA: (*With dignity.*) And I'm Mrs Helliwell.

LOTTIE: (*Shaking her head.*) *No*, if we're all going to be on our dignity, let's get it *right. You're* not *Mrs Helliwell.* You're Miss Maria Fawcett.

CLARA: (*As MARIA is too stunned to speak.*) Now just a minute –

LOTTIE: (*Turning to her, with mock sweetness.*) Miss Clara Gawthorpe, isn't it? Gawthorpe's, Greengrocer's, corner of Park Road. (*Turning to ANNIE.*) I'm afraid I don't know your maiden name –

ANNIE: I'm Mrs Parker to you.

LOTTIE: Please yourself, I don't care. I'm broad-minded. (*Surveying them with a smile.*)

CLARA: (*Angrily.*) I suppose that Mrs Northrop's been talking to you.

LOTTIE: Certainly. Met in the old Hare and Hounds, where I used to work. She's an old friend of mine.

CLARA: (*Angrily.*) If you've come 'ere to get money out of us –

LOTTIE: Who said anything about money?

MARIA: Well, you must have some idea in coming to see us.

LOTTIE: (*Coolly.*) Oh – I didn't come here to see any of you three.

ANNIE: Well, who did you come to see then?

LOTTIE: (*Smiling.*) A gentleman friend, love.

CLARA: (*Angrily.*) *Gentleman friend! You'*ll find none o' your gentleman friends in *this house*, will she, Maria?

MARIA: (*Indignantly.*) I should think not!

ANNIE: Just a minute, Clara. I'd like to hear a bit more about this.

LOTTIE: Very sensible of you. You see, if a gentleman friend gets fond of me – then tells me – more than once – that if he wasn't married already, he'd marry me.

CLARA: (*Grimly.*) Well, go on.

LOTTIE: Well – then I suddenly find out that he isn't married already, after all, then you can't blame me – can you? – if I'd like to know if he's still in the same mind. (*Beams upon them, while they look at each other in growing consternation.*)

CLARA: (*Astounded.*) Well, I'll be hanged.

ANNIE: Now we *are* getting to know something.

MARIA: (*Flustered.*) Clara – Annie. (*Pause. Suddenly to LOTTIE.*) Who was it? (*Front door bell rings.*)

ANNIE: Just a minute, Maria, there's somebody else here now.

CLARA: (*Angrily.*) Oh – for goodness' sake – can't you keep 'em out?

RUBY: (*Appearing, importantly.*) The Rever-ent Clem-ent Mer-cer! (*All three wives look startled, as MERCER, a large grave clergyman, enters, and RUBY retires.*)

MERCER: (*Sympathetically.*) Mrs Helliwell?

MARIA: (*Faintly.*) Yes?

MERCER: (*Taking her hand a moment.*) Now, Mrs Helliwell, although you're not a member of my congregation, I want you to realise that I feel it my duty to give you any help I can.

MARIA: (*Confused.*) I'm afraid – I don't understand – Mr Mercer.

153

MERCER: Now, now, Mrs Helliwell, don't worry. Let's take everything calmly. May I sit down? (*Takes chair and brings it down.*)

(*MERCER sits down, smiling at them. MARIA sits.*)

ANNIE: Did somebody ask you to come here?

MERCER: Yes, madam. A working man I know called Northrop stopped me in the street and told me to go at once to Alderman Helliwell's house as a clergyman's presence was urgently required here. So here I am – entirely at your service.

(*LOTTIE, in danger of exploding, rises and goes quickly towards conservatory, where she stands with her back to the others. MERCER gives her a puzzled glance, then turns to the other three.*)

Now what is it? Not, I hope, a really dangerous illness?

MARIA: (*Blankly.*) No.

MERCER: (*Rather puzzled.*) Ah! – I hurried because I thought there might be. But perhaps you feel some younger member of your family is in urgent need of spiritual guidance. An erring son or daughter?

(*A noise from LOTTIE.*)

CLARA: (*Forcefully.*) No.

MERCER: (*Puzzled.*) I beg your pardon?

CLARA: I just said No. I mean, there aren't any erring sons and daughters. Just husbands, that's all.

MERCER: (*Rises.*) Husbands?

(*LOTTIE suddenly bursts into a peal of laughter, turning towards them. MERCER looks puzzled at her.*)

LOTTIE: (*Laughing.*) You've got it all wrong.

MERCER: (*Rather annoyed.*) Really! I don't see –

LOTTIE: I think they want you to marry 'em.

MERCER: (*Looking astounded.*) Marry them!

ANNIE: (*Rising, with spirit.*) 'Ere, Maria, come on, do somethin'. (*To MERCER.*) You'd better talk to Mr Helliwell –

MARIA: (*Who has risen.*) He's in the dining-room – just across – (*Almost leading him out.*) Ask him if he thinks you can do anything for us – (*Now outside room.*) Just in there – that's right –

CLARA: (*To LOTTIE.*) Which one was it?

(*MARIA returns, flustered, shutting door, as LOTTIE returns to her seat, still smiling.*)

LOTTIE: I think you missed a chance there, at least, two of you did.

MARIA: Two of us!

LOTTIE: Well, you remember what I told you? (*Smiling reminiscently.*) I'd known him here in Cleckleywyke, but it was at Blackpool we really got going. He said he was feeling lonely – and you know what men are, when they think they're feeling lonely, specially at Blackpool.

CLARA: (*Hastily.*) It couldn't have been Herbert. He's never been to Blackpool without me.

ANNIE: Yes, he has, Clara. Don't you remember – about four years since – ?

CLARA: (*Thunderstruck.*) And he said he hadn't a minute away from that conference. I'll never believe another word he says. But your Albert was with him that time.

ANNIE: (*Grimly.*) I know he was.

MARIA: So was Joe. Said he needed a change.

LOTTIE: (*Sweetly.*) Well, we all like a change, don't we?

(*SOPPITT enters, rather hesitantly. CLARA sees him first.*)

CLARA: (*Sharply.*) Now, Herbert Soppitt –

SOPPITT: Yes, Clara?

LOTTIE: (*Going to him.*) Well, Herbert, how are you these days? (*Playfully.*) You haven't forgotten me, have you?

SOPPITT: Forgotten you? I'm afraid there's a mistake –

CLARA: (*Grimly.*) Oh – there's a mistake all right.

MARIA: Now, Clara, don't be too hard on him. I expect it was only a bit o' fun.

SOPPITT: What is all this?

LOTTIE: (*Playfully.*) Now, Herbert –

SOPPITT: (*Indignantly.*) Don't call me Herbert.

CLARA: (*Angrily.*) No, wait till I'm out o' t'way.

ANNIE: I expect he didn't mean it.

SOPPITT: (*Annoyed.*) Mean *what?*

(*ALBERT PARKER now enters, rather wearily. SOPPITT turns to him.*)

I found that Mrs Northrop, Albert.

LOTTIE: Oh – hello, Albert!

PARKER: (*Staring at her.*) How d'you mean – *Hello, Albert!*

LOTTIE: (*Playfully.*) Now, now – Albert!

(*PARKER looks at her in astonishment, then at the three women, finishing with his wife.*)

ANNIE: (*Bitterly.*) Yes, you might well look at me, Albert Parker. You and your cheap holiday at Blackpool! I only hope you spent more on her than you've ever done on me.

PARKER: (*Vehemently.*) Spent more on *her?* I've never set eyes on her before. *Who is she?*

(*ANNIE and CLARA now look at one another, then at MARIA, who looks at them in growing consternation.*)

MARIA: I don't believe it. I *won't* believe it.

(*RUBY looks in, excitedly.*)

RUBY: There's a motor-car stopping near t'front gate.

CLARA: (*Shouting as RUBY goes.*) Well, tell it to go away again.

(*HELLIWELL comes out of dining-room, bumping into RUBY as she goes out, and begins speaking early.*)

HELLIWELL: (*Who is flustered.*) What with a photographer who's drunk and a parson who's mad – ! (*He sees LOTTIE now, and visibly wilts and gasps.*) Lottie!

MARIA: (*Furiously.*) Lottie! So it was *you*, Joe Helliwell.

HELLIWELL: Me what?

MARIA: Who said you'd marry her –

HELLIWELL: (*Shouting desperately.*) That was only a bit o' fun.

MARIA: (*Bitterly.*) You and your bit o' fun!

RUBY: (*Importantly.*) Mayor o' Cleckleywyke, Yorkshire Argus, Telegraph and Mercury.

(*MAYOR enters, carrying case of fish slices, with REPORTERS behind.*)

MAYOR: (*Pompously.*) Alderman and Mrs Helliwell, the Council and Corporation of Cleckleywyke offers you their heartiest congratulations on your Silver Wedding and with them this case of silver fish slices.

(*He is now offering the case to MARIA, who has suddenly sunk down on the settee and is now weeping. She waves the case away, and the bewildered MAYOR now offers it to HELLIWELL, who has been looking in exasperation between his wife, LOTTIE and the MAYOR. HELLIWELL takes the case and opens it without thinking, then seeing what is in it, in his exasperation, shouts furiously.*)

HELLIWELL: An' I told yer before, Fred – I don't like fish. (*Quick curtain.*)

End of Act Two.

ACT THREE

Scene: as before. About quarter of an hour later. RUBY is tidying up the room, and also eating a large piece of pasty. She continues with her work several moments after rise of curtain, then NANCY makes cautious appearance at conservatory, sees that nobody but RUBY is there, then turns to beckon in GERALD, and they both come into the room.

NANCY: What's been happening, Ruby?

RUBY: What 'asn't been 'appening! Eee – we've had some trade on what wi' one thing an' another.

NANCY: (*Mischievous rather than reproachful.*) You see what you've done, Gerald.

RUBY: What! He didn't start it, did he? 'Cos if he did, he's got summat to answer for.

NANCY: Did – anybody ask where I was, Ruby?

RUBY: No, an' I'll bet you could stop out all night and they'd neither know nor care.

GERALD: But what *has* been happening, Ruby?

RUBY: (*Confidentially.*) Place 'as been like a mad-'ouse this last half-hour. To start with, mayor o' Cleckleywyke's been and gone –

NANCY: The mayor?

GERALD: (*Amused.*) Why did they want to bring the mayor into it?

RUBY: Nobody brought him. He come of his own accord – with a case o' fish things an' wearing t'chain – like a chap in a pantymime. He soon took his 'ook. But reporters didn't –

GERALD: Reporters, eh?

RUBY: Ay, an' there were plenty of 'em an' all an' they didn't want to go, neither, not like t'mayor. So Mr Helliwell an' Mr Parker took 'em into t'kitchen an' give 'em bottled ale an' for all I know they may be there yet. Mrs Helliwell's up in t'bedroom – feeling poorly – an' Mrs Soppitt's with her. Mr Soppitt an' Mrs Parker's somewhere out in garden –

NANCY: I told you there was somebody there.

RUBY: Ah, but let me finish. Now there's a woman wi' dyed 'air washing herself in t'bathroom upstairs – an' nobody knows what she wants – beyond a good wash. Down in t'dining-room there's a photographer who's right tidily tryin' to argue with gert big parson – an' I'll bet he's makin' a rare mess – an' that'll be to do next.
(*Exit RUBY.*)

GERALD: Sounds all very confused to me.

NANCY: Yes, and I'd better slip upstairs while nobody's about. Oh – Gerald.

GERALD: Nancy!

NANCY: Do you still love me?

GERALD: Yes, Nancy – still – even after a whole hour.
(*They kiss. Enter SOPPITT and ANNIE PARKER from conservatory.*)

SOPPITT: Here, I say! You two seem very friendly!

ANNIE: I believe you were the girl he was seen with.

SOPPITT: Were you?

NANCY: Yes. We're practically engaged, you know. Only – I was frightened of saying anything yet to Uncle Joe.

SOPPITT: Well, don't start tonight –

ANNIE: Why shouldn't she? He won't be quite so pleased with himself tonight as usual – just as I know another who won't.

NANCY: Good night.

ANNIE: Good night. Why don't you go outside and say good night properly? You're only young once.
(*NANCY and GERALD exit to conservatory.*)
Yes, you're only young once, Herbert. D'you remember that time, just after you'd first come to Cleckleywyke, when we all went on that choir trip to Barnard Castle?

SOPPITT: I do, Annie. As a matter of fact, I fancy I was a bit sweet on you then.

ANNIE: You fancy you were! I know you were, Herbert Soppitt. Don't you remember coming back in the wagonette?

SOPPITT: Ay!

ANNIE: Those were the days!

SOPPITT: Ay!

ANNIE: Is that all you can say – Ay?

SOPPITT: No. But I might say too much.

ANNIE: I think I'd risk it for once, if I were you.

SOPPITT: And what does that mean, Annie?

ANNIE: Never you mind. But you haven't forgotten that wagonette, have you?

SOPPITT: Of course I haven't.

(*He has his arm round her waist. Enter CLARA.*)

Hello, Clara.

CLARA: How long's this been going on?

ANNIE: Now, don't be silly, Clara.

CLARA: Oh – it's me that hasn't to be silly, is it? I suppose standing there with my 'usband's arm round you bold as brass, that isn't being silly, is it? I wonder what you call that sort of behaviour, then?

SOPPITT: It was only a bit of fun.

CLARA: Oh – an' how long have you been 'aving these bits o' fun – as you call them – Herbert Soppitt?

ANNIE: You've a nasty mind, Clara.

CLARA: Well – of all the cheek and impudence! Telling me I've got a nasty mind. You must have been at it some time getting Herbert to carry on like that with you. Don't tell me he thought of it himself, I know him too well.

ANNIE: Oh – don't be so stupid, Clara. I'm going into the garden. I want some fresh air.

(*She goes out.*)

CLARA: Well, Herbert Soppitt, why don't you follow her and get some fresh air, too? Go on, don't mind me. Come here.

(*SOPPITT doesn't move.*)

You 'eard me, come here!

SOPPITT: Why should I?

CLARA: Because I tell you to.

SOPPITT: I know. I heard you. But who do you think you are?

CLARA: Herbert Soppitt – you must have gone wrong in your head.

SOPPITT: No. Not me. I'm all right.

CLARA: (*Sharply.*) You'd better go home now an' leave me to deal with this business here.

SOPPITT: (*Bravely.*) Certainly not.

CLARA: In my opinion it's awkward with both of us here.

SOPPITT: (*Pause.*) Well, *you* go home then!

CLARA: What did you say?

SOPPITT: (*Bravely.*) I said, *you* go home. You are doing no good here.

(*Very angry now, she marches up to him and gives him a sharp slap on the cheek.*)

CLARA: Now then! (*Steps back and folds arms.*) Just tell me to go home again!

SOPPITT: (*Slowly, impressively, approaching her.*) Clara, I always said that no matter what she did, I'd never lift a hand to my wife –

CLARA: I should think not indeed!

SOPPITT: But as you aren't my wife – what about this?

(*He gives her a sharp slap. She is astounded.*)

CLARA: Herbert!

SOPPITT: (*Commandingly.*) Now sit down. (*Pointing.*)

(*She does not obey. In a tremendous voice of command.*)

Sit down!

(*She sits, staring at him. Then when she opens her mouth to speak.*)

Shut up! I want to think.

(*A silence, during which she still stares at him.*)

CLARA: (*In a low voice.*) I don't know what's come over you, Herbert Soppitt.

SOPPITT: (*Fiercely.*) You don't, eh?

CLARA: (*Gaping at him.*) No, I don't.

SOPPITT: (*Severely.*) Well, you don't think I put up with women coming shouting and bawling at me and smacking my face, do you?

CLARA: Well – you've never gone on like this before.

SOPPITT: Yes, but then before you were my wife –

CLARA: (*Hastily.*) I'm your wife now.

SOPPITT: Oh, no – you're not. (*Produces letter.*)

CLARA: Give me that letter!

SOPPITT: *Sit down* – and *shut up, woman!*
(*Enter ALBERT PARKER.*)

PARKER: Where's Annie?

SOPPITT: She's out there somewhere – why don't you look
for her?

CLARA: Perhaps she's hiding her face – and if you'd seen
what I'd seen tonight, Albert Parker –

SOPPITT: Hold your tongue before it gets you into
mischief!

CLARA: I'm only –

SOPPITT: *Shut up.*

PARKER: Here, but wait a minute – I'd like to hear a bit
more about this.

SOPPITT: Then you're going to be disappointed. (*To
CLARA.*) You get back to Maria Helliwell, go on!

PARKER: Here, Clara, you're not going to –

SOPPITT: *You* mind your own business! (*To CLARA.*) Go on
– sharp.
(*CLARA exits.*)

PARKER: Herbert, 'ave you been 'aving a lot to drink?

SOPPITT: I had a few, trying to find that Mrs Northrop.

PARKER: I thought as much.

SOPPITT: And I may possibly have some more, but
whether I do or not, I'll please myself – just for once –
and if any of you don't like it, you can lump it.

PARKER: Where did you say my wife was?

SOPPITT: She's out there in the garden.

PARKER: (*Disapprovingly.*) What – at this time o' night?
(*Looking to garden.*)

SOPPITT: Yes – and why not?

PARKER: (*With dignity.*) I'll tell 'er that. I've no need to tell
you. You're not my wife.

SOPPITT: No, and she isn't, either. Don't forget that.
(*PARKER goes to the door and calls.*)

PARKER: Annie! Hey – Annie!

SOPPITT: Why don't you go out and talk to her, instead o' calling her like that – as if she were a dog or something?

PARKER: 'Cos standing about in damp grass this time o' night is bad for me. I don't want to start a running cold on top of all this. (*Calls again.*) Hey – Annie! (*Turns to SOPPITT.*) I came in to 'ave a few words in private with her –

SOPPITT: Oh – I'll leave you.

PARKER: In my opinion, there's been a lot too much talk among us altogether, too much noisy 'anky-panky about this daft business. You might think we were a meeting o' t'gas committee way we've gone on so far. What's wanted is a few serious words i' private between us chaps an' our wives, an' less o' this public argy-bargy an' 'anky-panky. (*ANNIE PARKER enters through conservatory.*)

Ah – so there y'are.

SOPPITT: (*Going.*) Well, best o' luck, Annie!

PARKER: (*Suspiciously.*) How d'you mean?

SOPPITT: (*Turning at door.*) Hanky-panky!

(*He goes out.*)

PARKER: He's 'ad a drop too much, Herbert 'as! Comes of running round the town after that charwoman!

ANNIE: (*Amused.*) Well, Albert?

PARKER: (*Pompously and complacently.*) Well, Annie, I'm going to set your mind at rest.

ANNIE: (*Demurely.*) Thank you, Albert.

PARKER: (*Pompously and complacently.*) Yes, I don't want you to be worrying. Now I think you'll admit I've always tried to do my duty as a 'usband.

ANNIE: Yes, Albert, I think you've always tried.

PARKER: (*Suspiciously.*) What do you mean?

ANNIE: (*Demurely.*) Why – just what you mean, Albert.

PARKER: (*After another suspicious glance, returns to former tone, and is insufferably patronising.*) Of course, as nobody knows better than you, I'm in a different position altogether to what I was when I first married you –

ANNIE: When you *thought* you married me, Albert.

PARKER: Well, you know what I mean! In them days I was just plain young Albert Parker.

ANNIE: And now you're Councillor Albert Parker –

PARKER: Well, an' that's something, isn't it? And it isn't all, by a long chalk. I've got on i' business, made money, come to be a big man at chapel, vice-president o' t'cricket league, on t'hospital committee, an' so forth – eh?

ANNIE: Yes, Albert, you've done very well.

PARKER: (*Complacently.*) I know I 'ave. An' mind you, it's not altered me much. I'm not like some of 'em. No swank about me – no la-di-dah – *I'm a plain man.*

ANNIE: (*Rather sadly.*) Yes, Albert, you are.

PARKER: (*Looking at her suspiciously.*) Well, what's wrong wi' it? You're not going to tell me that at your time o' life –

ANNIE: (*Indignantly cutting in.*) My time of life!

PARKER: Well, you're no chicken, are yer? And I say, you're not going to tell me now, at your time o' life, you'd like a bit o' swank an' la-di-dah!

ANNIE: (*Wistfully.*) I've sometimes wondered –

PARKER: (*Brushing this aside.*) Nay, nay, nay, nobody knows better than me what you'd like. An' you know very well what a good husband I've been: steady –

ANNIE: (*Rather grimly.*) Yes, you've been steady all right, Albert.

PARKER: (*Complacently.*) That's what I say. Steady. Reliable. Not silly wi' my money –

ANNIE: (*Same tone.*) No, Albert, your worst enemy couldn't say you'd ever been silly with your money.

PARKER: (*Complacently.*) And yet at the same time – not stingy. No, not stingy. Everything of the best – if it could be managed – everything of the best, within reason, y'know, within reason.

ANNIE: Yes, within reason.

PARKER: (*In a dreamy ecstasy of complacency.*) Always reasonable – *and* reliable. But all the time, getting on, goin' up i' the world, never satisfied with what 'ud do for most men – no, steadily moving on an' on, up an' up – cashier, manager, share in the business – councillor this year, alderman next, perhaps mayor soon – that's how it's been an' that's how it will be. Y'know, Annie, I've sometimes thought that right at first you didn't realise just what you'd picked out o' t'lucky bag. Ay!

(*Contemplates his own greatness, while she watches him coolly.*)

ANNIE: (*After a pause.*) Well, Albert, what's all this leading up to?

PARKER: (*Recalled to his argument.*) Oh! – Well, yer see, Annie, I was just saying that I thought I'd been a good husband to you. An', mind yer, I don't say you've been a bad wife – no, I don't –

ANNIE: (*Dryly.*) Thank you, Albert.

PARKER: (*With immense patronage.*) So I thought I'd just set your mind at rest. Now don't you worry about this wedding business. If there's been a slip up – well, there's been a slip up. But I'll see you're all right, Annie. I'll see it's fixed up quietly, an' then we'll go an' get married again – properly. (*He pats her on the shoulder.*) I know my duty as well as t'next man – an' I'll see that you're properly married to me.

ANNIE: Thank you, Albert.

PARKER: That's all right, Annie, that's all right. I don't say every man 'ud see it as I do – but – never mind – I know what my duty is.

ANNIE: And what about me?

PARKER: (*Puzzled.*) Well, I'm telling yer – you'll be all right.

ANNIE: How d'you know I will?

PARKER: (*Hastily.*) Now don't be silly, Annie, If I say you'll be all right, you ought to know by this time yer *will* be all right.

ANNIE: (*Slowly.*) But I don't think I want to be married to you.

PARKER: (*Staggered.*) *What!*

ANNIE: (*Slowly.*) You see, Albert, after twenty-five years of it, perhaps I've had enough.

PARKER: (*Horrified.*) 'Ad enough!

ANNIE: Yes, had enough. You talk about your duty. Well, for twenty-five years I've done my duty. I've washed and

cooked and cleaned and mended for you. I've pinched
and scrimped and saved for you. I've listened for hours
and hours to all your dreary talk. I've never had any
thanks for it. I've hardly ever had any fun. But I thought
I was your wife and I'd taken you for better or worse,
and that I ought to put up with you –

PARKER: (*Staring, amazed.*) Put up with me!

ANNIE: (*Coolly.*) Yes, put up with you.

PARKER: But what's wrong with me?

ANNIE: (*Coolly.*) Well, to begin with, you're very selfish.
But then, I suppose most men are. You're idiotically
conceited. But again, so are most men. But a lot of men
at least are generous. And you're very stingy. And some
men are amusing. But – except when you're being
pompous and showing off – you're not at all amusing.
You're just very dull and dreary –

PARKER: Never!

ANNIE: (*Firmly.*) Yes, Albert. *Very* dull and *very, very* dreary
and stingy.

PARKER: (*Staring at her as if seeing a strange woman.*) 'As
somebody put you up to this?

ANNIE: No, I've thought it for a long time.

PARKER: How long?

ANNIE: Nearly twenty-five years.

PARKER: (*Half dazed, half indignant.*) Why – you – you –
you little serpent!

ANNIE: (*Ignoring this.*) So now I feel it's time I enjoyed
myself a bit. I'd like to have *some* fun before I'm an old
woman.

PARKER: (*Horrified.*) Fun! Fun! What do you mean – fun?

ANNIE: (*Coolly.*) Oh – nothing very shocking and terrible –
just getting away from you, for instance –

PARKER: (*In loud pained tone.*) Stop it! Just stop it now! I
think – Annie Parker – you ought to be ashamed of
yourself.

ANNIE: (*Dreamily.*) Well, I'm not. Bit of travel – and
liveliness – and people that are amusing – and no wool
business and town councillors and chapel deacons –

PARKER: (*Shouting angrily.*) Why don't you dye your hair
and paint your face and go on t'stage and wear tights – ?

ANNIE: (*Wistfully.*) I wish I could.

(*As PARKER groans in despair at this, RUBY looks in.*)

RUBY: (*Loudly and cheerfully.*) Mr Soppitt says if you haven't
finished yet yer better 'urry up or go somewhere else to
'ave it out 'cos they're all coming in 'ere.

PARKER: (*Angrily.*) Well, we 'aven't finished.

ANNIE: (*Coolly.*) Yes, we have.

(*RUBY nods and leaves the door open.*)

PARKER: (*Loudly.*) Now listen, Annie, let's talk a bit o'
sense for a minute –

ANNIE: They'll all hear you – the door's open.

PARKER: Nay – damn it – !

(*Goes to shut door, but SOPPITT and CLARA enter.*)

SOPPITT: (*Amused.*) Hello, Albert – what's made you look
so flabbergasted?

PARKER: (*Annoyed.*) If I want to look flabbergasted, then
I'll look flabbergasted, without asking your advice,
Herbert.

SOPPITT: Hanky-panky!

PARKER: Now shut up! 'Ere, Clara, yer wouldn't say I was
stingy, would yer?

CLARA: Well, you've never been famous for getting your
hand down, have you, Albert?

PARKER: (*Indignantly.*) I've got my 'and down as well as
t'next man. I've always paid my whack, let me tell yer.
Call a chap stingy just because he doesn't make a big
show – 'cos he isn't – er –

ANNIE: (*Burlesqueing his accent, coolly.*) La-di-dah!

SOPPITT: Now stop tormenting him, Annie.

PARKER: (*Indignantly.*) Tormenting me! Nobody'll torment
me. And I like that coming from *you*, Herbert, when
you've been a by-word for years.

CLARA: (*Angrily.*) A by-word for what?

PARKER: For years.

CLARA: Yes, but a by-word for years for what?

PARKER: Oh! Hen-pecked! Ask anybody who wears
trousers in your house!

ANNIE: Albert, don't be so vulgar!

PARKER: Why, a minute since you wanted to wear tights.

ANNIE: Only in a manner of speaking.

PARKER: How can it be in a manner of speaking? – 'cos either you're wearing tights or you're not.

(*Enter LOTTIE and HELLIWELL.*)

LOTTIE: What's this about tights?

PARKER: Now you'll clear out right sharp – if you'll take my tip.

LOTTIE: And I'll bet it's the only kind of tip you do give, too. (*To ANNIE.*) He looks stingy to me!

PARKER: Stingy! If anyone says that again to me tonight – I'll – I'll give 'em jip.

(*Exit PARKER.*)

HELLIWELL: For two pins I'd either leave this house myself or else clear everybody else out. I've never seen such a place – there's folk nattering in every damn corner!

ANNIE: Where's poor Maria?

SOPPITT: Clara!

(*Exeunt SOPPITT, CLARA and ANNIE.*)

HELLIWELL: Now, Lottie, be reasonable. A bit o' devilment's all right, but I know you don't want to make real mischief.

LOTTIE: Where's the mischief come in? Didn't you say – more than once – that if you hadn't been married already?

HELLIWELL: (*Urgently to her.*) Now, you know very well that were only a bit o' fun. When a chap's on a 'oliday in a place like Blackpool an' gets a few drinks inside 'im, you know very well he says a lot o' damn silly things he doesn't mean –

LOTTIE: (*Indignantly.*) Oh – I see. Just tellin' me the tale an' then laughing at me behind my back, eh?

HELLIWELL: (*Urgently.*) No, I don't mean that, Lottie. Nobody admires you more than I do. You're a fine lass and a good sport. But you've got to be reasonable. Coming 'ere *like this*, when you know as well as I do, it were just a bit o' fun!

(*MARIA enters. She is dressed to go out, and is carrying some housekeeping books, some keys, and several pairs of socks.*)

MARIA: (*At door, leaving it open; grimly.*) Just a minute, Joe Helliwell!

HELLIWELL: (*Groaning.*) Oh – Christmas! (*Then sees she has outdoor things on.*) 'Ere, Maria, where are yer going?

MARIA: (*Determined, but rather tearful.*) I'm going back to me mother's.

HELLIWELL: Your mother's! Why, if you go to your mother in this state o' mind at this time o' night, you'll give her a stroke.

LOTTIE: That's right. She must be about ninety.

MARIA: (*Angrily.*) She's seventy-two. (*Pauses.*) And mind your own *business*. I've got some of it 'ere *for you*.

LOTTIE: What do you mean?

MARIA: (*Indicating things she's carrying.*) Some of your new business, an' see 'ow you like it. You'll find it a change from carrying on wi' men behind the bar.

HELLIWELL: What in the name o' thunder are you talking about?

MARIA: I'm talking about 'er. If she wants my job, she can 'ave it.

LOTTIE: (*Simultaneous with HELLIWELL.*) 'Ere, just a minute –

HELLIWELL: (*Simultaneous with LOTTIE.*) Now listen, Maria –

MARIA: (*Silencing them by holding up keys and rattling.*) There's all t'keys, an' you'd better start knowing where they fit. (*Puts them on table behind settee.*) An' don't forget charwoman's just been sacked, an' I don't expect Ruby'll stay. You'll have to manage by yourself a bit. An' greengrocer calls at ten and the butcher calls at half-past –

HELLIWELL: (*Shouting.*) What does it matter when t'butcher calls?

MARIA: (*Calmly.*) I'm talking to 'er, not to you. (*To LOTTIE, who looks astonished.*) These is the housekeeping books an' you'll 'ave to 'ave 'em straight by Friday or he'll make a rumpus. 'Ere you are.

LOTTIE: (*Backing away.*) I don't want 'em.

HELLIWELL: (*Harassed.*) 'Course she doesn't –

MARIA: She can't run this house without 'em. You said so yourself. (*Throws books on to settee.*)

HELLIWELL: I know I did, but it's nowt to do with 'er.

MARIA: Then what did she come 'ere for? (*To LOTTIE, producing socks.*) An' look, 'ere's five pairs of his socks and one pair of woollens (*Hangs them on back of settee.*) that wants darning, and you'd better get *started* on 'em. An' upstairs you'll find three shirts and two more pairs of woollens you'll 'ave to do tomorrow, an' you'd better be thinking o' tomorrow's dinner, 'cos he always wants something *hot* an' he's very *particular*. (*Turns towards door.*)

LOTTIE: (*Aghast.*) 'Ere, what do you think I am?

HELLIWELL: Now, Maria, you're getting it all wrong. Nobody knows better than me what a good wife you've been. Now 'ave a bit of sense, love. It's all a mistake.

MARIA: And there's a lot of other things you'll have to manage, but while you're trying to manage them and him, too, I'll be at Blackpool.
(*She goes, followed by HELLIWELL.
Enter ORMONROYD.*)

ORMONROYD: I know that face.

LOTTIE: Harry Ormonroyd.

ORMONROYD: Lottie, my beautiful Lottie. And you haven't forgotten me?

LOTTIE: Forgotten you! My word, if you're not off I'll saw your leg off. 'Ere, you weren't going to take their photos?

ORMONROYD: Yes, group for Yorkshire Argus. Make a nice picture – very nice picture.

LOTTIE: Nice picture! Don't you know? Haven't they told you?
(*Roars with laughter.*)

ORMONROYD: Here now, stop it, stop it. Have a drink of port.

LOTTIE: Well, I suppose I might.

ORMONROYD: Certainly, certainly. Liberty 'All here tonight.

LOTTIE: Oh – it's Liberty Hall right enough. Chin – chin.

ORMONROYD: All the best, Lottie.

LOTTIE: Nice drop of port wine this. Joe Helliwell does himself very well here, doesn't he?

ORMONROYD: Oh, yes, Lottie, you'll find everything very comfortable here. 'Ere, somebody told me you were back at the Talbot.

LOTTIE: I was up to Christmas. Who told you? Anybody I know?

ORMONROYD: (*Solemnly.*) Yes – now just a minute. You know him. I know him. We both know him. I have him here on the tip of my tongue. Er – (*But can't remember.*) no. But I'll get him, Lottie, I'll get him.

LOTTIE: Then I had to go home. Our Violet – you remember our Violet – she married a sergeant in the Duke of Wellington's – the dirty Thirty-thirds – and now she's in India.

ORMONROYD: (*Remembering, triumphantly.*) Tommy Toothill!

LOTTIE: What about him?

ORMONROYD: (*Puzzled by this.*) Nay, weren't you asking about 'im?

LOTTIE: No, I've something better to do than to ask about Tommy Toothill.

ORMONROYD: (*Still bewildered.*) Quite so, Lottie. But what were we talking about him for? Didn't you say he'd gone to India?

LOTTIE: No, you fathead, that's our Violet. Oh – I remember, it must have been Tommy Toothill 'at told you I was working at the Talbot – d'you see?

ORMONROYD: (*Still bewildered.*) Yes, I know it was. But what of it, Lottie? Aren't you a bit argumentative tonight, love?

LOTTIE: (*Good-naturedly.*) No, I'm not, but you've had a couple too many.

ORMONROYD: Nay, I'm all right, love. 'Ere, what's happened to your Violet?

LOTTIE: (*Impatiently.*) She married a sergeant and went to India.

ORMONROYD: (*Triumphantly.*) Of course she did. Somebody told me – just lately.

LOTTIE: I told you.

ORMONROYD: (*Reproachfully.*) Yes, I know – I can 'ear. But so did somebody else. I know – Tommy Toothill!

LOTTIE: You've got him on the brain. Then at Whitsun – I took a job at Bridlington – but I only stuck it three weeks. No life at all – I told 'em, I says, 'I don't mind work, but I do like a bit of life.'

ORMONROYD: I'm just the same. Lot's 'ave a bit of life, I say. An' 'ere we are, getting down in dumps, just because Tommy Toothill's gone to India.

LOTTIE: He hasn't, you pie-can, that's our Violet. Nay, Harry, you're giving me the hump.

ORMONROYD: Well, play us a tune, just for old times' sake.

LOTTIE: Aaaa, you silly old devil, I'm right glad to see you.

ORMONROYD: Good old times, Lottie, good old times. (*They sing. Interrupted by entrance of HELLIWELL, PARKER and SOPPITT.*)

HELLIWELL: Now what the hangment do you think this is – a taproom? Yorkshire Argus wants you on telephone.

LOTTIE: Come on, love, I'll help you.

HELLIWELL: And then get off home.

ORMONROYD: See you later. (*ORMONROYD and LOTTIE exit.*)

PARKER: Now, what's wanted now is a few serious words in private together.

HELLIWELL: Yes, yes, Albert. I know. But give a chap time to have a breather. I've just had to persuade Maria not to go back to her mother's.

PARKER: Why, what can her mother do?

HELLIWELL: Oh – don't start asking questions – just leave it, Albert, leave it, and let me have a breather. (*Enter the three wives, all with hats and coats on.*)

ANNIE: Now then – Albert – Joe – Herbert –

HELLIWELL: What is this – an ultimatum?

MARIA: Joe Helliwell, I want you to answer one question.

HELLIWELL: Yes, Maria?

MARIA: Joe, do you love me?

HELLIWELL: (*Embarrassed.*) Now what sort of a question is that to come and ask a chap – here? Why didn't you ask me upstairs?

MARIA: (*Solemnly.*) Once and for all – do you or don't you?

HELLIWELL: Yes, of course I do, love.

MARIA: Then why didn't you say so before?

(*All three women sit down, take off hats.*)

PARKER: (*As if beginning long speech.*) And now we're all by ourselves it's about time we started to put our thinking caps on, 'cos we're not going to do any good running round the 'ouse argy-bargying –

MARIA: That's right, Albert.

PARKER: Yes, but let me finish, Maria. We –

(*He is interrupted by RUBY appearing round door.*)

RUBY: (*Loudly, cheerfully.*) She's back!

MARIA: Who is?

RUBY: That Mrs Northrop. (*Withdraws, leaving door open.*)

HELLIWELL: (*Loudly, in despair.*) Oh – Jerusalem – we don't want 'er 'ere.

MRS NORTHROP: (*Appearing, still carrying bag, and flushed.*) If you don't want me here why did you send 'im round chasing me and askin' me to come back? Yer don't know yer own minds two minutes together. (*To MARIA.*) You 'aven't settled up wi' me yet, y'know.

HELLIWELL: (*Annoyed.*) Outside!

PARKER: (*Hastily, anxiously.*) Half a minute, Joe, we can't 'ave her telling all she knows – we'll be t'laughing stock of Cleckleywyke tomorrow.

MRS NORTHROP: (*Contemptuously.*) Yer've bin that for years, lad. I'd rather ha' Joe Helliwell nor you. Joe 'as 'ad a bit o' fun in his time, but you've allus been too stingy.

PARKER: (*The word again.*) Stingy! If anybody says that again to me tonight, they'll get what for, an' I don't care who it is.

HELLIWELL: (*To MRS NORTHROP.*) I told you – outside – sharp!

MRS NORTHROP: (*Full of malice.*) Suits me. I reckon naught o' this for a party. You can't frame to enjoy yourselves. But then there's one or two faces 'ere that 'ud stop a clock, never mind a party. But wait till a few of 'em I know 'ears about it! You'll 'ear 'em laughing at back o' t'mill right up 'ere.

PARKER: Now we can't let her go i' that state o' mind.

CLARA: You ought to charge 'er with stealin'.

MRS NORTHROP: (*Horrified.*) Stealin'! Why – for two pins – I'll knock yer lying 'ead off, missis. Never touched a thing i' my life that wasn't me own!

(*RUBY looks in, and MRS NORTHROP sees her.*)

What is it, love?

RUBY: (*Loudly, chiefly to HELLIWELL.*) That photographer's asleep an' snoring be telephone.

HELLIWELL: (*Irritably.*) Well, waken him up an' tell him to go home.

(*RUBY withdraws. MRS NORTHROP takes charge again.*)

MRS NORTHROP: (*Significantly.*) An' I *could* keep me mouth shut if it were worth me while –

CLARA: (*Almost hissing.*) That's blackmail!

SOPPITT: (*Hastily.*) Shut up, Clara!

MRS NORTHROP: (*Looking at him.*) Hello, *you've* come to life, 'ave yer?

HELLIWELL: (*To MRS NORTHROP.*) How much d'you want?

MARIA: (*Angrily.*) I wouldn't give her a penny.

CLARA: (*Quickly.*) Nor me, neither.

PARKER: (*Quickly.*) Can we trust 'er – we've no guarantee?

SOPPITT: (*Quickly.*) She could sign something.

ANNIE: (*Quickly.*) That'ud be silly.

MARIA: (*Quickly.*) Not one single penny!

HELLIWELL: (*Angrily.*) Will you just let *me* get a word in – an' be quiet a minute? Now then –

RUBY: (*Looking in.*) Mr Helliwell!

HELLIWELL: (*Impatiently.*) What?

RUBY: I wakened 'im an' told 'im to go 'ome. But 'e says 'e *is* at 'ome.

(*Withdraws as HELLIWELL bangs and stamps in fury.*)

HELLIWELL: (*At top of his voice.*) What *is* this – a bloody mad-'ouse?

MERCER: (*Off, but approaching.*) Mr Helliwell! Please!

HELLIWELL: (*Groaning.*) Oh! – Jehoshaphat! – another of 'em!

(*MERCER enters.*)

MERCER: (*Sternly.*) Mr Helliwell, I cannot allow you to use such language. It's quite unnecessary.

HELLIWELL: (*Protesting.*) You wouldn't think so if –

MERCER: (*Cutting in.*) *Quite* unnecessary. A little patience – a little quiet consideration – that's all that is needed.

HELLIWELL: What – with folk like her? (*Pointing to MRS NORTHROP.*)

MERCER: (*Surprised and disapproving.*) Mrs Northrop! What are *you* doing here?

MARIA: (*Quickly.*) Making trouble!

MERCER: (*Before MRS NORTHROP can speak.*) Making trouble? (*He stoops a little, near her.*) And you've been drinking again.

MRS NORTHROP: (*Humble, crestfallen.*) Only a drop or two – just because I was a bit upset –

MERCER: (*Accusingly.*) And then you come and make a nuisance of yourself here. *T-t-t-t-t!* What's to be done with you? I am ashamed of you after all your promises.

MRS NORTHROP: (*Humble and flattering.*) Oh – Mr Mercer – you're a wonderful man – an' you're t'only preacher i' Cleckleywyke worth listening to. (*To the others, roundly.*) Aaaa! – he's a fine preacher is Mr Mercer. Like – like a – gurt lion of a man! (*To MERCER, admiringly.*) Ay, y'are that an' all.

MERCER: (*Briskly, masterfully.*) Now, Mrs Northrop, flattery won't help. You've broken all your promises. I'm ashamed of you.

MRS NORTHROP: (*Almost tearful now.*) Nay – Mr Mercer –

MERCER: Now – go home quietly –

MARIA: (*Quickly.*) She'll tell all the town about us.

MERCER: We cannot allow that. Mrs Northrop, you must make me a solemn promise.

MRS NORTHROP: (*Looking up at him, humbly.*) Yes, Mr Mercer.

MERCER: Now promise me, solemnly, you will tell nobody what you've heard here tonight. Now promise me.

MRS NORTHROP: (*In solemn quavering tone.*) I promise. (*Making suitable gestures.*) Wet or dry…may I die.

MERCER: T-t-t-t. But I suppose that will do. Now off you go, quietly home, and be a good woman. Good night, Mrs Northrop.

MRS NORTHROP: (*Humbly.*) Good night, Mr Mercer, and thank you very much. (*Turns at door to address the company.*) Aaaa! – he's a gurt lion of a man – (*Fiercely, a parting shot.*) Worth all you lot put together. (*She goes.*)

HELLIWELL: (*With relief.*) Well, we're rid o' one. (*To MERCER.*) Now have you studied that letter, Mr Mercer?

MERCER: (*Producing it.*) I've considered it very carefully. (*Impressively.*) And you know what I think?

SEVERAL OF THEM: (*Eagerly.*) No. Tell us. (*Etc.*)

MERCER: (*Slowly.*) This letter – in my opinion – is perfectly genuine.

HELLIWELL: (*Disgustedly.*) I thought you were going to tell us summat we didn't know.

MERCER: (*Ignoring this.*) I am sorry to say it – but – quite obviously – you are, none of you, really married.

PARKER: (*Bitterly.*) 'Ere, don't rub it in. (*Hopefully.*) Unless, of course, you're prepared to marry us yourself – quietly – now.

MERCER: (*Indignantly.*) Certainly not. Quite impossible.

HELLIWELL: (*Impatiently.*) Well – what the hangment are we going to do, then?

MERCER: (*Turning to him impressively.*) My dear sir – (*Then quickly.*) I don't know.

HELLIWELL: (*Disgusted.*) Oh – Christmas!

MERCER: But if you want my final opinion, I think that if there were less bad temper and bad language in this house, and a little more patience and quiet consideration, you would have a better chance of settling your affairs.

HELLIWELL: (*Exasperated.*) And *I* think I'm getting a bit tired o' you, Mr Mercer.

MERCER: (*Very angry, towering over HELLIWELL.*) What! After wasting my time, you now have the audacity – Here!

(*HELLIWELL flinches, but it is the letter he is being given.*) *Good night, sir.* Good night, ladies.

(*He marches out and bangs doors. HELLIWELL breathes heavily and wipes his face.*)

HELLIWELL: Well, that's another we're rid of.

PARKER: (*Beginning in his usual style.*) And now what's wanted –

CLARA: (*Cutting in, mimicking him.*) Is a few serious words. We know. But what's really wanted now is a bit o' brainwork, and where we're going to get it from I don't know.

HELLIWELL: (*Severely to CLARA.*) You'll get it from me if you'll keep quiet a minute.

(*They concentrate hard, and now ORMONROYD, still carrying a large glass of beer, comes in and sits down in the chair centre, while they stare at him in amazement and disgust.*)

ORMONROYD: (*Cheerfully.*) Now – let's see – what were we talking about?

PARKER: (*Angrily.*) We weren't talking about anything to you.

ORMONROYD: (*Ignoring this.*) I wouldn't object to a nice hand at cards. (*To HELLIWELL, who is looking exasperated.*) I like a game o' solo, don't you?

HELLIWELL: No. And I told you to get off 'ome.

ORMONROYD: (*Reproachfully.*) Nay, but you want your photo o' t'group, don't you?

PARKER: You'll take no photos 'ere tonight.

ORMONROYD: Now it's a funny thing you should ha' said that. I'm a chap 'at notices things – I 'ave to be in my profession – an' I've been telling meself there's people

'ere in this 'ouse tonight who isn't easy in their minds.
No, there's summat a bit off 'ere – just you see.

CLARA: Oh – for goodness' sake –

ORMONROYD: (*To HELLIWELL.*) And people has to be
easy in their minds to be photographed. Nobody ever
comes with the toothache, y'know, to 'ave their photos
taken.

SOPPITT: (*Seriously.*) No, I don't suppose they do. It never
occurred to me – that.

ORMONROYD: Name, sir?

SOPPITT: Soppitt.

ORMONROYD: Ormonroyd 'ere. There's thought in this
face. I'd like to do it some time in a nice sepia finish.
Remind me, Mr Soppitt.

(*LOTTIE enters.*)

Ah, there y'are, Lottie. Join the company.

MARIA: (*To LOTTIE.*) I thought you'd gone long since.

HELLIWELL: You know very well you promised to go,
half an hour since.

CLARA: (*Rises.*) We ought to put police on you.

ORMONROYD: Now what's the idea of picking on Lottie?
Why don't you live and let live? We're all in the same
boat. We all come 'ere and we don't know why. We all go
in our turn and we don't know where. If you are a bit
better off, be thankful. An' if you don't get into trouble
an' make a fool of yourself, well be thankful for that, 'cos
you easily might. What I say is this – we're all human,
aren't we?

ANNIE: Yes, and thank you, Mr Ormonroyd.

PARKER: What yer thanking him for? Who's he to start
telling us what we ought to do?

CLARA: Impudence, I call it.

(*Telephone rings.*)

ORMONROYD: Oh, me? I'm nothing much. But in case
you want to be nasty, Councillor Albert Parker, just
remember though I may be nothing I 'appen to work for
a newspaper. Behind me stands the Press, don't forget
that, an' the Press is a mighty power in the land today –

(*RUBY enters.*)

RUBY: Telephone went and when I says: 'Who is it?' chap
said: 'Yorkshire Argus – is Ormonroyd, our
photographer there?' an' when I says, 'Yes, he's still 'ere,'
he says, 'Well, tell him he's sacked.' You're sacked. I'm
sorry.

(*RUBY exits.*)

ORMONROYD: (*Suddenly crushed.*) So am I, lass. I left a
bag in 'ere somewhere.

LOTTIE: You must have left it down at Lion, lad.

PARKER: I thought 'e couldn't carry corn.

ANNIE: Shut up, Albert.

LOTTIE: Nay, Harry, you silly old devil, it's not so bad.

ORMONROYD: It's not so good. Hard to know where to
turn.

LOTTIE: Come on, lad, never say die. We've seen a bit of
life an' we'll see some more before they throw us on the
muck heap. (*To others.*) For two pins, I'd take him away
now, and leave you to settle your own troubles – if you
can.

HELLIWELL: Why – what's he got to do with our
troubles?

LOTTIE: Plenty. Now, Harry, tell 'em where you were
married.

ORMONROYD: Nay, Lottie, they don't want to hear about
my bad luck.

PARKER: We've enough of our own, without his.

ANNIE: No, Albert. Come on, Mr Ormonroyd.

LOTTIE: Tell 'em where you were married.

ORMONROYD: Lane End Chapel – five an' twenty years
since.

HELLIWELL: 'Ere, he must be in t'same boat with us then.

ORMONROYD: Just another o' my bits of bad luck.

CLARA: We can understand that all right.

LOTTIE: Yes, but Harry 'ere had separated from his wife
and they wanted to be free.

HELLIWELL: Well, what were they worrying for? They
were free. Parson hadn't proper qualifications.

LOTTIE: Hold on a minute…go on, Harry.

ORMONROYD: I know he hadn't. Wife found that out. But what she'd forgotten, till I got a copy o' t'certificate, is that in them days – twenty-five years since – chapel wedding – registrar had to be there an' all – to sign certificate.

PARKER: Joe, he's right.

ORMONROYD: I know damn well I'm right. I've been carrying certificate for months trying to find a loophole in it – see for yourself.

CLARA: Are we married after all?

HELLIWELL: Yes, of course we are. If parson didn't tie us up, registrar did – all legal – as right as ninepence.

CLARA: Aaaaa, thank God!

MARIA: Mr Ormonroyd, this is best night's work you ever did. Thank you.

LOTTIE: Now then, Harry, buck up, lad. Why don't you take that little photo shop in Blackpool again?

ORMONROYD: Nay, it 'ud cost me about a hundred pound to start it again – and I haven't a hundred shillings – an' I know you haven't.

LOTTIE: No, but there's folk here who'd never miss it.

PARKER: 'Ere, steady.

ANNIE: Albert, stingy again?

PARKER: Nay, never – if that's how you feel –

HELLIWELL: We'll soon fix you up, Ormonroyd lad, leave it to me. By gow, you've taken a load off my mind – Aaaaa – now then, everybody, let's brighten up. (*At door.*) Who'll give us a song? Ruby… Ruby…bring some more drinks, lass. Owt you've got.

ANNIE: Let's sing a bit.

ORMONROYD: Lottie's the one. Come on, Lottie, play us a tune.

CLARA: Now then, Herbert Soppitt, you see, I am your wife after all.

SOPPITT: Yes, Clara, and I hope we'll be very happy. But we won't be if you don't drop that tone of voice. I don't like it.

CLARA: Yes, Herbert.

(*SOPPITT begins to sing.*)

PARKER: 'Ere, Joe, you wouldn't say I was dull and dreary, would you?

HELLIWELL: Ay, a bit, Albert.

PARKER: Well, that beats me. I've always seemed to myself an exciting sort of chap. (*To ANNIE.*) Anyhow, stingy or whatever I am, I'm still your husband.

ANNIE: So it looks as if I'll have to make the best of you.

MARIA: We'll all have to make the best of each other. But then, perhaps it's what we're here for.

HELLIWELL: That's right, love.

PARKER: Well, we'd better see if we can have some of this fun of yours you talk about.

ANNIE: Aaaa, it doesn't matter, Albert.

PARKER: It does. I say we'll have some fun.

(*Takes her hand and begins singing. They are all singing now.*)

ORMONROYD: (*Loudly.*) All in your places. We'll have this group yet, and to hell with the Yorkshire Argus! Now, steady – steady – everybody.

(*Enter RUBY. The flashlight goes off and RUBY drops her tray. But they are all singing as curtain falls.*)

The End.

MR KETTLE AND MRS MOON

A Comedy in Three Acts

Characters

GEORGE KETTLE

MRS TWIGG
the housekeeper

MONICA TWIGG
Mrs Twigg's daughter

ALDERMAN HARDACRE

SUPERINTENDENT STREET

DELIA MOON

HENRY MOON
her husband

MR CLINTON

DR GRENOCK

Mr Kettle and Mrs Moon was first performed on 1 September 1955 at the Duchess Theatre, London, with the following cast:

GEORGE KETTLE, Clive Morton

MRS TWIGG, Phyllis Morgan

MONICA TWIGG, Wendy Craig

ALDERMAN HARDACRE, Julian Somers

SUPERINTENDENT STREET, Richard Warner

DELIA MOON, Frances Rowe

HENRY MOON, Raymond Francis

MR CLINTON, Beckett Bould

DR GRENOCK, John Moffatt

Director, Tony Richardson

Set, Paul Mayo

The action of the play passes in the living-room of George Kettle's flat in Brickmill, a town in the Midlands, on a wet Monday in November.

Act One – Morning
Act Two– Afternoon
Act Three – Early evening

Time – the present

ACT ONE

The living-room of George Kettle's flat in Brickmill, a town in the Midlands. A wet Monday in November. The flat consists of the ground floor of a solid Victorian villa. The living-room has a door right leading to the hall, a door down left to the kitchen and an arch in an alcove up right giving access to the bedroom. A large window in a deep bay up left overlooks the street. The fireplace is presumed to be in the 'fourth wall'. The room is furnished in a shabby-comfortable masculine style. There is a big sofa right centre with a small table by it; an easy chair; a dining-table with two chairs; a cabinet for drinks; a powerful radiogram upstage of the door down right, and a business-like desk and telephone up centre. At night the room is lit by a standard lamp right of the desk, and electric-candle wall-brackets right and left. The switch for the brackets is below the door left.

When the curtain rises, GEORGE KETTLE, an attractive man in his forties, is discovered sitting on the sofa, finishing his breakfast which is set on a small collapsible table. He is in dark formal clothes. The rain can be heard outside the window. There are some lights on. With a fixed resigned melancholy look, which never changes, KETTLE takes a last sip of tea, wipes his mouth and then folds his napkin, rises and goes into the hall for his hat, coat, umbrella and scarf. He re-enters and places the umbrella on the dining-room table and his hat on the settee table, and throws his coat over the back of the sofa. He puts on his scarf and coat, picks up his hat and goes to the mirror and adjusts the hat – he brushes some specks off his coat, picks up the papers, switches off the lights, and goes out. We hear the slam of the outer door off. It is important that he should perform every action very smoothly and carefully, and without moving a muscle of his face.

Just after the slam, MRS TWIGG, a mournful-looking working woman in her fifties, enters and immediately switches on the radio, from which there comes the sound of a very noisy cinema organ. She takes the breakfast tray and the small folding table on which it was placed into the kitchen, returning at once with a duster. She begins dusting in a sketchy routine fashion. The telephone rings. She tries to answer it but the radio organ is making too much noise. Putting

down the receiver by the side of the telephone, she goes to switch off
the radio. But when she picks up the receiver again, shouting 'Hello
– Hello!' clearly the caller has rung off. She now switches on the
radio again, but just as she has moved a step or two away from it the
telephone rings again. This time she switches off the radio first, then
answers the telephone.

MRS TWIGG: (*Into the telephone.*) Yes it is – but he isn't
here... I don't know... What name?... Hardacre?
Alright, Mr Hardacre. (*She puts down the receiver and*
continues with her work. After a few moments, the telephone
rings again. She answers it.) Yes – this is Mr Kettle's flat...
No, he isn't. He's at the bank, same as usual... (*Surprised.*)
You *are* the bank? Well then, I don't know where he is...
All I can tell you is he had his breakfast same as usual
and set off same as usual... No, he didn't seem any
different... Well, I'll be going home soon – I don't give
him his lunch on Mondays, 'cos I have my washing to do
at home... Yes, I could leave him a note. (*She replaces the*
receiver and continues with her work. She moves to the
window, closes it, then switches on the wall-brackets. The
telephone rings. She moves to the telephone and lifts the
receiver. Into the telephone.) Yes, it is – but he isn't here... I
don't know. Bank's just rung up to ask where he was, and
I told 'em I couldn't say. What name?... Hardacre?... All
right, Mr Hardacre. (*She replaces the receiver, then moves to*
the sofa and dusts it.)
(*The sound of the front door closing and of cymbals being*
clashed is heard. GEORGE KETTLE enters. He carries a
box containing a child's shooting game, and a drumstick. He
moves to the easy chair, puts the box, his hat and the drumstick
on it. He then removes his coat.)
(*Surprised.*) Mr Kettle? What's the matter? Have you
been taken bad?
KETTLE: No, I've been taken good. (*He hits his hat with the*
drumstick.)
MRS TWIGG: (*Puzzled.*) How do you mean?
KETTLE: Never mind, Mrs Twigg. (*He goes out to the hall*
and hangs his coat on the hall-stand.)

MRS TWIGG: Bank's been asking for you. So has Mr Hardacre – Hardacre's Stores, I suppose?

KETTLE: (*Off.*) That's the chap.

MRS TWIGG: But didn't you go to the bank the same as usual?

KETTLE: (*Off.*) No.

MRS TWIGG: But you set off the same as usual.

(*KETTLE enters from the hall. He carries a pair of cymbals.*)

KETTLE: (*Crossing to MRS TWIGG.*) After that it stopped being the same as usual. (*He clashes the cymbals in her face, then puts them on the table by the sofa and crosses to the arch.*) Now I'm going to change these clothes.

MRS TWIGG: (*Puzzled.*) Why, Mr Kettle?

KETTLE: (*Stopping and speaking over his shoulder.*) Because I don't like them, Mrs Twigg.

(*KETTLE goes into the bedroom. MRS TWIGG looks uncertainly after him.*)

MRS TWIGG: (*Calling.*) If you're not feeling well, Mr Kettle, I think you ought to say so.

KETTLE: (*Off.*) I'm feeling fine.

MRS TWIGG: But you can't be – coming back like this...

KETTLE: (*Off.*) Never felt better.

MRS TWIGG: (*After a pause; worried.*) But what about the bank?

KETTLE: (*Off.*) What about it?

MRS TWIGG: (*Moving to the arch.*) Well, they're asking for you.

(*There is no reply.*)

(*After a pause.*) They don't know where you are. You'll have to let 'em know, won't you?

KETTLE: (*Off.*) No.

(*The telephone rings. MRS TWIGG moves to the telephone.*)

(*Off. He shouts.*) Don't answer it, Mrs Twigg. Just take the receiver off and put it down.

(*MRS TWIGG, bewildered, lifts the telephone receiver to stop it ringing, and lays the receiver on the desk.*)

MRS TWIGG: (*After a pause.*) I suppose you know what you're doing, Mr Kettle?

KETTLE: (*Off.*) Yes, I know what I'm doing. What are *you* doing?

MRS TWIGG: Just tidying up. I like to get back home soon on Mondays.

KETTLE: (*Off.*) Off you go, then.

MRS TWIGG: There's no lunch here for you, y'know, Mr Kettle. Don't forget you always have it at the club on Mondays. (*She dusts the desk.*) I suppose I could nip out an' get you something?

(*KETTLE enters from the bedroom. He is now loosely and comfortably dressed, in old corduroy trousers and a jersey, or whatever the actor prefers. He is in his socks. He looks different from the formal type who went into the bedroom: a relaxed, free-and-easy man.*)

KETTLE: No, thank you, Mrs Twigg. (*He moves to the desk and picks up the receiver. Into the telephone.*) Good-bye. (*He puts the receiver on the desk. To MRS TWIGG.*) Now you go home.

(*During the following dialogue he sits on the sofa, puts on a pair of casual shoes which are on the floor in front of the sofa, takes his pipe and tobacco from his pocket and fills and lights his pipe. MRS TWIGG watches anxiously, clearly baffled by KETTLE's conduct.*)

MRS TWIGG: What about the telephone?

KETTLE: That's all right.

MRS TWIGG: But nobody can talk to you if it's like that. It's engaged all the time.

KETTLE: (*Rising and crossing to the cabinet.*) Probably it likes to be engaged. (*He pours a whisky and soda for himself.*)

(*MRS TWIGG, puzzled, stares at KETTLE, then notices the parcel.*)

MRS TWIGG: What is this, sir?

KETTLE: A shooting game.

MRS TWIGG: A shooting game?

KETTLE: I happened to see it in the toyshop window – so I bought it. You shoot at jungle animals and knock them over. I had one – oh – thirty-five years ago – and it seemed to me about time I had another one. (*He sips his drink.*)

MRS TWIGG: (*Looking disapprovingly at the drink.*) Mr
Kettle, I don't want to say anything I oughtn't – but I
must tell you straight I don't like to see you drinking
like this in the morning.

KETTLE: Jolly good health! (*He drinks and puts his glass on
the table by the sofa, then crosses to the easy chair.*)

MRS TWIGG: It isn't right. You don't know what it'll lead
to. You're known to be one of the steadiest and
best-respected men in Brickmill...

KETTLE: (*Picking up the bowler hat and drumstick and handing
them to MRS TWIGG.*) Mrs Twigg, never mind about that.
Tell me something. Do you like Brickmill? (*He unties the
string of the box.*)

MRS TWIGG: Well, I've lived here all my life – and...

KETTLE: (*Cutting in.*) Now give me a plain answer. *Do you
like it?*

MRS TWIGG: No, not much. But we have to put up with it.

KETTLE: Have we?

MRS TWIGG: (*Surprised.*) Well, haven't we?

KETTLE: No. (*To avoid further argument. Gently but firmly.*)
Now, off you go, Mrs Twigg.

MRS TWIGG: (*Putting the drumstick on the table by the sofa; a
routine question.*) Same time in the morning, I suppose,
Mr Kettle?

KETTLE: (*Considering this.*) I don't know.

MRS TWIGG: (*Astonished.*) You don't know?

KETTLE: No. Perhaps I shan't be here.

MRS TWIGG: Why, where are you going?

KETTLE: (*Without emphasis.*) I don't know. I haven't any
plans. I don't want to have any plans. I'm tired of plans.

MRS TWIGG: You're in a queer state of mind, aren't you,
Mr Kettle?

KETTLE: (*Thoughtfully.*) No, I don't think so, Mrs Twigg.

MRS TWIGG: Perhaps you'll feel better in the morning.
Anyhow, I'll come at the usual time. (*She hesitates.*) You
wouldn't like a nice cup of tea and then a nice lie down,
would you?

KETTLE: No, I wouldn't. But you would, wouldn't you?
(*Almost coaxingly.*) Now, why don't *you* have a nice cup of
tea and then a nice lie down?

MRS TWIGG: (*Wistfully.*) I wish I could.

KETTLE: Why not, then?

MRS TWIGG: (*Severely.*) I've too much to do – Monday an'
all. Really – I'm surprised at you, Mr Kettle.
(*KETTLE takes his bowler hat from MRS TWIGG.*)
Where would we be if everybody started behaving like
that?

KETTLE: I don't know. But where are we now? Good
morning, Mrs Twigg.

MRS TWIGG: (*Disapprovingly.*) Good morning, Mr Kettle.
(*MRS TWIGG crosses and goes into the kitchen.*
KETTLE kicks his bowler hat off through the arch, then
opens the box and the game on the easy chair. The game consists
of cardboard lions, tigers, etc. that can be knocked over by
rubber-tipped darts fired from little spring pistols. He then
tries his hand and shoots three times from various positions.
MONICA TWIGG enters. She is a girl of eighteen, dressed
in cheap finery, and a rather absurd mixture at the moment
of cheap glamour and the woe-begone bedraggled. She wears
a raincoat and head-scarf.)

MONICA: (*Calling as she enters.*) Ma! Ma! (*She sees*
KETTLE.) Mr Kettle.

KETTLE: Yes. You're Mrs Twigg's daughter?

MONICA: That's right. Monica. Isn't my mother here?

KETTLE: No, you've just missed her.

MONICA: I thought I might do. But I didn't think you'd be
here. Aren't you supposed to be at the bank all day?

KETTLE: Yes. But this morning I'm big-game hunting
instead. (*He indicates the game.*)

MONICA: (*Astonished.*) Why – that's just a kid's game.

KETTLE: Yes, but I wanted to try it again.

MONICA: (*Amused.*) You don't mean instead of going to the
bank?

KETTLE: Yes, I do. But what about you?

MONICA: (*Confidentially.*) I've just got the push again –
right off, beginning of the week. The manageress took

one look at me – she was right out of temper of course, everybody is on a wet Monday morning – an' she says, 'I thought I told you Friday we didn't want you.' So I says, 'Well, I thought you didn't mean it,' I says. So she says, 'Well, I mean it you know an' you can go an' get your card,' she says. (*She breaks off and looks inquiringly at KETTLE.*) Well, if I'm going to stay here talking any longer, I'd like to take my coat off an' dry it. But, of course, I'll go if you like. Only it's no use standing here in a wet coat.

KETTLE: Take it off and dry it then.

MONICA: (*Crossing to the kitchen door.*) Okay. It'll dry quickest in the kitchen.

(*MONICA goes into the kitchen. KETTLE picks up his glass and sips his drink. MONICA re-enters from the kitchen. She has removed her raincoat and head-scarf and is dressed in a skimpy frock that emphasises her youthful but fairly full figure, of which she is highly conscious. She has done her best, in this brief time, to make herself look attractive. She notices KETTLE's drink.*)

I'll bet that's whisky.

KETTLE: It is.

MONICA: (*Perching herself on the back of the sofa.*) You wouldn't like to give me some, I suppose?

KETTLE: No, I shouldn't.

MONICA: I've had some, you know, more than once – out with chaps, though I don't really fancy it. (*She puts her leg up on to the back of the sofa.*) I'm more for cocktails. But why wouldn't you give me any whisky? You're not mean, are you?

KETTLE: (*Thoughtfully.*) I don't know – yet. I haven't really started exploring myself. But I'm dead against letting you have any whisky. How old are you? (*He moves to MONICA and removes her leg from the back of the sofa.*)

MONICA: Eighteen.

KETTLE: You're far too young. (*He continues round the sofa, crosses and picks up a pistol and a dart.*) It's wasted on anybody under thirty, in my opinion. By the way, aren't you always changing jobs?

MONICA: That's right. I'll bet my mother's told you that, hasn't she? Trust her! She gets right fed up with me. But I tell her what does it matter. You might as well have a change. One thing's as good as another here in Brickmill. (*She indicates the game.*) How do you do this?

KETTLE: I'll show you. (*He goes to the sofa and fires a dart.*) Now you have a try. (*He hands a pistol and dart to MONICA.*) What do you want to do, Monica?
(*During MONICA's following speech, she fires twice.*)

MONICA: (*Confidentially.*) I'd like to be a model – or on television – or a film star. And if I can't be one of them, something with some glamour in it; I don't care what I do – it's all the same. (*Dreamily.*) I want to have my photo taken at a night club – wearing a backless evening gown – holding a glass of champagne wine – 'Miss Monica Twigg seen at the Caffy de Paris' – it'll say underneath. And I'd keep flying to places – like they all do – Rome and New York and Hollywood.

KETTLE: You'd probably get tired of flying to places.

MONICA: Well, if I did – I'd pack it up. 'Monica Twigg resting in the country' – it'ud say underneath the photo. Or I'd be wearing a bathing costume at Cap What's-it – where they all go. And I've got as good a figure as most of 'em – better than some. I've had trouble enough with it already – chaps pawing me about – it's got me the sack twice – but so far that's all it has got me. (*She fires again.*)

KETTLE: Don't you want to get married?
(*MONICA puts the pistol on the table by the sofa, collects the darts and sets up the animals.*)

MONICA: Not in Brickmill, I don't – no fear. It's murder here. What about you, Mr Kettle?

KETTLE: What about me?

MONICA: My mother says you never seem to have any girls here. And you're not married. Don't you go in for sex?

KETTLE: I seem to have been off it for some time, Monica. I was married once, but it didn't work. That was before I came to Brickmill. (*He fires.*)

MONICA: Bank send you to different places, I suppose?

KETTLE: Yes, you move around.

MONICA: Well, you picked a bloody awful place when you came here, I must say. As soon as my brother Ted's done his National Service, I'm off...

KETTLE: 'Miss Monica Twigg boards the bus for Birmingham' – it'll say underneath the photograph.

MONICA: (*Giggling appreciatively.*) You're a bit livelier than I thought you'd be, Mr Kettle.

(*KETTLE lies on the sofa and prepares to fire.*)

You don't look bad either, dressed like that.

(*The front door bell rings.*)

Somebody at the door.

KETTLE: Can't help that.

MONICA: Aren't you going to answer it?

KETTLE: No. If anybody really wants to see me, he must walk in.

(*There is a sharp knock at the door. ALDERMAN HARDACRE bursts in. He is a severe-looking elderly man, dressed in a rather old-fashioned dark business style. He is very angry. KETTLE fires as HARDACRE enters.*)

HARDACRE: Look here, Kettle – what's happening? They told me at the bank you must be ill.

KETTLE: (*Mildly.*) Well, I'm not.

HARDACRE: So it seems. What on earth are you doing?

KETTLE: (*Blandly.*) I'm playing the 'Jungle Shooting Game' with Miss Monica Twigg. Miss Twigg – Alderman Hardacre – Jungle Shooting Game.

MONICA: (*Impressed.*) Hardacre's Stores?

HARDACRE: Yes, young woman – and a very busy man. I don't know what you're supposed to be doing here, but I'll be much obliged if you'll leave us – unless of course you're living here. (*He eyes MONICA suspiciously.*)

MONICA: Here – here – none o' that. I came to tell my mother, who works for Mr Kettle, I'd got the sack.

HARDACRE: That wouldn't surprise me.

MONICA: I've had the sack from your Stores, too, in my time. And not sorry, either. You've got some stinkers there, let me tell you.

HARDACRE: (*Angrily.*) How d'you mean – stinkers?

MONICA: I could tell you a thing or two.

KETTLE: (*Helpfully.*) She probably could, you know, too.

HARDACRE: (*Removing his hat.*) I wouldn't listen to a word a girl of that type had to say. And if you've any sense, Kettle, you won't. Or let anybody catch you playing silly children's games with her. A man in your position...

MONICA: (*Over the back of the sofa.*) I think I'll pop round to the Labour Exchange – an' see what's doing. (*She crosses to the kitchen door.*) Bye-bye, Mr Kettle.

KETTLE: Bye-bye, Monica.

HARDACRE: Now, look here, Kettle...

MONICA: (*To HARDACRE; severely.*) You want to tell one or two o' them old floor managers of yours to keep their hands to themselves. A bit o' fun's all right – but...

HARDACRE: (*Angrily.*) Nonsense! Don't tell me...

MONICA: (*Shouting him down.*) Nobody can tell you anything, can they? You know it all. So I won't tell you what they call you. But it isn't Hardacre. (*MONICA exits triumphantly to kitchen.*)

HARDACRE: (*Staring disapprovingly at KETTLE; severely.*) If you want my opinion, Kettle, you're more to blame than she is for that piece of impudence. She doesn't know any better. You do. (*He moves to the desk and puts his hand on it.*) And you're encouraging her.

KETTLE: (*Mildly.*) 'Jungle Shooting Game'? I don't see any connection between that and the behaviour of your floor managers, Hardacre. Not that I'd be too hard on them. Monica's obviously charged full of sex – and rather unscrupulous – and when you think of the lives your middle-aged floor managers must lead...

HARDACRE: (*Cutting in.*) Don't talk rubbish! My floor managers have all been with me for years – thoroughly decent respectable men...

KETTLE: (*Cutting in.*) That's what I'm saying – think of the barren lives...

HARDACRE: (*Angrily.*) Drop it. I've wasted enough time this morning. Let's get to business. (*He is severe now, rather wildly angry.*) And let me remind you that I represent one of the biggest accounts the London and North Midland Bank has in this district. I could have arranged our Extension Loan directly through the Head Office. But I decided to deal with them through you and our local branch, chiefly as a favour to you. At the time you were very grateful. I call this morning to see you – and what happens? You're not there – and nobody knows if you're ill or gone up to London – or what's going on. I come here – and what are you doing?

KETTLE: (*Smiling.*) Playing the 'Jungle Shooting Game'.

HARDACRE: With that little – whatever-she-is? And you're not ill.

KETTLE: I never said I was.

HARDACRE: (*Baffled and angry.*) Well, what do you think you're doing? Fooling about – dressed like that – Monday morning. What do you think they'd say if I reported it to your Head Office? And I've half a mind to – I really have.

KETTLE: (*Sympathetically.*) If you feel like that, I think you ought, y'know, Hardacre.

HARDACRE: (*Amazed.*) You think I ought? What's the matter with you, Kettle? Have you been drinking – or what?

KETTLE: I'm having one now. Can I offer you one?

HARDACRE: (*Angrily.*) No, you can't offer me one. I don't drink at any time, and certainly not on Monday morning when I'm up to my eyes in work. As you ought to be, Kettle, and always have been since I've known you.

KETTLE: I'll try to explain.

HARDACRE: I should think so.

KETTLE: (*Relaxed and easy.*) I woke up at the usual time this morning. Had my bath, shaved, put on my usual bank uniform. Had breakfast. Looked at The Times and the Birmingham Post. Set out for the bank as usual. It was raining – a wet Monday morning in Brickmill. Still, nothing unusual in that. I remembered that you'd be coming in – and some other people with important accounts. I wondered who I'd be lunching with at the club. And then – suddenly – a voice spoke to me.

HARDACRE: (*Grimly.*) I see. A voice spoke to you.

KETTLE: Now you're going to ask me whose voice it was...

HARDACRE: No, I'm not. You were talking to yourself.

KETTLE: In a way. But it's rather complicated...

HARDACRE: No, it isn't. You told yourself to stay away from the bank, from your work, and to come back here and drink whisky and play at shooting lions.

KETTLE: (*Mildly protesting.*) I thought you wanted me to try to explain.

HARDACRE: (*Contemptuously.*) Yes – if you've anything sensible to say. But if you haven't, *I'll* say something. (*KETTLE ignores HARDACRE and fires at the animals.*) (*Very angrily.*) Will you stop that nonsense and listen to me for a minute? It'll be for your own good.

KETTLE: (*Rising.*) How do you know what my own good is? I don't know much about that myself yet. In fact you might say I'm only just starting to find out.

HARDACRE: I'm an older man than you...

KETTLE: I'm only about an hour old.

HARDACRE: (*Shouting.*) Stop that!

KETTLE: Alderman Hardacre, for the last three years I've been tormented by a desire to throw something at you. And now – unless you clear out at once – I'm going to do it. (*He looks around for something to throw.*) (*HARDACRE moves hastily to the desk and picks up his hat.*) A man ought to keep something handy for times like this. One of those custard pies they used to have in the old comic films.

HARDACRE: (*Crossing to the door and turning.*) I'm going. But you realise I came here to discuss important bank business. And this is what I get. Very well, I'm going to ring up your district Head Office. (*HARDACRE goes out. KETTLE, unperturbed, hums a tune, crosses to the radiogram and puts on a record of Borodin's 'Polovtsian Dances' from 'Prince Igor', after one or two false starts, getting the third theme starting with the heavy drum.*

He turns it on at full blast, then collects his drumstick and experiments happily, trying the stick on various plant pots, etc. Finally, he sits on the sofa and uses the coal scuttle as a drum. He is delightfully absorbed in this.

SUPERINTENDENT STREET enters. He is a heavily-built man in his fifties. He is astonished at what he sees and hears.)

STREET: (*Shouting.*) Mr Kettle! Mr Kettle!

(*KETTLE sees STREET, rises, moves to the radiogram and switches it off.*)

KETTLE: Hello, Superintendent.

STREET: (*Reproachfully.*) I rang and knocked but couldn't make you hear, Mr Kettle. I couldn't think what was going on in here. Something the matter with your coal scuttle?

KETTLE: I'm using it as a big drum.

STREET: A big drum?

KETTLE: Yes, a big drum. I've always wanted to join in those dances from Prince Igor – but never got round to it before. You wouldn't like to try putting in the drum bits while I do the cymbals, would you?

STREET (*Severely.*) I've something better to do this morning, Mr Kettle, even if you haven't.

KETTLE: (*Sitting on the sofa at the left end.*) No, I haven't, not at the moment.

STREET: (*Suspiciously.*) I called at the bank – and they said I might find you here. Off-colour, are you?

KETTLE: (*Smiling.*) No. I'm on-colour.

STREET: What?

KETTLE: On-colour.

STREET (*Suspiciously.*) Are you all right, Mr Kettle?

KETTLE: I'm fine, Superintendent. How are you?

STREET: (*Not liking this.*) Busy. So I'll come to the point. You'll remember you wrote to us about our parking regulations at your bank corner. You asked if we couldn't see our way to modifying them a bit for the convenience of your customers. Especially on Tuesdays and Saturday mornings – remember?

KETTLE: Superintendent, I'll be frank with you. I don't care.

STREET: (*Astonished.*) You don't care?

KETTLE: Not a rap. Let 'em all park there – or run 'em all in for parking there – just as you please.

STREET: (*Aggrieved.*) It's not a question of just as I please, Mr Kettle. Don't get that into your head. I carry out my instructions, that's all.

KETTLE: You don't sound very happy about it.

STREET: Happy about it. Why should I be happy about it?

KETTLE: But who *is* happy about it?

STREET: (*Exasperated.*) I don't know what you're talking about. Happy about *what?*

KETTLE: Well – about parking near the bank and Alderman Hardacre's loan for his extension, and the way his floor managers behave to girls, and Monica Twigg always getting the sack and Mrs Twigg wanting to get home early on Mondays...

STREET: (*Exasperated.*) What *is* all this?

KETTLE: (*Earnestly.*) Almost everything that goes on really, isn't it? And I say – who *is* happy about it? Who is it who's enjoying it all?

STREET: (*Moving behind the sofa and leaning over the back; confidentially.*) Oh – you're feeling like that, are you? Well, I'll admit there've been times when I've had one of them days that go on for ever – and everybody you have anything to do with seems half daft with fuss and worry and vexation – I've asked myself that sort of question. Tried it on the wife, too, when at last I got home, but she could never see what I was driving at, having a very female point of view.

KETTLE: It's not quite that, Superintendent. I tried to tell Hardacre that I heard a voice this morning, just before I got to the bank. Now that voice, I think, belonged to me as I am now and spoke to him – that is, to me as I was then – and it simply said, 'Why, George?' And I said, 'Do you mean all this – going to the bank on a wet Monday in Brickmill?' And the voice said 'Yes. What's it all for? And how long's it going on?'

STREET: I see. And how long have these voices been going on, Mr Kettle?

KETTLE: No, no. That won't do. One voice. Just this morning. And really – you must grasp this, Superintendent – make an effort now – really *my* voice. I – the man who's talking to you now – asked the question.

STREET: (*Humouring.*) Where's the other one then?

KETTLE: He's gone.

STREET: (*Clearly humouring KETTLE.*) Now let's get this straight. The George Kettle who was the manager of the Brickmill branch of the London and North Midland Bank has gone – just vanished.

KETTLE: Yes. That was easy. He was only a sort of a ghost.

STREET: Well, I don't know. Seemed a solid dependable kind of chap the three years or so I've known him.

KETTLE: I dare say.

STREET: Well respected in the town. That doesn't suggest a sort of ghost.

KETTLE: Unless it's a ghost town. Have you ever read about those ghost towns near Death Valley in California? They still have railway stations, streets, hotels, shops, banks, houses – but no people, no life there. Now perhaps Brickmill is another kind of ghost town. You're a solid dependable sort of chap, but suddenly you wake up in the main street and you see there isn't anything real.

STREET: But you're the one who woke up.

KETTLE: Yes – I didn't put that very clearly. I woke up and took over – and your solid dependable chap vanished.

STREET: I've got it now. Well, I hope you're as friendly as the other George Kettle was.

KETTLE: More friendly, I'd say.

STREET: Then you wouldn't object to doing me a small favour?

KETTLE: I hope not, Superintendent. What is it?

STREET: (*Earnestly.*) Just promise me you won't go out until you see me again. You won't be missing anything. It's a nasty day. You're snug in here. I feel you'd enjoy yourself a lot better staying indoors. What do you say? Just as a favour?

KETTLE: (*Rising.*) As a matter of fact, I'd no intention of going out again this morning. But, as you insist upon it, I'll stay in this afternoon, too. But I may have to go out before the shops close, you know.

STREET: Yes, yes, I'll be back before then. (*He crosses to the door.*) Well – er…

(*KETTLE picks up one of the pistols and moves up to the table by the sofa.*)

KETTLE: (*Threatening STREET with the pistol; casually.*) By the way, Superintendent, I'd like to make one thing clear before you go. Because it might save you a good deal of trouble.

STREET: (*Moving slowly and cautiously to KETTLE.*) And what's that?

KETTLE: (*Smiling.*) I haven't gone mad, you know.

STREET: (*With false heartiness.*) Bless my heart and soul, Mr Kettle, I've never imagined such a thing for a minute. You're as sane as I am.

KETTLE: I'm saner than you are. *Now.*

STREET: (*Heartily.*) I wouldn't be surprised. (*He suddenly disarms KETTLE and realises the pistol is a toy. He notices the shooting game and, anxious to change the subject, points to it.*) Now what's that you've got there?

KETTLE: The 'Jungle Shooting Game'. Like to try it?

(*He loads the pistol for STREET, then loads the other for himself. STREET sits on the sofa, at the right end. KETTLE sits on the left arm of the sofa and during the ensuing dialogue is always prevented from firing by STREET taking the pistol from him after he has reloaded it.*)

STREET: I used to be a bit of a marksman at one time – but it's years ago. Don't suppose I can do anything with these things. Now then. I'll have a go at that lion first. Never thought I'd do a bit of lion shooting on a wet Monday morning in Brickmill.

KETTLE: (*Gravely.*) No – you owe that to me.

STREET: I do indeed. (*When he shoots, he must appear to shoot very well; if necessary this can be easily faked. He is very pleased with himself.*) Down he goes! And another of 'em.

(*He names the particular animals as he knocks them down.*)
Some slaughter in the jungle this morning, Mr Kettle.

KETTLE: But no screams – no blood – no agony – no life
ebbing out.

(*The front door bell rings.*)

STREET: Your door, isn't it? (*He rises.*) Now don't you
bother about this, Mr Kettle. Ten to one it's somebody
wanting me – and if it isn't, I can deal with 'em. (*He
crosses to the door.*) You don't want to trouble yourself
about people this morning.

(*STREET goes out. KETTLE rises and packs up the shooting
range in its box. STREET re-enters and moves to the easy
chair.*)

Well, it was for you, not for me. Mrs Henry Moon. She'd
been to the bank – and they'd told her to try here. She's
the chairman of some fund committee – Infirmary
Wireless Fund, isn't it? – that you're treasurer of. But I
did say you wouldn't be up to adding her Wireless Fund
figures for her this morning – so she popped off. She'd
come in her red sports car – so it was no trouble. I did
right, didn't I? You wouldn't want to be bothered with
her this morning, would you?

KETTLE: (*Moving to STREET; thoughtfully.*) Why should Mrs
Moon have a red sports car?

STREET: Why shouldn't she? Henry Moon can afford to
keep two or three cars. And a nippy little car like that is
just right for a woman to drive herself – shopping and so
forth.

KETTLE: (*Still thoughtfully.*) Yes, but why should a cold
severe woman like Mrs Moon choose a bright red sports
car. Something's wrong.

STREET: (*Heartily.*) Oh – they all have their little fancies.
Well, I'm off – till I get back. Don't forget your promise.
(*STREET goes out. KETTLE puts the game on the dining
table then moves to the desk and looks up a number in the
directory pad, humming the tune of the record to himself. He
lifts the receiver and dials a number.*)

KETTLE: (*Into the telephone.*) Moon and Francis?... Henry
Moon there, please? George Kettle... Yes, I think it's *very*

important. (*He waits.*) Mr Moon?... This is George Kettle... No, it won't take a minute. It's about that red sports car that Mrs Moon drives... No, there's nothing gone wrong with it that I know of... That's not the point. What I want to know is this. Did you give it to her or did she choose it herself?... No, I'm not trying to be funny... Well, this *is* what I rang you up about... Bought it herself, did she? No, it isn't bank business – nothing wrong there... Damned impudence? Oh, I don't know, Mr Moon. Fascinating name, by the way. Perhaps that's why she married you.

(*He replaces the receiver to break the call, then removes the receiver and lays it on the desk. He has the air of a man who has just done a good job. He moves to the radiogram and switches on the record. He then collects the cymbals and drumstick and sits on the sofa. He attempts to beat time on the coal scuttle and clash the cymbals at the same time. He ends by putting the cymbals on his feet.*

DELIA MOON enters. She is a good-looking but severe-looking woman in her middle or later thirties, well but severely dressed. The look of cold severity is increased by her wearing diamond-shaped or similar spectacles. She is clearly rather pleasantly surprised by KETTLE's unusual appearance. KETTLE finds keeping time to the record too difficult, so removes the cymbals from his feet, rises, crosses to the radiogram and switches it off. He turns and sees DELIA.)

Hello, Mrs Moon.

DELIA: Good morning, Mr Kettle. I did ring and knock...

KETTLE: Too much noise here – yes.

DELIA: You look quite different in those clothes. What are you trying to do?

KETTLE: I'm trying to join in this thingummy dance from Prince Igor, but it's very difficult to work both the big drum – that's the coal scuttle – and the cymbals. It needs two people. We might try in a minute.

DELIA: (*Not unpleasantly but not committing herself.*) Oh – might we?

KETTLE: (*Gravely.*) I'm appealing now to the bit of you that chose the red sports car.

DELIA: I see. But let's talk about you for a minute, shall we? I've had three different accounts of you this morning. I went to the bank and they said you were probably ill. Then Alderman Hardacre came in – in a filthy temper – and said you must have been drinking for days. I came here, and Superintendent Street said I'd better not come in because you seemed to him more than half dotty. So I pretended to drive away, but as soon I knew he'd gone, I hurried back, dying of curiosity. You don't seem to me ill, drunk or dotty.

KETTLE: I'm not. Those fellows don't understand, though I did my best with the Superintendent. By the way, I rang your husband just now about the red sports car.

DELIA: (*Amused.*) You rang up Henry. Why?

KETTLE: I had to know whether he'd given it to you or you'd chosen it yourself.

DELIA: I'll bet he was furious.

KETTLE: He was, after I'd told him it wasn't bank business.

DELIA: But why did you want to know, Mr Kettle?

KETTLE: When the Superintendent came back from shooting you off, he mentioned your red sports car, and I suddenly wondered how you came to have such a thing. Quite unlike my idea of you. And perhaps my idea of you was wrong. (*He collects the drumstick.*)

DELIA: And that's why you risked asking me to bang the coal scuttle for you?

KETTLE: Yes. But you can have the cymbals if you like.

DELIA: (*Taking the drumstick.*) No. I'll be on the big drum. But not for long, mind you.

KETTLE: Don't do it at all if you're against it.

DELIA: No, let's get it over with. You won't be happy until you hear what it sounds like, will you?

KETTLE: No. And that's the first sensible thing anybody's said to me this morning. I'm very glad I wondered about that red sports car. (*He moves to the sofa and picks up the cymbals.*) Now then – you remember how it goes – 'boom da da – boom da da – boom da da'?

DELIA: Yes – but I'll miss the very first *boom*, you know, because it'll have started before I know it's started, if you see what I mean. (*She sits on the sofa at the right end.*)

KETTLE: (*Moving to the radiogram and switching it on.*) Yes, of course. (*He moves to the sofa.*)

(*They have a go. DELIA hits the coal scuttle while KETTLE clashes the cymbals. During DELIA's following speech, to enable the words to be heard, the music is reduced in volume and increased at the end of the speech by off-stage control.*)

DELIA: (*After a dozen bars or so; shouting.*) Just a minute! Stop it! Don't you think it would be better if I bashed a cymbal with this stick when it gets to the top – 'diddle-diddle-diddle-diddle' – that part? You hold a cymbal out – and I'll bash it – um?

KETTLE: It's an idea. We'll try it again, then.

(*They have a good happy go now. DELIA hits the cymbal on the fifth bar, etc.*)

DELIA: (*Shouting.*) That's enough. Can't take any more just now.

(*KETTLE puts the cymbals on the sofa, crosses to the radiogram and switches it off.*)

KETTLE: Thank you very much, Mrs Moon. I think I've wanted to do that for years. Like a drink?

DELIA: (*With mock severity.*) I'm not in the habit of drinking in the morning, Mr Kettle. (*She puts the drumstick on the sofa seat.*)

KETTLE: (*Collecting his glass.*) You're not in the habit of playing the coal scuttle in the morning, either, are you, Mrs Moon? (*He crosses to the cabinet.*) So never mind about habits. Would you like a drink? I'm having one.

DELIA: All right, then.

KETTLE: I'm having a whisky. But there's sherry, if you'd prefer it.

DELIA: Yes, please.

(*KETTLE takes a decanter of sherry from the cabinet cupboard, pours a glass of sherry for DELIA and a whisky and soda for himself.*)

I went to the bank to ask you about the accounts of the Infirmary Wireless Fund. Are you interested?

KETTLE: (*Pleasantly.*) Not at all.

DELIA: Isn't that a shocking thing for a bank manager to say, Mr Kettle?

KETTLE: It's an impossible thing for a bank manager to say, Mrs Moon. (*He crosses to her and gives her the drink, then raises his own glass.*) Boom-da-da! (*He drinks.*)

DELIA: Diddle-diddle! (*She sips her sherry.*)

KETTLE: But I'm no longer a bank manager. I stopped this morning – about twenty-five past nine.

DELIA: Just like that?

KETTLE: (*Moving to the easy chair.*) It took about three seconds. There I was, on my way, nearly there in fact – and suddenly a voice said, 'Why, George?' 'Why! What's it all for? And how long's it going on?' I couldn't reply. So I packed it up. And that's why they all think I'm ill, drunk or barmy. But I'm not. I've just packed it up, that's all.

DELIA: And what are you going to do now?

KETTLE: Not a good question. Not coming from a coal scuttle drummer and a cymbal basher.

DELIA: You're probably right. But women can't help being tremendous planners, you know, Mr Kettle. I take it, you don't know yet what you're going to do?

KETTLE: Yes, I do. I'm just going to be *not* a bank manager. The opposite of what Superintendent Street calls a solid dependable chap. So you'd better ask young Morgan to be your treasurer until they've appointed another manager. I'm sorry in a way, Mrs Moon, because that was the only thing that really brought us together, and up to a point I enjoyed that.

DELIA: Up to what point, Mr Kettle?

KETTLE: (*With decision.*) No, Mrs Moon.

DELIA: Now why do you say that?

KETTLE: When I turned back this morning, I knew that one of the first things I must do was to stop pretending. I'd had years and years of it – and I'd had enough. Now if you begin asking me personal questions, I'll answer you truthfully – and you mightn't like that. I don't mind offending people I dislike – old Hardacre, for instance – but I don't want to offend you, if I can help it.

DELIA: But perhaps you won't offend me. After all, you said I was very sensible about the Prince Igor dance.

KETTLE: You were splendid, Mrs Moon.

DELIA: And in any case – as you ought to realise – you've now raised my curiosity to such a height that I've almost got a temperature.

KETTLE: You look the same as usual.

DELIA: And what's that?

KETTLE: Slightly sub-normal.

DELIA: (*Putting her glass on the table by the sofa.*) If you mean by that, I look cool and rather severe, let me tell you that's the way I try to look – and take quite a lot of trouble about it.

KETTLE: Very well. And this'll answer your question. When we used to meet on the Fund Committee, half-dead or asleep though I was then, I'd spend half the time wondering what it would be like to take off those damned spectacles of yours, ruffle your hair, change those sensible clothes, put you into frills and nonsense and make love to you.

DELIA: (*Rising; gasping a little.*) Oh!

KETTLE: That's what I meant when I said I enjoyed meeting you up to a point.

DELIA: Does something like that go on in your mind with most women you meet?

KETTLE: No. Chiefly with you.

DELIA: (*With decision.*) Well! (*She crosses to the door.*)

KETTLE: What are you going to do now? Fetch the Superintendent?

DELIA: No.

(*DELIA goes out. KETTLE makes as if to follow her, then checks himself, crosses to the cabinet, shrugs and refills his glass. He looks rather miserable. He makes one or two small restless movements, then stops, hearing something. The front door is heard to open, close, and the sound of it being locked follows. KETTLE, surprised and delighted, stares at the door. DELIA re-enters. She carries a basket of food parcels, and a dress box. She dumps the basket and parcel on the desk, picks up her sherry glass and drains it, then looks at KETTLE.*)
'Fetch the Superintendent!' That was a stupid thing to say, wasn't it? (*She puts her glass on the table by the sofa.*)

KETTLE: Yes. Easily the stupidest thing I've said this morning.

DELIA: Do you think you're the only person in this brute of a town who can stop pretending?

KETTLE: I'm hoping I'm not.

DELIA: Not that *you're* going to take off these damned spectacles of mine, ruffle my hair, change my suitable clothes, and put me into frills and nonsense. But *I am.* (*She picks up the dress box.*) Now where's a bedroom? (*She points to the arch.*) Through there?

KETTLE: Yes, the door at the end.

DELIA: Right.

(*DELIA goes out. KETTLE crosses to the standard lamp and switches it on. He then looks up a number in the telephone directory pad, picks up the receiver and dials a number, humming to himself.*)

KETTLE: (*Into the telephone.*) Hardacre's Stores?... This is London and North Midland Bank, wishing to speak to Alderman Hardacre... Yes, very urgent... (*He now uses a voice unlike his ordinary one.*) Alderman Hardacre?... Yes, this is the London and North Midland Bank... No, it's not about your Extension Loan... It's about life – L-I-F-E. We thought you'd like to know that we think it's *wonderful.* Good morning.

(*He replaces the receiver to break the call, then lifts the receiver and puts it on the desk. He then crosses to the light switch and switches off the wall-brackets, changing the lighting so that it is warm and intimate.*

DELIA enters from the bedroom. She looks very different. She is wearing some sort of soft loose housecoat; her hair is looser; the spectacles have gone, and she looks an extremely attractive, very feminine creature. KETTLE stares at her in astonished admiration.)

DELIA: (*Displaying the housecoat; smiling.*) Well?

(*KETTLE moves behind the easy chair.*)

Is this what you imagined?

KETTLE: (*Enthusiastically.*) No, this is much better. Crikey – woman – what a transformation. But tell me – which is you – this one or the other one?

DELIA: I don't know. Both probably.

KETTLE: Or somebody different from either.

DELIA: Yes.

KETTLE: Just as I'm not really either a bank manager, a solid dependable, or a purely anti-bank manager type, but probably different from either.

DELIA: Can I have a cigarette?

KETTLE: (*Crossing to the table by the sofa.*) You can. (*He offers her a cigarette from the box on the table.*) But there seems something all wrong about this settling down for a smoke – it's an anti-climax.

DELIA: (*Taking a cigarette.*) Yes, but we're both feeling self-conscious.

(*KETTLE lights DELIA's cigarette. She sits in the easy chair.*) Better to talk for a while – if it's honest talk.

KETTLE: I'll do my best. But remember – I'm new to it. We chaps deceive ourselves, you know. I imagine you don't – as a rule.

DELIA: No. We just indulge in one enormous piece of self-deception – about a father, a lover or husband, a son – and that's all. Now – I know you're not married...

KETTLE: (*Standing by the sofa.*) I was. We bust up during the war, when I was in the army. The Pay Corps, by the way – no heroics. She thought I was too dull. And she was right – I was.

DELIA: Did she find an exciting man?

KETTLE: He sells typewriters now in Manchester – and plays golf every weekend. But that proves nothing. He may still be all 'a wonder and a wild desire'.

DELIA: What I meant to ask was – have you a mistress?

KETTLE: No.

DELIA: I thought all you men had – even in Brickmill.

KETTLE: Some have, some haven't. I'm always being surprised. But then I alternate between believing that people are making illicit love all over the place and concluding that there isn't as much of it as we're apt to think.

DELIA: (*Amused.*) So do I. And just when I think it's one, something happens that seems to prove it's the other.

KETTLE: Yes. How about you and Henry Moon?

DELIA: It doesn't work. The trouble is – I don't even like him any more.

KETTLE: I hardly know him. But he always seems to me a little unreal. (*He transfers the ashtray from the left arm of the sofa to the right arm of the easy chair.*) Like a lot of estate agents. They themselves seem as unreal as their advertisements – 'charming old-world residence replete with all modern conveniences' – that sort of thing.

DELIA: Yes, Henry's like that. Even if you quarrel, you can't make him stop acting – he won't become real.

KETTLE: Is your cold severe performance for him – or for yourself?

DELIA: A bit of both. He thinks it's smart – and safe. And it's my reply to Brickmill. In another place I mightn't bother keeping it up. Or with another man.

KETTLE: Have you just bought that astonishing thing you're wearing?

DELIA: Yes, I saw it in Morley's – and bought it to wear in secret, just for my own pleasure.

KETTLE: And now for mine.

DELIA: I hope so. There's food in the other parcels – nice greedy food – that I also bought because it was raining and November in Brickmill and I was thirty-six and hadn't a lover. We'll eat it soon. (*She stubs out her cigarette.*)

KETTLE: Not yet – I think – don't you? And it isn't raining, it isn't November, we aren't in Brickmill, thirty-six is the perfect age, and you have a lover. Get up, please, Mrs Moon.

DELIA: If you prefer it, Mr Kettle. (*She rises and stands facing KETTLE, looking at him.*)

KETTLE: (*Very gently.*) You're very beautiful. You're what a man feels life ought to be when he dares to think like a man. For the last year or two, every time I stared at you and wondered, aching a little, I must have known somehow this moment was coming if I dared to meet it. Now I want anything you want, and don't want anything you don't want.

211

DELIA: (*Half laughing.*) You're very sweet. But all wrong. (*She moves slowly close to him.*) You're supposed to be more masterful than that.

KETTLE: Certainly.

(*KETTLE takes DELIA in his arms and they kiss passionately but do not hold each other long. They look at each other as the curtain falls.*)

End of Act One.

ACT TWO

The same. Afternoon.

*When the curtain rises, it is the middle of the afternoon. It is raining.
The lights are on and the window curtains are closed. The remains of
lunch are on the dining-table, on a folding table-tray below the sofa,
and various coffee cups, plates, etc. are scattered around, some on the
floor below the sofa. The stage is empty, but DELIA enters immediately
from the bedroom. She is dressed as she was for her first entrance in
Act One, and her housecoat is draped over the back of the sofa. She
crosses to the window, opens the curtains, then takes a look at the
lunch things scattered around, and with the instinct of a tidy woman,
but with a slight move of distaste, begins in a very leisurely fashion
to put them together before taking them in the kitchen. MONICA
enters from the kitchen. She is dressed as before, and is wearing her
raincoat, which is rather wet. The two stare curiously at each other.*

DELIA: (*Standing by the dining-table; surprised.*) Oh – good
afternoon.

MONICA: (*Cheerfully.*) 'Afternoon.

DELIA: (*Amused.*) Wasn't the back door locked, then?

MONICA: No. Ought it to have been? (*Getting no reply she
continues cheerfully.*) Well, I wouldn't know, would I?

DELIA: (*Obviously amused.*) And I wouldn't know who you
are.

MONICA: Monica Twigg. My mother looks after…

DELIA: (*Cutting in.*) Yes, yes. He told me.

MONICA: Where *is* Mr Kettle?

DELIA: (*Waving a hand towards the bedroom.*) He's asleep.

MONICA: He's not ill, is he?

DELIA: (*With mock gravity.*) No. He seemed to me in the best
of health.

MONICA: (*Confidentially.*) That's what I thought this
morning. My mother said he was ill and I said he wasn't.
Just fed up, like me, I said.

DELIA: It can happen to any of us on a wet Monday in
Brickmill, can't it?

213

MONICA: It's a wet Monday here all the week if you ask me. I think I'll dry my coat in the kitchen.

DELIA: Do. And take these with you, Monica.

(*She hands MONICA some lunch things from the dining-table. MONICA exits to the kitchen. DELIA stacks the coffee cups, then moves towards the arch. MONICA re-enters from the kitchen, without her raincoat, notices DELIA's housecoat on the back of the sofa.*)

MONICA: (*Indicating the housecoat.*) Is this yours?

DELIA: Yes. I bought it this morning, just to cheer myself up.

MONICA: I saw it in Morley's window. Can I have a look at it?

DELIA: Yes, of course.

MONICA: (*Picking up the housecoat.*) Smashing! (*She drapes it against herself.*) This is what I see myself in – when I've got somewhere. Under the photo it'll say – 'Miss Monica Twigg relaxes at home.' (*She falls into an ecstatic trance.*)

DELIA: (*Crossing and sitting on the left arm of the easy chair.*) A sort of Career Girl, aren't you, Monica?

MONICA: (*Rather gloomily.*) When I can get going. (*She puts the housecoat carefully over the back of the sofa.*) Though I can't make up my mind if I ought to go in for bein' a model – or films – television. Did you show this to Mr Kettle?

DELIA: Yes. I thought it might amuse him. Though I came to see him on Hospital Committee business. He's the treasurer.

MONICA: (*Darkly.*) If you ask me, it's not committee business he wants.

DELIA: Oh?

MONICA: (*Darkly.*) No. What he could do with is – *sex.*

DELIA: (*Half-laughing.*) Monica!

MONICA: (*Bursting out.*) I don't care – I'll bet it's true. I expect you're like my mum who says he doesn't go in for it. She says I've got it on the brain, and that lots of men don't go in for it. Well, all I can say is – every time I get a job they seem to me to be going in for it, good and proper. The trouble I have with 'em.

DELIA: Yes, I can see you might have, Monica. (*She rises, crosses to the sofa and picks up the housecoat.*) Some girls do. But where does Mr Kettle come in? Don't tell me...

MONICA: (*Cutting in; confidentially.*) No, he's never made passes at me. Not so much as one of those looks.
(*DELIA crosses and puts the housecoat on the chair by the dining-table. MONICA follows DELIA.*)
But I saw right off this morning, he's just as fed up as I am – he's in a Rebellious Mood – Mr Kettle is – ready to clear out of Brickmill for good an' all – (*Grandly.*) to wipe the dust from his shoes. And if he is, then I'm ready to go with him.
(*DELIA, during the ensuing dialogue, collects the remainder of the plates and dishes, piles them on the table-tray, and eventually sits on the left arm of the easy chair. MONICA moves and stands near the table by the sofa.*)

DELIA: No, Monica, I don't think...

MONICA: (*Cutting-in; with fine sweep.*) I'll say to him straight out, 'Take me with you, Mr Kettle.' Mind you, I'll warn him that he's only a stepping stone in my career. I'd be using him just as he'd be using me.

DELIA: It doesn't sound a very nice arrangement, Monica.

MONICA: (*Grandly.*) I'd be honest with him. He could regard me as a plaything of an idle hour – that's up to him – but all the time I'd be on the look-out for the next stepping stone. Because I'm more for Cold Glamour than just sex. It'll say in the papers, 'Miss Monica Twigg laughingly denied any rumours of romance. "We are just friends," she said.'

DELIA: Who are you with now?

MONICA: (*With careless grandeur.*) Oh – one of these rich Californian playboys – or Eastern princes.

DELIA: With poor Mr Kettle left far behind?

MONICA: (*Still in the part.*) Just one of those things. That's life, isn't it?

DELIA: (*Briskly.*) Not for most of us, it isn't. Suppose you help me to wash up?

MONICA: (*Deflated.*) Mum'll do it when she comes in tonight. She'd rather. She wouldn't thank us for doing it.

She likes to look after Mr Kettle. But I'll bet she doesn't know as much about him as I do.

DELIA: And I'll bet you don't know as much about him as *I* do, Monica. You're much too young. And if I were you, I wouldn't bother about running a career. It takes a lot of hard work and determination. It's much more fun just being nobody.

MONICA: Not in Brickmill it isn't. And I'm sure I'm good at *something* – even if I don't know what it is yet. And how can you know if they don't let you try? And anyhow, I've had enough of this lousy hole.

DELIA: But isn't there any nice boy who's interested in you, Monica?

MONICA: Yes, two or three. Trouble about nice boys is that I'm not interested in *them*. They're so *dull*. And the other sort, who aren't dull, mess you about so much. People think I'm a sexy type – that's how I lose jobs – but I'm not so gone on sex.

DELIA: Give it time. You'll be surprised.

MONICA: (*Indignantly.*) All these pieces in women's mags – they make me mad. All about what you must do to find him and keep him. 'Make yourself fresh and dainty for him.' And just look what you've got to keep yourself fresh and dainty for.

DELIA: (*Laughing.*) I quite agree. That's why I stopped reading those magazines.

MONICA: (*Indignantly.*) Why don't they have a go at keeping fresh and dainty for *us?* And what d'you get for it all? Your photo in the papers sitting in night clubs? Big cars and airplanes to de luxe hotels? No bloody fear! All you get is four kids, a kitchen full of washing, red hands an' flat feet an' Housewives' Choice. (*She breaks off, then looks at DELIA.*) I expect you *do* know Mr Kettle better than I do.

DELIA: (*Rising and picking up the loaded tray; firmly.*) Quite definitely, Monica.

MONICA: Then d'you think he'd just take me to Birmingham – to have late dinner an' wine – an' coffee in the lounge with liq-ures?

DELIA: (*Firmly.*) No, Monica. Mr Kettle is the quiet type –
he just doesn't like wild nights in Birmingham.

MONICA: (*Gloomily.*) It'll have to be that buyer at
Hardacres then.

DELIA: He sounds much more promising.

MONICA: Only – he's so fat.

DELIA: It's all those late dinners and wine, probably. But
that's the type.

(*The front door bell rings urgently.*)

Is that the front door?

MONICA: Yes.

DELIA: See who it is – that's a good girl. Don't let anybody
in until I know who it is. Unlock the door and peep out.

MONICA: (*Crossing to the door.*) Okay. I could do a turn as a
maid, couldn't I?

DELIA: Why not?

(*MONICA goes out.*

*DELIA goes out with the tray to the kitchen, re-enters, goes
out with the folding table to the kitchen, then re-enters.*

MONICA re-enters from the hall, full of excitement.)

MONICA: It's a Mr Moon – an' he says his wife's here.
You're not her – are you?

DELIA: Yes.

MONICA: (*Impressed and delighted.*) Oi – this could be
getting a bit hot. What shall I tell him?

DELIA: (*Moving towards the arch.*) He'd better come in. I'll
be back in a minute.

(*MONICA goes out.*

DELIA goes into the bedroom.

*HENRY MOON enters. MONICA follows him on. MOON
is a fairly large, stupid-looking man in his late forties, dressed
in the tweedy style of the estate-agent-County-gent. He stares
around in surprise.*)

MONICA: This way, please.

MOON: Nobody here.

MONICA: (*Handsomely overplaying the maid.*) Mrs Moon asked
me to tell you, Mr Moon, that she would be with you in a
minute. (*She closes the door.*)

MOON: (*Staring at MONICA.*) Oh – she did, eh?

MONICA: In the meantime, Mr Moon, would you care to be seated? (*She indicates the easy chair.*)

MOON: (*Still surprised.*) Oh, yes – certainly. (*He sits in the easy chair, and stares at MONICA.*)
(*MONICA returns MOON's stare for a few moments, then sits at the left end of the sofa.*)

MONICA: Not very pleasant weather we're having, is it, Mr Moon?

MOON: (*Irritated.*) What *is* this?

MONICA: What is what, Mr Moon?

MOON: What's the matter with you, girl? (*He looks in astonishment at MONICA.*)

MONICA: (*Solemnly.*) You think I'm the maid here, don't you, Mr Moon?

MOON: Well, aren't you?

MONICA: (*With immense dignity.*) Not at all.

MOON: Oh!

MONICA: (*Loftily.*) As a matter of fact, if you're interested, Mr Moon, I'm an actress – well known in films and television. I'm beginning rehearsals next week for the part of a maid – not a small part, quite important, actually – for a television play. So I thought I'd just try it out, y'know, Mr Moon.

MOON: You – you did, did you? Well, what are you doing here?

MONICA: Trying it out.

MOON: But why should you be trying it out here?

MONICA: (*Loftily.*) Oh – I see what you mean, Mr Moon. Well, I happen to be visiting relations in Brickmill. But, of course, I live in London.

MOON: And how long have you been living in London?

MONICA: Oh – several years. Why?

MOON: (*Triumphantly.*) Because – about a month or two ago, you served me with coffee in the cafe in Market Street.

MONICA: (*Rising, annoyed.*) Okay – what if I did?

MOON: (*Rising and moving about the easy chair; indignantly.*) Well, why tell me all that stuff about television and being an actress?

MONICA: (*Moving above the right end of the sofa.*) Just
hopeless trying to kid you, isn't it?

MOON: (*Complacently.*) Yes.

MONICA: (*Grimly.*) I'll bet.

(*DELIA enters from the bedroom, looking tidy and composed.
She wears her spectacles.*)

MOON: (*Acknowledging DELIA; without surprise.*) Delia.

DELIA: (*Composedly.*) Henry.

MONICA: (*Cheerfully.*) Well, I'll say good afternoon, Mr
and Mrs Moon.

(*MONICA exits to the kitchen.*)

MOON: (*Indignantly.*) Tried to stuff me with all kinds of
nonsense, that girl. Caught her out at once, though.
Made her look silly. Cheeky little devil!

DELIA: She is rather. (*She crosses and sits in the easy chair.*)

MOON: Quite. Bit fishy her being around here, isn't it?

DELIA: No, Henry. She's the daughter of George Kettle's
housekeeper.

MOON: (*Putting his hat and umbrella on the dining-table.*) Oh
– is she? Well, Delia, I guessed you were here because I
saw your car outside. Otherwise I wouldn't have known,
of course.

DELIA: No, Henry, you wouldn't.

MOON: No. Not the least idea you were here before that,
naturally. Saw your car outside.

DELIA: Yes, you said that. But what were you doing
outside?

MOON: I came to have a word with Kettle. He's here, isn't
he?

DELIA: Yes. In his bedroom.

MOON: Taken queer?

DELIA: No, he's just asleep.

MOON: (*Indignantly.*) Asleep? That's a bit much, isn't it?

DELIA: He felt sleepy – after lunch. He gave me lunch
here, you know.

MOON: Any particular reason?

DELIA: We were both hungry.

MOON: They told me at the bank you'd been asking for
him this morning. Hospital Fund business, wasn't it?

DELIA: In the first place, Henry – yes.

MOON: How do you mean – 'in the first place'?

DELIA: That's why I called to see him. What about you?

MOON: What about me?

DELIA: Why have you called to see him?

MOON: Oh – well, Kettle rang me up this morning. Told the girl it was very urgent. Then it turned out to be some dam' silly question about you and your car. Sounded fishy to me. Thought the tax people had been sniffling round. But when I lunched at the club, I heard some funny rumours about Kettle. Some very queer tales going round, Delia. Hardacre says he's drinking hard. Somebody else said he was half off his rocker. How did he strike you?

DELIA: He seemed to me fairly sober and quite sane, Henry.

MOON: He did, did he? But why is he asleep, then?

DELIA: Because he felt sleepy, Henry. I told you.

MOON: (*Indignantly.*) That's all very well, but he's not the only man who feels sleepy after lunch. What if we all turned in like that?

DELIA: Then you'd all feel less sleepy in the evening.

MOON: You must admit that it 'ud be a bit thick if we all slept after lunch. Besides, what about you Delia?

DELIA: What about me, Henry?

MOON: (*Indignantly.*) Well – dash it all – I mean to say – a chap oughtn't to give a woman lunch and then just turn in like that. What are *you* supposed to be doing while he's asleep?

DELIA: (*Thoughtfully.*) I think I'm supposed to be washing up.

MOON: Why? Can't the housekeeper wash up?

DELIA: Perhaps she's busy at home. It's Monday, you know, Henry.

MOON: (*Indignantly.*) Of course it's Monday. And that makes the whole thing dam' ridiculous.

DELIA: Why, Henry?

MOON: (*Angrily.*) Why? Why? Well, look at it. Not the weekend – or holiday time – or anything. But *Monday.* Monday!

DELIA: (*Dreamily.*) Moon Day really – I suppose.

MOON: I dare say – but what does that matter?

DELIA: It ought to matter to you Moons.

MOON: (*Indignantly.*) And that's another thing. Just remember it. When Kettle rang me this morning – and I found it wasn't bank business and gave him a rocket – damned impudence, I told him – he said Moon was a fascinating name – and perhaps that was why you'd married me.

DELIA: (*Smiling.*) Did he? How sweet!

MOON: Sweet? What's sweet about it? (*He stares suspiciously at DELIA.*)

DELIA: (*Smilingly.*) Yes, Henry?

(*MOON is about to say something, then checks himself.*)

MOON: No – never mind.

DELIA: (*Rising and crossing to the sofa.*) Did you have a nice lunch at the club? (*She sits on the sofa at the left end, removes her spectacles and puts them in her handbag.*)

MOON: No, liver and bacon – worse than usual. But that's beside the point.

DELIA: I didn't know there was a point.

MOON: Certainly there's a point. A fellow says an idiotic thing like that over the phone – girl on the switchboard listening, probably – and all you can say is, 'How sweet!' The same fellow has you to lunch – then goes to sleep – while you sit waiting here with your car outside.

DELIA: I could hardly bring it inside.

MOON: (*Angrily.*) You know what I mean.

DELIA: No, I don't. Do you?

MOON: (*Impressively.*) Delia.

DELIA: Yes, Henry?

MOON: (*Impressively.*) I'm going to put two straight questions to you – and I want two straight truthful answers.

DELIA: Are you sure?

MOON: Sure? Of course I'm sure. Why shouldn't I be?

DELIA: (*Gently.*) Because I've never felt you liked the truth, Henry.

MOON: (*Staggered.*) My godfathers! *Me!* Not like the truth? What are you talking about? Let anybody show me the facts, and I'm always ready to face them. Ask them at the office. Ask them at the club. Why, some people think I overdo it. 'You're too outspoken, Henry, old boy,' some people say.

DELIA: Don't let's bother about those people, Henry. You just be outspoken. Two straight questions – two straight truthful answers. Go on.

MOON: (*Impressively.*) Number one, then. Have I – or have I not – played the game with you, Delia?

DELIA: You've played *your* game with me, Henry – but not *my* game with me.

MOON: I don't know what that means – doubt if you do – but we'll leave it for the time being. The next question's more important. (*Very impressively.*) Are you playing the game, Delia?

DELIA: Do you mean – am I being unfaithful to you, Henry?

MOON: (*Perturbed by such plain speech; hastily.*) Certainly not. I'm not talking on those lines at all. I know what you want to do. You want me to say more than I mean – then you turn round and ask me what the devil I mean by accusing you of this, that and the other. Oh – no, I'm not having that. You don't catch me falling for that one, my dear girl. No fear! I'm just putting a simple straight question to you. Are you playing the game?

DELIA: (*Losing her temper.*) But it isn't a simple straight question at all. It just doesn't mean anything. What game? If you mean am I having an affair – why don't you say so?

MOON: (*Shouting.*) Because I'm not going to be jockeyed into a false position and have you making a fool of me. It's an old trick – and this time it won't work.

DELIA: (*Raising her voice.*) Then what on earth *are* you talking about?

MOON: (*Angrily.*) Well, for instance, your car's out there, isn't it? Been out there for two or three hours. Nobody

could miss it. As soon as I came round the corner, I
knew you must be here. There must be other people who
must be thinking the same thing. They'll start talking –
probably doing it now. That's not good enough, is it?
You can't call that playing the game – not in a town like
this.

DELIA: (*Goading him.*) You mean – they aren't playing the
game when they start talking?

MOON: (*Goaded: loudly and wildly.*) No, of course I don't –
and you know dam' well I don't, Delia. I mean *you* aren't
playing the game when you give 'em an excuse to talk –
or when you're just staying on here, when you don't
know who might come in, instead of clearing out, or for
that matter when you even have lunch with a fellow
who's behaving so queerly and other fellows are already
wondering about him. And I say I've played the game
with you – and now you're not playing the game with
me – that's all.

(*KETTLE enters from the bedroom. He looks pleasantly tousled
and relaxed, and is lighting his pipe. MOON moves above the
easy chair.*)

KETTLE: Oh – hello – Moon.

MOON: (*Indignantly.*) Hello, Kettle.

DELIA: (*Lovingly.*) Did you have a nice sleep?

KETTLE: (*Smilingly.*) Wonderful!

DELIA: (*Lovingly.*) I hope we didn't wake you.

MOON: (*Indignantly.*) And I must say this seems to me a bit
much. Did he have a nice sleep? I hope we didn't wake
him! Who is he, anyhow – the Shah of Persia? He ought
to be doing his job at the London and North Midland
Bank now – never mind his nice sleep. Now I'll put a
straight question to you, Kettle…

DELIA: (*To KETTLE.*) Henry's putting straight questions
this afternoon.

MOON: (*To KETTLE.*) What do you think you're up to?
(*KETTLE, comfortably smoking, looks from MOON to DELIA,
then back to MOON.*)

KETTLE: (*Slowly.*) Well, Moon, old chap…

MOON: (*Cutting in; indignantly.*) Never mind about the 'Moon, old chap' – we're not on those terms.

KETTLE: You prefer Mr Moon? I'm delighted. I like Mr Moon. Well, Mr Moon. I'm not up to anything at the moment, as you see. I'm just taking it easy – as you see, smoking – pure Latakia, too. I've always wanted to smoke pure Latakia.

DELIA: It has an enchanting smell.

KETTLE: It has, hasn't it? I never dared to smoke it before because it's supposed to be bad for one.

MOON: Bad for you?

KETTLE: That's why I'm smoking it now. And that's about all I'm up to at the moment, Mr Moon. What do you suggest?

MOON: I suggest you try what I've tried, Kettle. And what I've tried – is to play the game.

KETTLE: (*Interested.*) I overheard you talking about that. Which game? You know, I bought a Jungle Shooting Game this morning…

MOON: (*Cutting in; loudly.*) I'm talking about doing the Decent Thing.

(*DELIA laughs. MOON glares at her.*)

DELIA: I'm sorry, Henry. You looked so funny, that's all.

MOON: (*With dignity.*) As soon as you're ready to listen properly, I'll carry on.

KETTLE: Delia, behave yourself.

DELIA: (*Meekly.*) Yes, George.

MOON: (*Indignantly.*) And I must say – it's a bit much when a fellow has to listen to another fellow telling his wife to behave herself…

KETTLE: (*Cutting in; gravely.*) Quite right, Mr Moon. It *is* a bit much. But you were talking about doing the decent thing.

MOON: I expect other people to try and do what I've always tried to do, to play the game. What I have done, in spite of temptations.

DELIA: (*Interested.*) Really, Henry. And you never told me.

MOON: Naturally not. But you can take my word for it – they were there.

KETTLE: (*With immense mock gravity.*) Isn't that rather too vague, Mr Moon? Oughtn't you to give us a definite example?

DELIA: Of course he ought. Especially as this is the first I've heard of them.

KETTLE: (*With immense mock gravity.*) Remember – unless you can convince us on this point, your whole argument falls to the ground.

DELIA: (*Encouragingly.*) Now, Henry. Who, for instance? (*She moves along the seat of the sofa to the right end.*)

MOON: (*Crossing and sitting on the sofa at the left end; doubtfully.*) All very like a cad, y'know.

DELIA: I don't mind. I like cads' talk.

KETTLE: (*Moving to the easy chair and sitting.*) And I *am* a cad from now on. So…?

MOON: Well – for example – there's a Miss Carson in our office – often acts as my assistant…

DELIA: (*Interested.*) Is that the bulgy red-haired one?

MOON: (*With dignity.*) Miss Carson *has* auburn hair – and an unusually fine figure. She's – er – rather devoted to me. At least my partner Jack Francis always says so – pulls my leg about it.

KETTLE: (*Encouragingly.*) Good! I pass Miss Carson as a temptation.

MOON: Well, several times Miss Carson and I have had to spend a night away from Brickmill – on important business. And what's happened?

DELIA: (*Enjoying this.*) Yes, what *has* happened, Henry?

MOON: (*With massive anti-climax.*) Nothing.

KETTLE: Nothing?

MOON: Nothing. After a hard day's work together, I've stood her a spot of dinner and perhaps a few drinks afterwards, but we've been jolly good pals, that's all – just jolly good pals.

DELIA: I'll bet Miss Carson hates being a jolly good pal.

MOON: That's not the point. I appeal to you, Kettle.

KETTLE: Quite right, Moon. Not the point. We're talking about you now, not Miss Carson. She's merely the temptation you've resisted.

MOON: Quite. The point is – I've stuck to my guns.

KETTLE: A very happy way of putting it, too.

MOON: Delia and I may not have been getting along as well as we might – though I don't think we've made a bad show of it – but if she played the game with me, I was ready to play the game with her.

KETTLE: If she stuck to her guns, you would stick to your guns.

MOON: Absolutely.

DELIA: (*Impatiently.*) I wish you'd stop sticking to your guns, Henry, and simply tell me what you think.

MOON: That's the point. What am I to think?

KETTLE: (*Sympathetically.*) Well, what would you like to think, Mr Moon?

MOON: (*Angrily.*) It isn't a question of what I think but of what other people will think. Just remember that. (*He glances at his watch and rises.*) I must go. (*He collects his hat and umbrella.*)

(*KETTLE rises, moves to the door and opens it.*)

Got an important appointment at four. Two fellows coming from London to look at the Murchison factory – fine property. Very big deal, if it comes off. (*He looks appealingly at them.*) Let's try and keep our heads, shall we? There's a right and a wrong way even in this sort of thing. After all, none of us can afford a scandal, can we?

KETTLE: Yes, I can. One of the few things I can afford, from now on.

MOON: (*Crossing to the door.*) If you'll take my tip, Kettle – you'll be careful – very, very careful. You're going too far along the line. You going home, Delia?

DELIA: No, not yet, Henry.

MOON: Talk things over, eh? Quite right. Well, I must run. (*Goes out.*)

(*DELIA and KETTLE wait for a moment, looking meaningly at each other.*)

DELIA: (*Softly.*) Well, that's Henry. You see what I meant?

KETTLE: (*Crossing to the desk.*) I do. What's the telephone number of his office?

DELIA: Eight-three-five-seven. Why?

KETTLE: (*Lifting the receiver.*) I have an urgent message for Miss Carson. (*He dials and listens.*) Number engaged. (*He holds the receiver and waits.*)

(*DELIA rises and moves above the sofa. MONICA enters from the kitchen.*)

DELIA: Hello – I thought you'd gone, Monica.

MONICA: Raining too hard. So I washed up. But I thought I'd tell you I get the idea now. I was a bit dumb, wasn't I? I'm going now but I'll be back. I want to know what happens – an' there might be something I can do. Boy, is my face red?

(*MONICA exits to the kitchen. KETTLE, still at the telephone, looks inquiringly at DELIA.*)

KETTLE: What's that about?

DELIA: (*Half-laughing.*) She had designs on you.

KETTLE: (*Dialling.*) Nonsense! She's only a kid.

DELIA: She's a full-grown female, complete with assorted designs.

KETTLE: (*Into the telephone.*) Is that Moon and Francis?... I want to speak to Miss Carson, please – Yes, yes, very important... (*He waits.*)

(*DELIA moves to the dining-table, collects the table mats, puts them in the table drawer and finds a revolver in the drawer, which she takes out.*)

Miss Carson?... This is a friend – a well-wisher. Now don't you take any more of that 'jolly good pal' nonsense from Henry Moon. That man's crazy about you. Yes, you ought to have seen the look in his eye when he described your figure. He's raving and drooling. All the best, Miss Carson. (*He replaces the receiver to break the call, then puts the receiver on the desk.*)

DELIA: (*Showing him the revolver; seriously.*) Why this thing?

KETTLE: (*Carelessly.*) The bank gave every manager one some time ago when the crime wave started. But it doesn't work very well and it's doubtful if I could hit anything with it.

DELIA: I could. My father taught me...

KETTLE: (*Cutting in.*) Give it to me, my pet. (*He takes the revolver from DELIA, puts it in the desk drawer, then leads DELIA to the easy chair.*) Let's talk about ourselves – or even Henry.

DELIA: (*Sitting in the easy chair.*) I don't want to talk about Henry.

(*KETTLE sits on the right arm of the easy chair.*)

You see, though, what I meant – about nothing being real.

KETTLE: I'm not sure you're very real yet. But better, not worse.

DELIA: That's the wrong way to talk, darling. I'm very real.

KETTLE: Of course. But we've allowed ourselves to be bullied out of any genuine belief in happiness. So we think it can't be real.

DELIA: That's men, not women.

KETTLE: Then women should never have let it happen to men. They ought to have stopped it. (*He looks smilingly at her.*) When do we go, Delia? Tonight?

DELIA: (*Looking steadily at him.*) Go? Where?

KETTLE: I don't know. Anywhere. Just go.

DELIA: But, darling, why should we go?

KETTLE: (*Astonished.*) But – but – you don't imagine I'm staying on here, do you? I thought it was obvious from the first I was clearing out.

DELIA: This morning – yes.

KETTLE: Well – what's happened since...?

DELIA: (*Cutting in; smilingly.*) Me. Us.

KETTLE: (*Rising.*) You. Us. Certainly – but I tell you, I've finished with the bank – and with this town and any town that looks like this – with all this sort of life.

DELIA: But what does it matter *now?* I know how you felt – I felt it, too – but now we can laugh at it together – so everything's different.

KETTLE: Not for me it isn't.

DELIA: In other words, loving me isn't enough for you – though loving you would be enough for me?

KETTLE: That's not a fair question.

DELIA: (*Impatiently.*) Oh – don't be like Henry.

KETTLE: That's – just what I'm trying not to be – like Henry. What are you asking me to do – pretend all day long?

DELIA: Women have to do it – all day long and half the night.

KETTLE: I thought you didn't want to be that sort of woman.

DELIA: (*Rising.*) I didn't say I did. But I'm trying to be sensible for both of us.

KETTLE: (*Rather heatedly.*) Don't bother about me. I've stopped being sensible.

DELIA: (*Not taking his tone; pleading.*) That was all right this morning. And I loved you for it. But one of us *has* to be sensible. You talk about going – but you don't know where you want to go – or what you want to do when you get there.

KETTLE: (*Heatedly.*) That doesn't matter at this moment.

DELIA: (*Sharply.*) Of course it does. We're not children. Nobody's going to look after us.

KETTLE: (*Urgently.*) I tell you, Delia, all that matters is this. Do we go together – or do I go alone? (*Firmly.*) Because I'm not staying here. I've done with it all.

DELIA: (*Hotly.*) Which means that I haven't enough to keep you here.

KETTLE: (*Hotly.*) I never thought for a moment you'd want to stay.

DELIA: And what do we do if we don't? Try for a job as cook and barman at a third-rate hotel?

KETTLE: (*Heatedly.*) I'd rather be a barman in a fifth-rate hotel than a Brickmill bank manager enjoying another man's wife. I'd feel a rat and very soon I'd *be* a rat. Delia, this isn't you. It's putting those dam' clothes on again that's done it.

DELIA: (*Furiously.*) You needn't remind me that I took them off for you!

KETTLE: (*Angrily.*) Well – there are some I've taken off for ever – black coat, striped trousers, stiff collar.

DELIA: (*Turning to him; angrily.*) I suppose I'm not even worth a stiff collar now.

(*There is a ringing and knocking at the front door off.*)
Oh – damn! Now there's somebody here. (*She stands above right end of the sofa.*)

KETTLE: We ought to have locked that door again. (*He moves towards the door left.*)
(*There is a sharp rap on the door. STREET and HARDACRE enter left.*)

STREET: (*Closing the door; heartily.*) Back again, you see, like promised.

KETTLE: Go away.

HARDACRE: (*Pointedly.*) I think we passed your husband in his car, Mrs Moon.

DELIA: He's just been here, so don't bother throwing him at me.

KETTLE: In fact, don't bother about anything, Alderman Hardacre. Just go away.

STREET: Now – now – now, Mr Kettle.

HARDACRE: (*Angrily.*) I'm not going away until I've said what I've come to say. There's nobody at that bank of yours understands about my Extension Loan.

KETTLE: (*With obvious controlled fury.*) I'm in the middle of the most important, the most urgent argument I ever had in my life – (*Letting go.*) and you have to come blundering in, blathering about your Extension Loan. *Go away!*

HARDACRE: (*Loudly and angrily.*) You may think you're smart, Kettle, but I know it was you that rang me up this morning telling me life's wonderful. Well, now I'll tell you something, Kettle. I got on to your district Head Office this morning, and the chief inspector, Mr Clinton, has come to Brickmill specially – to talk to you. Now make something wonderful out of *that.*

STREET: It's quite true. I came to tell you…

HARDACRE: (*Triumphantly.*) But seeing as I'd fixed it for him to come over, I thought I'd have the satisfaction of telling you myself.
(*KETTLE ignores STREET and HARDACRE and crosses to left of DELIA.*)

KETTLE: (*To DELIA.*) Now – do you see what you're asking me to do?

DELIA: What does it matter about *them?* The point is, I asked you to do something for *me.*

KETTLE: It isn't for you – not as I see you.

DELIA: Perhaps you aren't seeing me.

HARDACRE: (*Angrily.*) What he will be seeing soon is Mr Clinton, his boss. And Mr Clinton'll be asking him what he's playing at.

DELIA: (*Crossly.*) Oh – shut up about Mr Clinton.

HARDACRE: (*Nastily.*) I'd like to know where you come into it. I must say, if I was Henry Moon…

KETTLE: (*Threatening HARDACRE.*) Go away!

HARDACRE: I *am* going. But you haven't finished with me yet.

DELIA: (*In disgust.*) Oh – surely!

HARDACRE: I'll see you later, Superintendent.

(*HARDACRE exits left, slamming the door behind him. STREET shakes his head, makes a tutting sound, then sits in the easy chair.*)

STREET: (*Cheerfully.*) He's a bit short-tempered and hasty, Alderman Hardacre is. But don't you worry about him, Mrs Moon. And don't worry about *me.* You get on with your argument.

KETTLE: (*Beginning with controlled fury.*) As you noticed this morning, Superintendent, I've become rather eccentric. And one form it takes is this – strange as it may seem, I don't seem to know how to conduct an intimate argument with a woman – (*Letting go now; furiously.*) if a police superintendent's listening to us.

STREET: Sorry about that, Mr Kettle. You see, I arranged to meet Mr Clinton here.

DELIA: (*Smoothly.*) George, how well do you know Superintendent Street?

KETTLE: Not very well. Why?

DELIA: (*Crossing below KETTLE to the window and picking up her housecoat.*) He's far more artful and dangerous than he appears to be. That's all. So be careful.

STREET: Be careful about what?

DELIA: (*Moving to KETTLE; ignoring STREET.*) He seems stupid. But he isn't. And I don't like that sly cat-with-a-mouse tone of his. So watch him. (*She crosses to the arch up right.*)

STREET: (*Slyly.*) That's not the way out, Mrs Moon.

DELIA: (*Sweetly.*) I'm going to the bathroom – do you mind?

(*DELIA exits up right, taking the housecoat with her. KETTLE looks after her then glares at STREET, who smiles broadly at him. During the ensuing scene, KETTLE paces irritably up and down.*)

STREET: Wonderful how the ladies soon make themselves at home, isn't it?

KETTLE: Couldn't you go and mind your own business?

STREET: Well, strictly speaking, you can't say anything isn't our business. There are so many ways of breaking the law now.

KETTLE: Too many ways, too many laws.

STREET: (*Heartily.*) Well, you're all right, Mr Kettle. Kept your promise I think, didn't you? Stayed in, eh?

KETTLE: (*Abruptly.*) Yes.

STREET: Not been lonely, I fancy.

KETTLE: (*Abruptly.*) I'm not lonely now. Thanks for calling. Good-bye.

STREET: We learn a lot in police work. Full of human nature, it is.

KETTLE: Very interesting. But some other time.

STREET: (*Expansively.*) I've noticed many a time the way some ladies, often seemingly the quietest, are attracted to a man the minute he goes a bit wild or a bit cracked. It doesn't last, of course – they've too much sense – but they can't help being fascinated.

KETTLE: You must have a lot of time to waste.

STREET: When a man gets to my position in police work, Mr Kettle, he doesn't charge in when the harm's done but does a bit of intelligent anticipation. Have you ever noticed how little trouble we have here in Brickmill?

KETTLE: I used to live near that big cemetery at Hendon. They'd very little trouble there, too.

STREET: Now, now, Mr Kettle. Let me make my point. Intelligent anticipation. Of course you've done nothing illegal – that we know of – but when a good steady man suddenly goes off the rails, I can't help being interested in him.

KETTLE: Before the pattern was quite fixed, they were probably talking like that in ant hills.

STREET: (*Shaking his head.*) That's far-fetched, Mr Kettle.

KETTLE: I'm all for the far-fetched, Superintendent. From now I want to be a fanciful unsound man.

STREET: You wouldn't if you'd seen what I've seen. I've helped to put dozens of 'em behind bars.
(*The front door bell rings off.*)
That might be your chief – Mr Clinton.

KETTLE: (*Moving to the door left.*) Well, this time I'll see for myself who it is. So you stay there.
(*STREET rises. KETTLE exits left.*
MR CLINTON and KETTLE enter left. CLINTON is a well-dressed man about sixty, with an easy fatherly manner, a dangerous type.)

CLINTON: Ah – Superintendent, we meet again.

STREET: We do, Mr Clinton. And what about your medical friend?

CLINTON: He'll be at our disposal in about a quarter of an hour or so.

KETTLE: What are you proposing to do – take my temperature?

CLINTON: Just whatever you'd like us to do, Mr Kettle. I'm here as your colleague. I work for the London and North Midland too. No doubt our friend Hardacre thinks I'm now shouting at you, threatening you with this and that. All right – let him think so. But the truth is, it's you I care about – not him. A good manager's more important to us than a good account. You see, I'm perfectly frank with you, Kettle.

STREET: And, if I may say so, it's a pleasure to listen to you, Mr Clinton.

KETTLE: It must be. And I'll tell you why. He's in your business, only further along and higher up.

(*DELIA enters from the bedroom. She wears her hat and is obviously ready to leave.*)

CLINTON: (*Rather surprised.*) Oh – good afternoon – Mrs Kettle.

DELIA: (*Dryly.*) I'm not Mrs Kettle.

KETTLE: (*Hastily.*) Mr Clinton – Mrs Moon.

CLINTON: How d'you do?

DELIA: How d'you do? (*She glances at KETTLE.*) I must go in a minute.

KETTLE: Mr Clinton's your spokesman. You'd better stay and listen to what he says, and what I have to say to him. Any objections, Mr Clinton?

CLINTON: (*Hesitating.*) It's – er – rather irregular...

DELIA: Oh – if it's irregular, I'll stay and listen. But, George, please, don't be childish.

STREET: Quite right, Mrs Moon.

DELIA: Don't *you* tell me that. You make me feel I must be wrong.

KETTLE: You *are* wrong. (*He indicates the easy chair.*)
(*CLINTON crosses to the easy chair and sits. DELIA stands above the right end of the sofa.*)
Well, Mr Clinton?

CLINTON: You've had a long training at the bank, long experience. You're known to be an excellent branch manager, the kind of man who would soon be promoted to a bigger branch.

DELIA: (*In dismay; involuntarily.*) Oh – no!

CLINTON: I beg your pardon?

DELIA: (*Moving below the sofa and sitting.*) No, go on.
(*KETTLE sits on the left arm of the sofa. STREET stands.*)

CLINTON: You're valuable to us, Kettle. We need you, my dear fellow. It's as simple as that.

KETTLE: Let's suppose it is. The bank needs me, but do I need the bank?

CLINTON: I'll come to that. You've taken a day off. All right. Take a week off. Take a month, if you give us a doctor's certificate. Only regard the bank as your friend.

KETTLE: But I don't want it as my friend. I've had enough of it.

CLINTON: What you do want is a break. You've gone stale.

KETTLE: I'm stale, so I have a break to freshen myself up. To become stale again. Perhaps to become stale for ever, sitting at the bottom of the Dead Sea. Or do I exaggerate, Mrs Moon?

DELIA: No, you just turn poetical at the wrong time, Mr Kettle.

CLINTON: (*Rising.*) You've been with us over twenty years. Why throw them away for a mood?

KETTLE: Why throw the rest of my life away for a bank?

CLINTON: You have to earn a living?

KETTLE: Certainly. I've only saved a few hundreds.

CLINTON: What do you propose to do then?

KETTLE: I've no idea. (*He looks at DELIA.*) Something fairly disreputable – with irregular hours.

CLINTON: We guarantee you enviable security, my dear Kettle – what everybody wants.

KETTLE: Perhaps they're wrong to want it.

CLINTON: Well, half the crimes are committed looking for it.

KETTLE: Perhaps *all* the crimes are committed looking for it. Perhaps that's where we've all gone wrong.

CLINTON: Very few people would agree with you.

KETTLE: (*Rising.*) That's the kind of man I want to be – that very few people agree with. I've spent years and years agreeing with everybody.

STREET: (*Heavily.*) Security's well worth having. It stands to reason.

KETTLE: Well, it can stop standing to reason. I've had my share of security. Now I'll take insecurity. Up one week, down the next. Tea and stale bread this Tuesday. Champagne and smoked salmon next Tuesday.

STREET: That's boys' talk.

KETTLE: Well, didn't you like being a boy?

STREET: Yes, but I had to grow up – to think and behave like a man.

KETTLE: Does that include taking the boy in you and wringing his neck?

STREET: It might have to.

KETTLE: Last week I didn't even feel I was a man. Today I do. A boy *and* a man – better still.

CLINTON: A conscientious boy? A responsible man? We have to keep the world going, you know, Kettle.

KETTLE: The world we enjoy, certainly. But there are different worlds.

CLINTON: There's only one that keeps *us* going.

KETTLE: I doubt it. But I know what you want to say. 'What would happen…?' Go on…

CLINTON: Very well. What would happen if every man walked away from his work as you did this morning?

KETTLE: How did you come here this morning?

CLINTON: I caught the twelve forty-five from Birmingham. Why?

KETTLE: What would have happened if everybody in Birmingham had tried to catch the twelve forty-five?

CLINTON: (*Protesting.*) Now, wait a minute…

STREET: (*Cutting in; puzzled.*) There's a catch there somewhere.

DELIA: I wonder if there is.

KETTLE: (*Turning to DELIA.*) Not as big a catch, Delia, as there's been in that 'What would happen if everybody did it?' line of argument. It's been one of the great flatteners, bleachers and dimmers of life. To hell with what would happen if everybody did it! Why not assume people are different? Even now some of 'em are.

CLINTON: But if the whole staff of our branch here had walked out as you did…

KETTLE: (*Cutting in.*) Why suppose anything of the kind? Young Morgan, for instance, is as anxious to be a bank manager as I am to stop being one. All right, let him. He goes in. I go out.

CLINTON: But why – Kettle – why?

KETTLE: Because I've had enough.

DELIA: (*Jumping up.*) And so have I.

KETTLE: (*Turning to her; alarmed.*) Delia!

DELIA: No. Not enough of you. But I want to think. Look!

(*She moves with deliberation to the telephone, replaces the receiver then turns to KETTLE.*) Don't take this off again. I'll ring you up.

KETTLE: To say what?

DELIA: I don't know yet. I tell you, I want to think. And I don't know what I'm thinking with you three men shouting at one another. (*She looks at the other two.*) You won't persuade him, you know. I see that now. Well, you won't succeed where I failed, that's one consolation.

KETTLE: Delia!

DELIA: No, George, don't let's say any more now.

(*DELIA crosses and exits hurriedly left. KETTLE makes a move to follow her, but the front door is heard to slam, before he can leave the room. He moves rather slowly and sombrely to the cabinet.*)

KETTLE: Anybody want a drink?

CLINTON: (*Crossing and sitting on the sofa at the right end; rather primly.*) Not at this time of day, thank you.

(*KETTLE pours a whisky and soda for himself.*)

STREET: Same here. And if you'll take my tip, Mr Kettle –

KETTLE: (*Cutting in; neatly but not rudely.*) I'm not taking your tip, Superintendent. I've no intention of turning into a drunk, but from now on when I feel like having a drink I'm going to have one. (*He raises his glass.*) Your health, gentlemen! God rest you – may nothing you dismay. (*He drinks. Slowly and reflectively.*) Y'know, I believe one of two things happens to men of my age who aren't really living. Either they die inside and Brickmill's full of men who died years ago – or they live in a fashion by turning into haters of a full warm existence, into large grey rats just gnawing away at the good life.

CLINTON: (*Dryly.*) Which are we, by the way, walking dead men or large grey rats?

KETTLE: (*Mildly thoughtful.*) I think you're rats. Enemies of what I take to be the good life.

CLINTON: And what's that?

KETTLE: I can't define it. If I could, I'd be able to see all round it, which would mean it would be smaller than I am. Therefore, not the good life.

STREET: (*Rather roughly.*) Your good life's going to be a nervous breakdown. Already you're irresponsible.

KETTLE: Certainly. From now on, gentlemen, I propose to dodge by every possible means all the responsibilities and commitments of the decent sound British citizen – poor devil!

CLINTON: (*Dryly.*) Do you indeed?

KETTLE: (*Expanding.*) I do. Money previously spent on taxes, rates, insurance premiums, subscriptions, will now be spent on constant travel, food and drink, gorgeous clothes for the woman I'm living with, and occasional evenings with symphony orchestras. I shall hobnob almost entirely with cheerful riff-raff – be polite only to nice pleasant people, and be downright rude to bigwigs, stuffed shirts and pompous busybodies. (*He moves to the desk and puts his drink on it.*) And now, gentlemen, no more argument. You can have a drink, play a shooting game or the drum and cymbals with me – or go away.

STREET: See what I mean, Mr Clinton? Everything topsy-turvy.

CLINTON: (*Rising.*) Our friend's probably outside now, waiting for one of us.

KETTLE: If you mean your medical friend, you're wasting your time. I haven't felt better for years. (*He lights his pipe.*)

STREET: (*With sinister intonation.*) Sometimes a doctor's certificate will excuse something that otherwise might get a man into serious trouble.
(*During the dialogue leading to the knock-out, CLINTON and STREET advance slowly towards KETTLE.*)

CLINTON: (*With sinister intonation.*) The bank isn't very happy about branch managers who suddenly walk out and begin expressing extremely subversive sentiments. We wonder what's behind it all.

KETTLE: (*Dreamily.*) I was quite right. Large grey rats.

CLINTON: Your accounts may be in order, Kettle, and then again they may not. Some men need more money than they're entitled to – to spend on travel, food and drink.

STREET: (*Tapping KETTLE on the shoulder; nastily.*) Or clothes for another man's wife. I noticed she took a dress in there that never came out – new and very saucy.

KETTLE: (*Losing his temper.*) Oh – shut up – you damned lout!

(*He tries to hit STREET. STREET counters KETTLE's blow and knocks him clean out, so that KETTLE falls unconscious to the floor.*)

STREET: (*Standing over KETTLE; coolly.*) Thought he'd have a go for that last little packet I handed him. Worked out nicely, didn't it? You're a witness. I had to hit him in self-defence, didn't I, Mr Clinton?

CLINTON: You did. If Dr Grenock could do anything with him now…

STREET: That's what I had in mind, of course. Might be just right. You bring him in, while I keep an eye on our friend here.

CLINTON: Excellent.

(*CLINTON crosses to exit left. STREET bends over KETTLE, making sure he is out. MONICA enters hurriedly from the kitchen.*)

MONICA: (*As she enters.*) I say, Mr Kettle… (*She breaks off.*) Here, what's going on?

STREET: (*Angrily.*) You keep out of this.

MONICA: (*Angrily.*) I believe you knocked him out.

STREET: (*Angrily.*) Self-defence. Go on. Pop off, girl.

(*The telephone rings. STREET moves to the telephone and lifts the receiver.*)

(*Into the telephone.*) Yes?… Oh – it's you, is it, Mrs Moon? Superintendent Street here… No, I can't give you Mr Kettle… He's out…

(*MONICA moves to STREET, snatches the receiver from him and struggles with him to retain it.*)

MONICA: (*Shouting into the telephone.*) He's not out. He's knocked out. He's unconscious…

(*STREET recovers the receiver and pushes MONICA away. MONICA moves below the sofa. STREET replaces the receiver, then moves to MONICA and puts a heavy hand on her shoulder.*)

STREET: (*Angrily.*) What's your name?

MONICA: Monica Twigg.

STREET: (*Angrily.*) Well, Monica Twigg, you've obstructed a police officer in the course of his duty – and now you're under arrest.

MONICA: (*Excitedly.*) Shall I have my photo in the paper?

STREET: You might.

MONICA: (*Delighted.*) Oh – goody, goody, goody!

(*MONICA sits happily on the sofa and grins at STREET as the curtain falls.*)

End of Act Two.

ACT THREE

The same. Early evening.

When the curtain rises, it is about five minutes later. STREET is pacing up and down behind the sofa. KETTLE, still unconscious, is lying on the floor. MONICA is sitting on the sofa, at the right end.

STREET: (*With mock severity.*) How d'you like scrubbing floors?

MONICA: I don't.

STREET: Well, that's what you'll be doing soon.

MONICA: Who says so?

STREET: (*Exasperated.*) I say so. The magistrate'll say so. The matron of the Home'll say so. The warden'll say so.

MONICA: What about the Army an' Navy?

> (*DR GRENOCK and CLINTON enter left. The DOCTOR is a formally-dressed, portentous man in his forties. He is not carrying the usual doctor's bag. STREET meets CLINTON and the DOCTOR. MONICA rises.*)

CLINTON: (*Introducing.*) Superintendent Street – Dr Grenock.

DOCTOR: How d'you do? Excuse me for a moment.

> (*He makes a brief examination of the unconscious KETTLE and is obviously satisfied by what he has observed.*)

Seems in good physical condition – fortunately. (*He is about to continue when he notices MONICA.*) Who's this?

STREET: Don't bother about her, Doctor. Under arrest for trying to obstruct a police officer.

MONICA: (*Complacently.*) It'll say in the paper, 'Pretty Girl Fights Police'.

STREET: You be quiet. Is he all right for you like this, Doctor?

DOCTOR: If I treat him just when he's coming round. I understand he wouldn't have agreed to have hypnosis?

STREET: He'd never have allowed you to come near him. He's a rebel now – see?

MONICA: Good luck to him!

DOCTOR: It's not uncommon. A secondary suppressed self suddenly takes charge. A minor form of dissociated personality. Not major, otherwise the primary self wouldn't have functioned so efficiently. It would have been inadequate for his complete social integration. You wouldn't say he was inadequate, would you?

STREET: No. Good quiet steady citizen – well thought of – gave no trouble.

CLINTON: Excellent in his work for us.

DOCTOR: Quite so. Did he tell you what happened to him this morning?

STREET: Yes. He heard a voice asking him what it was all for.

MONICA: (*Complacently.*) I've heard that voice – and there's no answer, neither.

STREET: (*Shouting.*) What you'll hear in a minute, if you don't keep quiet, is a loud slapping noise.

(*The DOCTOR ignores the interruption.*)

DOCTOR: A voice – eh? Yes – yes – yes – the usual thing. If I catch him just when he's coming round, a little quick neat hypnosis will do all that's necessary. I can restore the control of the primary self, which will at once suppress, probably to a fairly deep level, the rebellious secondary self.

(*MONICA edges to right of the DOCTOR.*)

I can persuade him he's had some accident.

MONICA: So can I.

DOCTOR: Sh!

(*MONICA moves below the sofa.*)

An interesting case. As the strain of modern life increases, with some inevitable loss of instinctive satisfactions... Let's put him on his bed, shall we? (*He motions to STREET.*)

(*STREET moves to KETTLE and lifts him by the feet. DOCTOR moves to KETTLE and lifts him by the shoulders.*)

I say –

(*STREET and the DOCTOR move slowly towards the arch.*)

– with some inevitable loss of instinctive satisfactions, and a growing sense of frustration on the unconscious level, there are bound to be more and more of these partial dissociations. And if we find we can cure them by light hypnosis, following some shock like this, then we've achieved a method of treatment that might be generally followed.

(*The DOCTOR and STREET exit with KETTLE to the bedroom. MONICA watches them go, then sits on the sofa at the right end. CLINTON moves to the desk, consults the telephone directory-pad, lifts the receiver, dials a number. MRS TWIGG enters hurriedly from the kitchen and is astonished to see MONICA.*)

MRS TWIGG: Monica, what are you doin' 'ere?

CLINTON: (*To MRS TWIGG.*) Just a minute, please.

MRS TWIGG: Oo – I'm sorry.

CLINTON: (*Into the telephone.*) Inquiries?… When's your next train to Birmingham?… No, that's too soon. What's the next? Thank you. (*He replaces the receiver.*)

MRS TWIGG: I *do* beg your pardon, sir, but this is my daughter – and I can't think what she's doin' 'ere.

MONICA: (*Complacently.*) I'm under arrest.

MRS TWIGG: (*Staggered.*) Under arrest? My goodness me! Whatever have you done this time?

MONICA: How do you mean 'this time'? I've never been arrested before.

MRS TWIGG: I should think not indeed.

MONICA: I might have my photo in the paper.

MRS TWIGG: (*Appalled.*) An' then what will your Aunt Florrie say? We'll never hear the last of it. (*She turns to CLINTON.*) I never know whether she's tellin' the truth, these days. What's happened, sir?

CLINTON: Superintendent Street will be out in a minute. I don't think it's very serious.

MRS TWIGG: But where's Mr Kettle?

CLINTON: In his bedroom. The doctor's with him now.

MRS TWIGG: (*Triumphantly.*) What did I tell you, Monica Twigg? Right from the first, didn't I say he was poorly?

MONICA: Go on. That Superintendent knocked him out. And they're giving him what's-it – hypnotism – like I've seen at the pictures.

MRS TWIGG: (*Indignantly.*) Now stop it, Monica. An' if you wasn't always going to the pictures an' readin' them picture papers, you wouldn't get such ideas. An' when it isn't pictures – all sex – sex – sex.

CLINTON: Quite true.

MONICA: Go on! You talk as if we'd invented it. Been going on a long time, hasn't it?

MRS TWIGG: Not on your scale, it hasn't. You think people have nothing else to do. Look what you said about poor Mr Kettle, when I told you he's not interested in sex – just doesn't fancy it.

MONICA: If you'd seen that posh glamorous housecoat that woman must have put on for him, and the look in her eye, a cat full of cream, you wouldn't say he didn't fancy it.

MRS TWIGG: (*Angrily.*) I tell you it's out of all reason. A nasty Monday morning, too – when *nobody* fancies it. (*STREET enters from the bedroom.*)

STREET: When nobody fancies what?

MONICA: (*Promptly.*) Sex.

STREET: (*Moving above the sofa; disapprovingly.*) Well, now we *are* talking, aren't we? Haven't left school five minutes – and sitting there, bold as brass, talking about sex.

MONICA: I left school three years since.

MRS TWIGG: Don't take any notice of her, Superintendent. She doesn't know what she's saying half the time.

MONICA: Yes, I do. She only gets mad at me because I can't keep a job long.

STREET: And why can't you keep a job long?

MRS TWIGG: (*Innocently.*) Sex.

STREET: (*Indignantly.*) Are *you* starting now?

MRS TWIGG: I only came to see if Mr Kettle might want a bit of something to eat. I could make him a nice shape an' a drop of custard.

MONICA: An' serve him right if he stays here.

STREET: Call later, Mrs Twigg. You're in the way now. And take that daughter of yours with you.

MONICA: (*Rising; disappointed.*) D'you mean I'm not under arrest?

STREET: Not this time.

MONICA: (*Disgusted.*) Why – you don't know your own mind two minutes together.

STREET: (*Roaring.*) *Outside!*

(*MRS TWIGG hastily pulls MONICA off to the kitchen.*)

(*Confidentially.*) I left the doctor to get on with it. Smart chap, I'd say.

CLINTON: Very. I've used him before. We get nervous breakdowns now and again.

STREET: I have an idea he'll pull it off.

CLINTON: Then I'll be very grateful for the help you've given, Superintendent.

STREET: Don't mention it, Mr Clinton. Been a pleasure.

CLINTON: But I'll tell you frankly I don't quite understand your interest in the case. Not really quite in your line of duty, surely?

STREET: No. But when I left him here this morning – all free and easy, having actually enjoyed playing a kid's game with him, and him not caring tuppence – the thought of him suddenly put my back up. I'd got to get back to my work. And he ought to get back to his. Why, where would we all be if...?

CLINTON: (*Cutting in; smoothly.*) Quite so. Exactly my own argument.

STREET: (*Indignantly.*) And then you're called a large grey rat.

(*The telephone rings. STREET lifts the receiver.*)

(*Into the telephone.*) Yes?... Oh, Alderman Hardacre, this is Superintendent Street here... No, we think it's all under control... Yes, Mr Clinton's still here... Well, come round and see for yourself. (*He replaces the receiver.*) Alderman Hardacre's hopping mad. Something about the Press...

CLINTON: (*Cutting in; hastily.*) We don't want the Press brought into this.

STREET: That's what I thought. Well, you'll have to calm him down, Mr Clinton. He'll be here soon.

(*The front door bell rings.*)

No, that can't be him. Even Hardacre couldn't be that quick.

(*There is a tap on the door.*)

(*Calls.*) Come in.

(*MOON enters.*)

Oh hello, Mr Moon.

MOON: How are you, Superintendent?

STREET: Nicely. This is Mr Henry Moon – one of our leading estate agents. Mr Clinton – district head of the London and North Midland Bank.

MOON: (*Crossing to CLINTON and shaking hands with him.*) Great pleasure, Mr Clinton. Come to take charge? Quite right, quite right. (*He hesitates a moment.*) By the way, my wife's not here, is she?

STREET: She *was* here, then went. But then we had a telephone call from her, and it's my belief she's now on her way back. So if you want to see her, you'd better wait.

MOON: Very well. But what about Kettle?

STREET: He's here.

MOON: (*Solemnly.*) I've a bone to pick with him.

STREET: You'll have to wait. (*He indicates the bedroom.*) Doctor's picking a bone with him just now. But I don't think he'll be long.

MOON: Kettle's a sick man, is he?

STREET: In a manner of speaking.

CLINTON: (*Gravely.*) Some temporary nervous trouble, Mr Moon.

MOON: (*Portentously.*) You don't surprise me, you don't surprise me at all. I was here earlier, and I said to myself then, 'Henry, old boy, keep your temper,' I said, 'you're dealing with a sick man – unbalanced,' I said. Kept phoning my office – all kinds of dam' nonsense. Quite upset my assistant, Miss Carson. (*To CLINTON, earnestly.*) How d'you find business conditions, Mr Clinton?

CLINTON: (*Solemnly.*) Favourable on the whole, Mr Moon – very favourable.

MOON: Glad to hear you say so, Mr Clinton. Same trend here. Things are moving nicely in Brickmill. Just negotiated an option on the old Murchison factory – you know it, Superintendent...

STREET: (*Heartily.*) Know it well.

MOON: (*Complacently.*) Looks like being a very big deal – six figures. Between ourselves, of course.

STREET: (*Confidentially.*) Yes – and while we're talking between ourselves – Mr Moon – I think if I were you, I wouldn't let Mrs Moon stay here very long.

CLINTON: I quite agree, Mr Moon.

MOON: (*Looking from one to the other.*) Oh, you do, do you? Take a firm line there, you think?

STREET: (*Confidentially.*) That's my advice – unofficially, of course, as a friend. Just put your foot down, Mr Moon.

MOON: Shouldn't be necessary. Just a quiet word ought to do it. But – er – any particular reason?

CLINTON: (*Tactfully.*) It's a delicate situation here – you know, Mr Moon – men's business.

MOON: Quite, quite. See what you mean.

STREET: (*Confidentially.*) As soon as women come into the picture, you never quite know where you are, do you?

MOON: Never. Noticed it many a time.

CLINTON: I've sometimes had a notion that in a properly planned world, you'd have to set them apart somehow, where they couldn't make mischief, except among themselves.

MOON: It's a thought, old man. Very well – I'll just...
(*But we never learn what he will do because at that moment the door bursts open. DELIA enters. She is dressed in travelling clothes, but looks much less severe than she did originally. She is a fierce creature now, full of fire and determination.*)

DELIA: Where is he?

STREET: In the bedroom. A doctor's with him.

DELIA: You hurt him.

CLINTON: (*Hastily.*) No, don't worry.

STREET: He's all right.

DELIA: (*Crossing quickly to the arch.*) I'll go and see.
(*DELIA darts into the bedroom.*)

MOON: (*Rushing to the arch and calling.*) Delia! Delia!
(*The three men stare after DELIA, not knowing what to do. After a moment vague sounds are heard from the bedroom, of DELIA's voice and the DOCTOR's voice raised in expostulation. Then the DOCTOR's voice can be heard quite clearly.*)

DOCTOR: (*Off; calling urgently.*) Superintendent! Superintendent!
(*The DOCTOR rushes on from the bedroom.*)

STREET: (*Crossing to the arch.*) I'm here.
(*The DOCTOR and STREET exit to the bedroom. A scuffling sound is heard off.*)
(*Off.*) Now you just be sensible, Mrs Moon.
(*STREET and the DOCTOR, with DELIA between them, struggling a little, enter from the bedroom. CLINTON moves to the easy chair.*)

DOCTOR: (*Indignantly.*) I assure you, madam, that I can't possibly allow you to disturb us like that. I speak for the patient as well as for myself. If you'll just wait, you'll be able to see for yourself what my treatment has done for him. But we can't possibly be interrupted now. Otherwise I couldn't guarantee anything. Superintendent, please make sure we're not disturbed again.

STREET: Certainly.
(*The DOCTOR exits to the bedroom.
STREET releases DELIA.*)
Now, Mrs Moon…
(*DELIA glares at STREET, then moves away, ignoring CLINTON and MOON. STREET looks significantly at MOON.*)
Mr Moon?

MOON: (*Not happy about this.*) Yes, of course, old man.
(*Hesitantly.*) Delia. You ought to go home.

DELIA: (*Impatiently.*) Who says so?

MOON: (*Uncertainly.*) Well – I do.

DELIA: (*Dismissing him.*) Don't be silly, Henry.

MOON: (*Rather bolder now.*) And *they* do, too.

DELIA: (*More interested now.*) You mean – these two?

MOON: Delicate situation here. Men's business, old girl.

DELIA: Please be quiet, Henry.

(*MOON retires to the right of the sofa. DELIA looks hard at the other two.*)

Now tell me what happened. And no lies, please.

STREET: I don't tell lies, Mrs Moon.

DELIA: You do. You told me he'd gone out.

STREET: Not *gone* out. I said he *was* out. I'd had to knock him out.

DELIA: Why?

STREET: Because he attacked me.

DELIA: Why did he attack you?

STREET: Didn't like something I said, I suppose.

CLINTON: (*With authority.*) My dear Mrs Moon, you must know that Kettle had been mentally unbalanced all day…

STREET: Even called us horrible names.

DELIA: What names?

STREET: He said we were large grey rats.

MOON: Good Lord! I must say…

DELIA: Don't say anything, Henry. Leave this to me. (*To the other two.*) Perhaps you were behaving like large grey rats. I wouldn't put it past you. Where was this doctor when all this happened? Where does he come in?

CLINTON: He's a specialist we employ. It happened we had an appointment…

DELIA: Here?

CLINTON: Yes.

DELIA: To do what?

CLINTON: Really, I can't see that's any concern of yours. I'm here on bank business.

DELIA: And I'm here on personal business – much more important.

STREET: You just remember you've no reason to be here that would sound well in a court of law.

DELIA: For that matter, neither have you. You've been dodging in and out all day as if this was a police station and not a man's house. Did he ask you to come here and knock him out?

STREET: (*Angrily.*) Mr Moon, if you can't make her go, at least make her keep quiet.

MOON: (*Sitting on the sofa at the right end.*) Easier said than done, old man.

DELIA: (*Grimly enumerating her points.*) Calls you rats – unbalanced – gets knocked out – specialist on the spot – the thumping lie you told me on the telephone – this fishy committee of welcome – and you want me to clear out. Pooh! There isn't a woman on earth who'd be satisfied with this situation. What's that doctor supposed to be doing in there?

CLINTON: Giving Kettle some necessary treatment.

DELIA: Treatment for *what?*

CLINTON: We're all living under a considerable strain these days.

DELIA: Are we? Why?

CLINTON: (*Testily.*) Because, my dear madam we can't help it.

DELIA: Why? Who's making us live under a strain?

CLINTON: (*Testily.*) Circumstances – circumstances.

DELIA: Who's made the circumstances?

(*The front door is heard to slam. HARDACRE enters hurriedly.*)

HARDACRE: You must be Mr Clinton. I'm Hardacre – spoke to you on the phone. Glad you took action at once. It's the only way. Take action. Get on with it, I always say. I nearly took it up with your Head Office.

CLINTON: I'm glad you didn't. I...

HARDACRE: (*Cutting in; roughly.*) You understand how I'm fixed. This big loan for my Extension. I was doing it through Kettle. As a favour. We'd always got on nicely. Till today. (*He sits in the easy chair.*) I say – till today.

STREET: Now, Alderman Hardacre, Mr Clinton knows all...

HARDACRE: (*Cutting in; roughly.*) A complete understanding – never a wrong word – *till today.*

MOON: You're repeating yourself, old man.

HARDACRE: (*Indignantly.*) And I well might repeat myself; so would you if you were me. Do you know how much money's at stake with this Extension?

MOON: (*Keenly interested.*) No. I've been wondering. Tell me.

HARDACRE: (*Indignantly.*) I'm not going to tell you, Moon. And I'm surprised at you asking. It's my business, not yours.

MOON: You asked if I knew. No need to be so touchy.

HARDACRE: (*Angrily.*) Touchy? Who says I'm touchy? And what I'm talking to you for, I don't know, Moon. What you're doing here, I can't imagine. No place for you. And no place for her neither. If she were my wife...

DELIA: (*Cutting in.*) I can think of fifty replies to that – all very rude. Now stop shouting.

HARDACRE: (*Loudly and angrily.*) I'm not shouting. And anyhow, I haven't to take orders from you.

(*The DOCTOR enters from the bedroom.*)

DOCTOR: (*With authority.*) Just a moment, please.

HARDACRE: And who are you?

DOCTOR: (*With dignity.*) I happen to be the doctor in charge of this case. And I'd be very glad if you wouldn't raise your voice so much. It's disturbing the patient. (*To DELIA.*) Are you Mrs Moon, by any chance?

DELIA: Yes. Why?

DOCTOR: The patient is asking if you are here.

(*DELIA moves towards the DOCTOR.*)

No – no – you'll see him shortly. (*To CLINTON.*) Quite successful, I think, Mr Clinton.

(*The DOCTOR exits to the bedroom.*)

HARDACRE: (*In quiet but impressive tones.*) All right, I'll talk quietly. But just listen to what I have to say. (*He is chiefly addressing CLINTON.*) If I don't see Kettle in the next half-hour and get some attention from him – and an apology – the fat'll be in the fire. Because I've made an appointment to meet the editor of the Brickmill Herald – who's a very good friend of mine – at the Union Club in an hour's time. And unless I feel properly satisfied by that time, doctor or no doctor – I'll tell him all I know. And he'll print it.

CLINTON: (*Disturbed.*) Alderman Hardacre – I assure you...

HARDACRE: Don't bother assuring me. Just show me Kettle in his right mind, that's all. And don't take too long about it – or else...

STREET: That's a bit hard, isn't it?

HARDACRE: You keep out of this.

STREET: Now – now – now!

HARDACRE: (*Rising.*) Don't 'now – now – now' me. Who d'you think I am – a lorry driver on the wrong side of the road?

STREET: (*Annoyed.*) And who do you think I am – a constable on traffic duty?

MOON: Hardacre, old man, we know you've had a bad day...

HARDACRE: I don't think you've had a very good one, neither.

MOON: Nothing wrong with *my* day.

HARDACRE: (*Nastily.*) That's what *you* think.

MOON: (*Annoyed.*) Well, I ought to know, oughtn't I? I'm not going to ask *you* what kind of day I've had, am I?

HARDACRE: Perhaps it's as well.

MOON: What are you talking about?

DELIA: (*Quietly but impressively.*) He's talking about me, Henry.

HARDACRE: (*Sitting in the easy chair.*) Well, I'm not leaving you out.

DELIA: Not even out of the Brickmill Herald, probably. Unless George Kettle does a little grovelling, we all go into the Herald, do we? Well, I'm going to tell you something that will surprise you. It serves me right. I ought to have known better.

STREET: You mean this morning?

DELIA: (*With spirit.*) No, this afternoon. When I must have forgotten what a *man* – might have to put up with here. (*With a step towards HARDACRE.*) But though it'll serve me right, that doesn't excuse you. And now I'll tell *you* something – and you can publish this in the Herald, too. There are about a dozen of you here – all stinkers – and you're the chief reason why nobody in their senses ever

wants to stay here. It isn't the factories and the smoke
and the fog and the dirt and the dingy streets and the
dreary little shops and the rissoles in the Old Oak Café
and the Brown Windsor soup in the County Hotel – it's
you.

HARDACRE: (*Angrily.*) That'll do. We've heard enough
from you.

MOON: (*Loudly.*) Possibly, Hardacre, old man. But all the
same...

HARDACRE: (*Cutting in; roughly.*) Don't you start, Moon.
When you can't even stop her wearing the trousers.

MOON: (*Indignantly.*) Trousers? Who's talking about
trousers?

(*The DOCTOR enters suddenly from the bedroom.*)

DOCTOR: (*Moving behind the sofa.*) Gentlemen, please. I
would like your attention – before Mr Kettle joins us.
He's dressing – and will be with us in a minute. I need
your co-operation. This morning, a secondary self,
hitherto suppressed, asserted itself. With the result that
you found Mr Kettle saying and doing things that
seemed to you quite strange.

HARDACRE: (*Grimly.*) I'll say he did. I thought he was
drunk.

DOCTOR: A pardonable mistake, my dear sir. Alcohol
helps to remove many of our social inhibitions.

HARDACRE: (*Fiercely.*) I never touch it. Never a drop
passes my lips...

DELIA: (*Cutting in; coldly.*) Nobody's interested in your lips.
Go on, Doctor.

DOCTOR: (*Very portentously.*) I've been able to treat him
successfully, restoring the primary self. He is – you may
say – cured. But at this very early stage, please accept
him exactly as before this unfortunate lapse.

HARDACRE: 'Ere, what do you...?

DOCTOR: No reproaches, please. If you co-operate with
me, then your presence here will do more good than
harm. It subjects him to a useful test. Most successful, I
think we may say, Mr Clinton.

CLINTON: Very gratifying, Doctor.

DOCTOR: Thank you. A most promising method of treatment. And one that...

DELIA: (*Cutting in.*) Just a minute.

DOCTOR: (*Annoyed at being interrupted.*) Well – I don't know what your interest is here, madam...

DELIA: Strictly personal – not scientific. What was this treatment?

DOCTOR: Well – if you must know, madam – shock followed almost immediately by a light hypnosis.

DELIA: He's knocked out – then just when he's coming round – without asking his permission.

DOCTOR: In the circumstances – naturally I couldn't ask his permission. For his own good I had to help him to suppress the secondary self and to restore the primary.

DELIA: How do you know which is the real George Kettle?

DOCTOR: That's beside the point. The primary self is successfully adjusted to life, the secondary self isn't. It's maladjusted, irresponsible, fanciful, incapable of playing a proper part in the modern social order. So the decision to restore the primary self is inevitable.

MOON: Absolutely. Very interesting, Doctor. Makes a chap think, doesn't it?

DELIA: (*Grimly.*) It's making this chap think – very hard.

DOCTOR: Mrs – er – Moon, I've permitted you to stay because for some reason or other the patient particularly inquired if you were here. I must ask for your co-operation, too – for *his* sake.

DELIA: (*Grimly.*) Don't worry. He'll get it.

DOCTOR: (*Listening.*) Sh! He's here.

(*KETTLE enters slowly from the bedroom. He is dressed in his bank manager's clothes and looks rather pale. His manner is meek and rather servile, in the sharpest contrast to his manner before now. He smiles sheepishly and apologetically to the company. DELIA regards him with horror; the men regard him approvingly.*)

(*In the usual hearty style.*) Well – Mr Kettle – feeling all right now, eh? Very different from what you did when you first came round – um?

KETTLE: (*Humbly.*) Doctor, when I remember, I can't think
what had taken possession of me. It was awful. I could
hear myself saying the most shocking things. 'There's
that cunning old busybody, Superintendent Street,' I was
saying. 'That stuffed shirt, Clinton, from the district
Head Office. That idiot, Henry Moon,' I was saying.
'That bad-tempered miserable old skinflint, Hardacre.'

HARDACRE: (*Angrily.*) Here – what d'you mean...?

DOCTOR: (*Cutting in; with authority.*) No, no, no, please. It
may be necessary for him to explain...

DELIA: (*Cutting in.*) Then it's my turn. What were you
saying to yourself about me?

KETTLE: (*Alarmed and apologetic.*) Oh – Mrs Moon – please
don't ask me. I didn't really know what I was saying –
thinking...

DELIA: (*Commandingly.*) Go on. What about me?

KETTLE: It doesn't make sense. I was saying to myself,
'That lovely enchanting creature, Delia Moon – what a
pity she's such a coward.'

DELIA: (*Moving to KETTLE and staring hard at him;
suspiciously.*) George Kettle!

KETTLE: (*With a sickly smile.*) You see, Mrs Moon, I didn't
know what I was saying. I told you it didn't make sense.
Excuse me, Mrs Moon. Oh – Mr Clinton.

CLINTON: (*Shaking hands with KETTLE.*) Nice to see you,
Mr Kettle. I came here for the afternoon – and couldn't
leave without saying 'Hello'.

KETTLE: (*Humbly.*) It's very good of you, Mr Clinton. I do
appreciate it. I'm sorry I wasn't at the bank when you
called – but I had some sort of accident.

CLINTON: (*Heartily.*) Don't mention it, Kettle. These things
happen. All right now, I think?

KETTLE: Yes, thank you, Mr Clinton. But we don't often
see you at our Brickmill branch – and I was hoping to
talk things over.

CLINTON: (*Heartily.*) We'll have that talk, next time. Here's
Alderman Hardacre – wants to have a word with you.
(*HARDACRE rises.*)

KETTLE: (*Apologetically.*) Oh – Alderman Hardacre – you must be worrying about that Extension Loan, aren't you?

HARDACRE: (*Grimly.*) Of course I am, Kettle. Spent all day worrying about it.

DOCTOR: (*Quickly.*) Careful now.

KETTLE: (*Timidly eager.*) I meant to tell you this morning I had a message from Head Office – it comes before the Board on Wednesday.

HARDACRE: (*In a bullying tone.*) You've put it to 'em properly Kettle – hot and strong, eh?

KETTLE: (*Eagerly.*) I can assure you I have, Alderman Hardacre – and I'm sorry you've been put to so much trouble.

HARDACRE: (*Moving to the door; roughly.*) Well, just be careful in future, Kettle.

KETTLE: (*Humbly.*) You can depend on me, Alderman Hardacre.

DELIA: (*Unable to restrain herself; disgusted.*) Oh – my God!

KETTLE: (*Turning to face DELIA; rather reproachfully.*) Mrs Moon!

DELIA: Well, Mr Kettle?

KETTLE: (*Apologetically.*) I suppose you're worried about the Infirmary Wireless Fund account?

DELIA: No, I'm not.

KETTLE: Oh!

DELIA: I'm worried about *you.*

KETTLE: I'm sorry. But really – I don't think it'll happen again.

DELIA: Don't bother about me. There must be somebody else you can apologise to. (*She moves abruptly to the desk.*)

HARDACRE: Well, I'm off. Glad you've come to your senses, Kettle.

(*DELIA unobtrusively extracts the revolver from the desk drawer.*)

KETTLE: (*Moving towards HARDACRE.*) Thank you, Alderman Hardacre.

(*HARDACRE exits abruptly before KETTLE can open the door for him. KETTLE turns to STREET.*)

Superintendent, I'm very glad you're here. You'll remember I wrote to you about the parking regulations at our bank corner?

STREET: Came to see you about it this morning, Mr Kettle.

KETTLE: Oh – I hope I haven't inconvenienced you at all, Superintendent?

STREET: No, not much. But I don't know if the doctor wants us to talk about it now.

DOCTOR: Frankly, I'd rather you didn't.

KETTLE: Thank you, Doctor. I appreciate that, and I don't feel quite… (*He looks faint.*)
(*CLINTON moves to the easy chair, turns it slightly and KETTLE sits.*)

CLINTON: Quite right. Don't rush things, Kettle, though I know how keen you are. But Dr Grenock's speaking for the bank, too – he's another member of the family.

KETTLE: (*Humbly.*) I'm glad to hear it. And I'd like to say this before you go, Mr Clinton. The London and North Midland isn't just something that pays me money. I like to feel it's my friend.

CLINTON: It is, Kettle, it is.

KETTLE: (*Smiling apologetically.*) I don't want to sound far-fetched. But in a way – because I owe it so much – I feel it's like a father and mother.

DELIA: (*Savagely.*) Why don't you go and kiss it?
(*KETTLE leans back and looks half asleep.*)

DOCTOR: Please! Well, gentlemen, you probably want to be off – and I must spend a few minutes giving my patient some advice about diet, sleep, that sort of thing. (*He glances at KETTLE.*)

CLINTON: (*Heartily.*) Of course. Wonderful job, Dr Grenock. (*He glances at KETTLE and lowers his voice.*) He's all right, I suppose?

DOCTOR: (*Motioning them to the door.*) Yes – yes – a natural reaction.
(*CLINTON and STREET move to the door. MOON rises and crosses above the sofa to DELIA.*)

CLINTON: (*Heartily.*) Well, good night, Kettle.

DOCTOR: (*Crossing to CLINTON and STREET.*) Bound to be exhausted – quite a natural reaction – but nothing to worry about.

(*STREET, CLINTON and the DOCTOR go out.*)

MOON: Better go home now, hadn't you, Delia?

DELIA: (*Moving to the sofa and sitting; rather grimly.*) Not yet, Henry. But *you* go.

MOON: Well, as a matter of fact, I must do some work at the office – on this Murchison factory deal. They're waiting for me.

DELIA: Who's they? Miss Carson?

MOON: (*With dignity.*) As my assistant, Miss Carson will be there, of course.

DELIA: Off you go then, Henry.

(*The DOCTOR enters.*)

Don't keep Miss Carson waiting.

MOON: Good night, Kettle.

KETTLE: (*Sleepily.*) Good night, Moon.

MOON: (*Crossing to the door, to the DOCTOR.*) First-class, absolutely first-class. Wouldn't have missed it for anything. Wonderful what you fellows can do nowadays.

DOCTOR: Thank you, Mr Moon. Well – good night.

MOON: Good night. (*MOON goes out.*)

DOCTOR: (*Surprised that DELIA does not depart.*) Mrs Moon, aren't you going with your husband?

DELIA: No, he's going to be busy at the office.

DOCTOR: Yes – but –

DELIA: So I'm staying here.

DOCTOR: I don't think you ought.

DELIA: I do. But just – carry on.

(*The DOCTOR, after giving DELIA a reproachful stare, moves to the easy chair, and turns to KETTLE.*)

DOCTOR: Now, Mr Kettle, I don't want to tire you – and, I shan't be long – but please pay attention.

KETTLE: (*Opening his eyes.*) Yes, Doctor?

DOCTOR: That's it. Just keep looking at me. (*He turns and stares reproachfully at DELIA.*) Now what we must guard against is a sudden relapse. You wouldn't like that, would you?

KETTLE: No, I shouldn't.

DOCTOR: So I want you to follow my instructions very carefully. Now – lead your ordinary life, but avoid all excitement.

KETTLE: If I lead my ordinary life, there won't be any excitement.

DOCTOR: (*Ignoring this.*) Eat plain wholesome food. No alcohol. No late hours. Avoid all over-stimulating experiences – perhaps you ought to buy a television set. As you're not married, we can ignore sex.

DELIA: Let's pretend it doesn't exist and we're all neuters.

DOCTOR: (*Crossing to DELIA and standing over her; angrily.*) Mrs Moon, I must ask you either to go or to keep quiet. Don't you realise that any interference at this stage in a hypnotic treatment can be extremely dangerous.

DELIA: (*Rising and backing a step or two away from the DOCTOR.*) Yes, and this can be even more dangerous. (*She points the revolver at him.*)

DOCTOR: (*Alarmed.*) How dare you! Put down that revolver at once.

DELIA: (*Sharply.*) Sit down.
(*The DOCTOR sits reluctantly on the sofa. She moves behind the sofa and threatens the DOCTOR with the revolver.*)
Let me explain, first, that I'm not a bad shot. I shan't kill you, of course – but I'll aim at your kneecap and put you out for months. That is, *if* you don't do what I say.

DOCTOR: This is preposterous. Why should I do what you say? What's the meaning of all this?

DELIA: Haven't they ever told you anything about women, Doctor Thing? Y'know, on the whole, even now, we're very docile passive creatures, easily imposed upon by you men, ready to believe all your nonsense and obey your idiotic rules. But one thing can make us desperate, rebellious, prepared to risk anything. Love, Doctor.

DOCTOR: (*Uneasily.*) I'm quite aware that at times the impulse...

DELIA: (*Cutting in; ruthlessly.*) Shut up!

DOCTOR: (*Rising; indignantly.*) If you think, madam...

DELIA: (*Turning the revolver on him; fiercely.*) And *sit down.*
(*The DOCTOR sits reluctantly on the sofa.*)

I'd almost enjoy shooting you – you miserable little man. For years, I've waited to love – and be loved. And today it happened – we found each other. We were wonderfully happy together. But then I did a stupid, cowardly thing. He asked me to go away with him – and I refused. But when I came back, ready to go with him, I found *you* here – turning him into a sanctimonious snivelling dummy again. He'd stopped being like that. He'd come alive. Then, you got hold of him when he was half conscious and mesmerised him into misery again. He was awake – and you wanted him sleep-walking again, like the rest of you.

DOCTOR: (*Rising; desperately.*) Mrs Moon – I assure you I was only...

DELIA: (*Fiercely.*) Undo what you've done – or I'll pull the trigger – I swear I will.

DOCTOR: (*Desperately.*) Kettle – I appeal to you – as a decent law-abiding citizen...

KETTLE: (*Quietly.*) No, Doctor. It's between you two.

DELIA: (*Fiercely.*) Go on. Do whatever you ought to do to free him completely.

DOCTOR: (*Resigning himself.*) Very well. But first you must realise what you're wanting me to do. What you will have is an anti-social, childish, irresponsible type, incapable of playing a proper part in the modern social order.

DELIA: (*Enthusiastically.*) I know.

DOCTOR: (*Severely.*) An obvious misfit, rebellious, extravagant, liable to overindulgence in alcohol – sex...

DELIA: (*Delighted.*) I know – I know.

DOCTOR: (*Very severely.*) And you'll probably be as bad as he is.

DELIA: (*Delighted.*) I do hope so.

DOCTOR: (*Glaring at her; furiously.*) *Strumpet!*

DELIA: (*Wildly.*) And the strumpet shall sound. (*She points the revolver at him.*) This is your last chance – one – two…

DOCTOR: (*In a panic.*) Stop, stop. I'll try. (*He turns to KETTLE.*) Now – Kettle – look at me – please.

KETTLE: (*Rising; coolly.*) No, Doctor. I'm tired of looking at you.

(*The exterior lights brighten as the clouds clear and the rain ceases.*)

DELIA: (*Astonished.*) George!

(*KETTLE crosses to DELIA and they embrace.*)

KETTLE: Well, Delia darling, you've seen what it would be like if I stayed here – *now* when do we go?

DELIA: (*Delighted.*) Tonight. Now. But I'd made up my mind before. I rang up to tell you.

KETTLE: I didn't know. So I felt I had to make you understand.

DOCTOR: (*Tapping KETTLE on the arm; astonished.*) But what about the treatment I gave you?

KETTLE: My dear chap, you couldn't hypnotise a rabbit. (*He takes the revolver from DELIA.*) By the way, the revolver isn't loaded. (*He tosses the revolver into the easy chair.*) So don't go and make a fuss about it.

DOCTOR: I won't. So long as you won't say anything to Mr Clinton.

KETTLE: Clinton! I don't propose to set eyes on him again. Why?

DOCTOR: (*Confidentially.*) Between ourselves – I've only just qualified as a psychiatrist. I'm an ear, nose, and throat man really.

KETTLE: How are *my* ears, nose, and throat?

DOCTOR: (*Seriously.*) I had a good look round. All in excellent condition.

KETTLE: (*Leading the DOCTOR to the door.*) Thank you, Doctor. And I don't think we need keep you – good-bye.

DOCTOR: Good day to you.

DELIA: (*Calling.*) Good-bye.

(*The DOCTOR goes out.*)

We'll go off in my car, I packed two bags – they're in the car – and I could start packing for you while you change clothes.

KETTLE: (*Surprised.*) Clothes? (*He looks with disgust at his clothes.*) Oh – of course – I'm wearing these dam' things. (*He tears his collar clean off, then hurriedly removes his coat. DELIA exits to the bedroom. KETTLE crosses to the radiogram and switches on the record.*
MRS TWIGG enters from the kitchen. She wears her outdoor clothes and is carrying a blancmange.)

MRS TWIGG: (*Shouting over the music.*) Mr Kettle – I've made you a shape.

KETTLE: All right. But you'll have to eat it yourself. We're going. I'll write to you. And remember me to Monica. (*MONICA enters. She is wearing outdoor clothes.*)

MONICA: You can remember yourself to Monica. Did I hear you say you were going?

KETTLE: Yes. As soon as we've packed a few things. (*DELIA enters from the bedroom. She carries a suitcase, KETTLE's easy clothes, and a bundle of other clothing for packing.*)

DELIA: (*As she enters.*) Here you are, darling. (*She sees MRS TWIGG and MONICA.*) Oh! (*She hands the easy clothes to KETTLE, puts the case on the floor, kneels and commences packing.*)

MONICA: If you two are going, so am I. And you can give me a lift.

KETTLE: Now, wait a minute, Monica…

MONICA: Oh – don't worry – I know she's got you. I won't have another try. But if that Superintendent's gone away – all baffled – he'll try an' take it out of me next.

MRS TWIGG: I'm afraid she's right – an' I wish you could give her a lift – 'cos I don't trust them lorry drivers an inch.

KETTLE: All right, Mrs Twigg. (*KETTLE exits to the bedroom. MONICA kneels by the case and helps DELIA to pack.*)

MONICA: (*Scornfully.*) Catch me askin' one of them. Mrs Moon, how about me bein' a personal maid for a week or two?

DELIA: No, I couldn't live up to your performance,
Monica. But we can drop you at my sister's – for a night
or two – she lives just the other side of Birmingham.

MONICA: (*Suspiciously.*) Has she a lot of children – an' no
help?

DELIA: Her husband's a television producer.

MONICA: (*Ecstatically.*) Hurry up – let's get going.
(*The radiogram comes into a loud passage.*
KETTLE enters from the bedroom. He carries some clothes
for packing, which he hands to DELIA. He has changed into
his easy clothes. MRS TWIGG stares at them with her mouth
open for a moment.)

MRS TWIGG: (*Shouting.*) Well – there's one thing – it's
stopped raining. I say – it's stopped raining.
(*The curtain quickly falls.*)

The End.